ADDRESSING CHALLENGING BEHAVIORS AND MENTAL HEALTH ISSUES IN EARLY CHILDHOOD

A copublication with the Council for Exceptional Children (CEC), *Addressing Challenging Behaviors and Mental Health Issues in Early Childhood* focuses on research-based strategies for educators to address challenging behaviors of children during early childhood and elementary school years. Utilizing research from the fields of neuroscience, child development, child psychiatry, counseling, and applied behavior analysis, the author suggests simple strategies for teachers to manage behaviors and promote mental health and resilience in children with challenging behaviors.

Addressing Challenging Behaviors and Mental Health Issues in Early Childhood provides a framework for best practices that are empirically based and have been successfully utilized in the classroom. An appreciation of the deep understanding of culture as it affects curricular approaches, family engagement, and child growth and development is utilized throughout this comprehensive, multidisciplinary resource. Bayat references the most recent research in the field of child mental health and provides educational and intervention approaches that are appropriate for all children with and without disabilities.

Mojdeh Bayat is Associate Professor of Education at DePaul University, USA. She has a BA in Law and Society from The American University, an MA in Early Childhood Special Education from Northeastern Illinois University, and a PhD in Child Development from Erikson Institute in Chicago.

ADDRESSING CHALLENGING BEHAVIORS AND MENTAL HEALTH ISSUES IN EARLY CHILDHOOD

Mojdeh Bayat

Routledge
Taylor & Francis Group

NEW YORK AND LONDON

First published 2015
by Routledge
711 Third Avenue, New York, NY 10017

and by Routledge
2 Park Square, Milton Park, Abingdon, Oxon OX14 4RN

Routledge is an imprint of the Taylor & Francis Group, an informa business

Library of Congress Cataloging in Publication Data
Bayat, Mojdeh.
Addressing challenging behaviors and mental health issues in early childhood / Mojdeh Bayat.
pages cm
Includes bibliographical references and index.
ISBN 978-1-138-01290-5 (hardback) -- ISBN 978-1-138-01291-2 (pbk.) -- ISBN 978-1-315-79562-1 (ebook) 1. Early childhood education. 2. Mentally ill children--Education (Early childhood) 3. Problem children--Education (Early childhood) 4. School children--Mental health services. 5. Child mental health. I. Title.
LB1139.25.B39 2015
372.21--dc23
2014046527

ISBN: 978-1-138-01290-5 (hbk)
ISBN: 978-1-138-01291-2 (pbk)
ISBN: 978-1-315-79562-1 (ebk)

Typeset in Bembo
by Saxon Graphics Ltd, Derby

To my daughter Naseem, who reminds me how resilient children can turn into strong, brilliant, and wonderfully creative adults who make their parents proud every day.

To my son Seena, who proves to me over and over again that there are no bounds to a child's strength in overcoming developmental obstacles and living a happy, healthy, and productive adult life.

CONTENTS

FIGURES

TABLES

PREFACE

My motivation for writing this book was a course titled Understanding Children's Behavior, which I designed and have taught in the Early Childhood Education Program at DePaul University in Chicago for the past eight years. Each of my students, who are undergraduate- and graduate-level early childhood teacher candidates, is required to work with a child with challenging behaviors over a period of time to support the child and address those behaviors. Teacher candidates are required to design a behavior intervention plan using techniques and methods that I teach in the course for this purpose. At the end of the term, students showcase their behavior intervention plans along with the results of their interventions.

After the first couple of years of teaching this course, the overwhelming success of my students' interventions became obvious, and their own expressed amazement of their success convinced me that the simple strategies I teach might be a great support to teachers in the field. I have taught the course as an in-service training for teachers in the field and found similar results. To make sure of the efficacy of the techniques, I conducted two survey studies. The result of my surveys confirmed my students' report, in that there was a clear reduction and/or elimination of challenging behaviors in a great number (about 93.1 percent) of all children whom my students worked with after using the taught strategies. In the last survey of in-service training participants, about 94.4 percent of teachers who took the course reported having successfully addressed the challenging behaviors of children they worked with after they had utilized those techniques. Thus, the course became the inspiration for writing this book. Though this is not a step-by-step guide for implementing a series of techniques, it does provide a basic framework for practice, as well as key strategies that my students used in the field. In particular, Chapters 7 and 9 of this book focus on these techniques.

My goal is that this book will be able to fill in an existing literature gap and provide needed support for educators in terms of addressing behavioral and mental health issues of children in early childhood education settings. I believe that understanding the underlying causes of mental health and developmental issues and related behavioral manifestations during early childhood is the foundation for best teaching practices. Therefore, I present research about the underlying causes of challenging behaviors, which shapes the foundation of strategies I recommend. Although the audience for this book is likely to be early childhood professionals, clinicians and educators, the strategies recommended are easily adaptable for parents to use at home with their children.

In preparing this book, I have utilized research from multiple disciplines, particularly from the fields of child development, early childhood education, special education, infant mental health, neuropsychology, child psychiatry, social work, child and family counseling, parenting and family studies, and American history. Additionally, I have drawn upon my own personal research and practice with children with developmental disabilities and challenging behaviors, as well as my work in early childhood teacher preparation. I hope this book will bring much needed attention to the mental health needs of young children.

Book Chapters

The first four chapters are related to providing an introduction and background information to the central topic of the book – early childhood mental health and related issues, such as factors contributing to children's emotional and behavioral problems as well as health. Chapters 5, 6, and 7 are devoted to early childhood prevention practices and intervention approaches for addressing behavioral and mental health issues in children (e.g. developmental child-centered play therapy and positive behavior support). Chapter 8 examines issues surrounding current ineffective school and classroom discipline procedures, such as suspension, expulsion, timeout, and corporal punishment. Chapter 9 focuses on practical, structural, and management strategies for early childhood classrooms, as well as a case example of successful interventions for a child with challenging behaviors. Chapter 10 examines the topic of parenting as it relates to culturally diverse families in the United States. Finally, Chapter 11 examines issues related to family–educator partnership and collaboration in early childhood and special education.

Most chapters include historical background related to the development of research and/or the theoretical approaches under discussion. Case examples presented throughout the book are of actual children with challenging behaviors whom my pre-service teacher candidates successfully worked with in the field. The names and identifying information of children and professionals have been changed to protect the privacy of children, their families, and their teachers.

ACKNOWLEDGMENTS

First and foremost, I am indebted to my colleague, Dr. Gayle Mindes. She was elemental in encouraging me to undertake this work, and further supported me in developing chapter manuscripts by reviewing each chapter and making recommendations for improvement. Gayle was particularly instrumental in the development of Chapter 1. I am grateful to have a colleague who is not only a prolific writer and one of the most insightful early childhood education leaders, but also is a wonderful mentor, whose constant encouragement and wise advice has made me a better educator and scholar. She is a valued colleague, a great friend, and a peerless mentor. I am forever in her debt!

I also would like to acknowledge my early childhood education pre-service teacher candidates in the course Understanding Children's Behavior, at DePaul University. I have used the cases of children they successfully worked with throughout this book. Their examples of successes in working with children with challenging behavior should be an encouragement to all early childhood educators entering the field.

Finally, in preparing this manuscript, I relied on the editorial talent of my daughter, Naseem. In all my writings, Naseem is the first person who reads my roughest drafts, and makes my language – which she describes as "foreign" – more Americanized.

1

CHILDREN WITH CHALLENGING BEHAVIORS AND THEIR EARLY EDUCATION

> I am at an impasse with Jacob. He is aggressive toward other children and doesn't get along. Jacob does not listen to me and throws tantrums if he doesn't get his way. I am always putting out fires with him. I have tried everything, but nothing works. Jacob takes all of my time and attention away from other children. I really don't know what to do with him. Can you give me some ideas about how to work with him?

This is a common story I hear in my work with teachers. Teachers are usually very stressed and desperately seeking solutions to help them work successfully with children who display challenging behaviors in their classrooms. Many teachers have the common belief that a solution is simple, easy, and fast. They may think that perhaps they can learn some useful behavior guidance strategies during a conversation, in an one-hour workshop, or via an email from an expert. Indeed, they ask if I can help them find easy and quick solutions to work with what many have, unfortunately, come to term as the "problem child." I cannot answer this question without raising others. Who are children with challenging behaviors? And why do they resort to these behaviors? In this chapter I will define challenging behaviors, and present issues related to early education and intervention for children with challenging behaviors.

A Historical Reflection

Young children with challenging behaviors were not the focus of scholarly attention until the last two decades. Instead, it was adolescents with challenging behaviors who typically captured the interest of scholars. For example, John Bowlby, whose groundbreaking work on attachment (1969, 1973, 1980) changed our understanding of children's emotional development, attributed the reason for his choice of career and research in child psychiatry to his after-college volunteer work with youth enrolled in a school for children who were described as maladjusted (Bretherton, 1992). Bowlby and other scholars of his time, such as Erikson (1968), focused on maladjustment in youth, and believed that the challenging behaviors of adolescents had roots in negative early caregiver–child relationships. However, despite seeing the relationship between early childhood and later behavior, addressing challenging behaviors in early childhood was mostly ignored.

In fact, until the 1990s, parents who approached professionals with their concerns about their young children's behaviors may have been told that it was natural for young children to have challenging behaviors, and that their child would outgrow those typical behavioral difficulties in time (Powell, Fixsen, Dunlap, Smith, & Fox, 2007). In the 1990s, several studies (Campbell, 1990; Cicchetti & Cohen, 1995; Cicchetti & Richters, 1993) correlated early behavioral difficulties with later challenges, if those initial behaviors were not corrected. This inspired an interest in studying young children's mental health, finding ways to address challenging behaviors, and possibly preventing further diminished cognitive outcomes, and other developmental difficulties, as well as social-emotional adjustment issues. Children's mental health problems were studied further in the 1990s, and it was established that early childhood challenging behaviors predicted a negative developmental and behavioral trajectory in later stages of life (Fergusson, Lynskey, & Horwood, 1996; Moffitt, Caspi, Dickson, Silva, & Stanton, 1996). For example, inconsolable tantrums, excessive crying, screaming, uncontrollable anger bouts, physical or verbal aggression, self-injury, noncompliance, disruptive behaviors, and withdrawal or social isolation are now considered signs of social-emotional or developmental issues that may lead to future conditions, such as conduct disorder. These behavioral challenges are linked to future academic failure, adolescent conduct problems, peer and relationship problems, and poor emotional regulation (Powell et al., 2007).

What is a Challenging Behavior?

I cannot discuss challenging behaviors of children without first defining what a challenging behavior is. Terms such as *behavior problems* or *problem behaviors*, *emotional and behavioral problems*, *behavioral difficulties*, or *challenging behaviors* are commonly used to describe behaviors that interfere with an individual's care and education, as well as with socialization and interactions with peers. The term *challenging behavior* is the preferred term because unlike the other terms, the former not only defines the behavior within the child, but also considers the child's environments and their related demands (Lyons & O'Connor, 2006). For example, a behavior is deemed challenging according to the social and cultural rules of an environment or a system, as opposed to considering the child as being the problem.

Therefore, in order to define *challenging behavior*, I adopt a definition that brings into account considerations of environmental factors (also used by Gebbie,

Ceglowski, Taylor, & Miels, 2012; Kaiser & Rasminsky, 2012; Powell et al., 2007; Williams, Perrigo, Banda, Matic, & Goldfarb, 2013). A challenging behavior is any behavior which: 1) interferes with the development, learning, and pro-social engagement and interactions of children with their peers and adults; 2) harms or may harm the child or others; and 3) may therefore put the child at risk for later social-emotional or learning problems.

Given this definition, a constellation of behaviors can be considered challenging. In young children, these behaviors may include prolonged tantrums, oppositional behaviors and angry reactions to others, verbal or physical aggression toward self or others, self-injury, disruptive behaviors, withdrawal, excessive crying, and anxious behaviors. Of course, it is typical in development for children in their early years to display some degree of these behaviors. However, most children respond positively to adults' guidance and are able to internalize self-discipline.

As they grow from toddlerhood to school age, children usually learn to control their behaviors internally and display appropriate social-emotional and behavioral responses based on different social situations. However, in some children, patterns of challenging behaviors may be severe or persistent over time. Early childhood teachers frequently report a range of challenging behaviors that may start from the toddler years but continue during preschool, kindergarten, and beyond (Brown & Conroy, 2011; Fox, Carta, Strain, Dunlap, & Hemmeter, 2010; Gardner et al., 2009; Gilliam, 2005; Sobanski et al., 2010). Such early and persistent patterns of challenging behaviors can be indicative of neurological, social-emotional, or other developmental issues, which can be prevented and addressed effectively in early childhood. In fact, when children with significant challenging behaviors are not identified in a timely manner, nor are they given any appropriate intervention, their problems will become more intense over time. This may predict not only poor academic outcome, but also peer rejection, adult mental health concerns, and adverse effects on their families (Dunlap et al., 2006).

Types of Challenging Behaviors

In a seminal work, Achenbach (1978) created the topography of challenging behaviors. For this topography, he constructed two categories of challenging behaviors: *externalizing* and *internalizing* behaviors. Externalizing behaviors are usually easy to pinpoint. These are behaviors that manifest in interpersonal interactions and relationships with others and often occur in response to external environmental events (Campbell, Shaw, & Gilliom, 2000). These may include explosive anger, verbal or physical aggression, or uncontrollable tantrums in response to a statement or event that is disliked by the child. Externalizing behaviors often occur as a reaction to a phenomenon and involve difficulties in interpersonal relationships with peers and adults (Dunlap et al., 2006). Internalizing behaviors, on the other hand, are more difficult to observe and pinpoint. These are behaviors that are intrapersonal. They often result from an internal emotional conflict, such as depression and anxiety. Examples of these behaviors are sadness, social isolation, and fearful reactions to specific or general situations. No matter what kind, challenging behaviors in early childhood often signal other serious mental health issues in the child (Brown & Conroy, 2011; Carter, Briggs-Gowan, & Davis, 2004; National Scientific Council on the Developing Child, 2008).

Prevalence of Children with Challenging Behaviors

There are varying estimates on the numbers of children with challenging behaviors; these differences are due to the range of methodologies and the population used for study. Some studies include all young children in the age range who may be receiving an intervention; others focus on young children in childcare settings where they may be newly diagnosed. Finally, others estimate the numbers based on statistical projections. Pastor, Reuben, and Duran (2012) report 3.1 percent of all children aged 4 to 14 years have been formally identified as having serious social and emotional problems between 2001 and 2007 in the United States. Other studies focusing on early childhood years report higher estimates. For example, statistical reports vary from indicating 10 percent to 15 percent (Raver & Knitze, 2002) to 10 percent to 30 percent of all children in early childhood to have challenging behaviors (Hemmeter & Fox, 2009). Preschoolers living in poverty or in low-income families seem to exhibit a higher rate of challenging behaviors than the general population, with an estimate of up to 31 percent having internalizing behaviors, and 57 percent having externalizing behaviors (Beyer, Postert, Muller, & Furniss, 2012). Aside from these numbers, survey studies of early childhood educators report that up to 60 percent of children in early childhood classrooms have behavioral issues, such as aggression and defiance (Anthony, B., Anthony, L., Morrel, & Acosta, 2005). Kindergarten teachers consider social and emotional problems a major impediment to learning and school readiness (Gilliam, 2005). In fact, it is reported that more than 65 percent of children with emotional and behavioral disorders in early childhood drop out of school in later school years due to challenging behaviors (Hemmeter & Fox, 2009). These statistics are alarming and make addressing children's mental health and early challenging behaviors a priority among other issues in early childhood education.

Having provided some historical context and recent incidence figures for the concept of challenging behaviors and children, I will briefly look at the systemic issues, which may have an influence on understanding and addressing challenging behaviors in children in a societal and cultural context.

Early Care and Education in United States: A Fragmented System

The system of early education of children in the United States is a fragmented and often confusing system. An explosion of different early childhood disciplines and professional categories contributes to the creation of this fragmentation (Gable,

2014; Lillas & Turnbull, 2009; Zigler, Gilliam, & Barnett, 2011). Professionals working with young children and their families come from a variety of disciplines, professional backgrounds, and expertise. Professional backgrounds include education, social work, counseling, developmental psychology, psychiatry, pediatric medicine, as well as allied health sciences such as occupational therapy, physical therapy, speech and language pathology, and nursing. Similarly, early childhood programs may be provided under different systems such as childcare, healthcare, early childhood education, child welfare, early intervention, and special education (Turnbull, Stowe, Klein, & Riffel, 2012). These early childhood programs may have different funding sources, different specialties and different configurations of service delivery for children and their families.

It would be ideal for these disciplines to come together to offer coordinated and widespread identification, prevention, and intervention programs for children and their families under a unified system of early care and education. However, the reality is far from this ideal. Indeed, individual programs usually operate independently and often without much communication or collaboration with one another. Because of differences in scope of services, not all children with mental health issues who are enrolled in these programs are necessarily identified early. For example, while some programs offer screening, identification, and diagnostic services for children with developmental and behavioral concerns, others do not include such services (Powell et al., 2007; Turnbull et al., 2012; Williams et al., 2013). Even though federal legislation requires public programs to provide services and offers families the availability for access to such early intervention services, there are various access and family preference issues that influence family participation in them (Turnbull et al., 2012).

Early Intervention and Special Education for Children with Disabilities

The term Early Intervention (EI) is used to refer to services for children with disabilities from birth to age three. These services are guaranteed under Public Law 94-142. Originally passed in 1975 as the All Handicapped Education Act, this law was renamed in 1990 as the Individuals with Disabilities Education Act (IDEA) and reauthorized in 2004 as the Individuals with Disabilities Education Improvement Act (IDEA, 2004). IDEA articulates the provision of services and provides funding for states for early intervention and education of all children from birth to age three who have disabilities, under Part C. Identification services via screening, evaluation, and diagnostic services are also funded by the states under IDEA of 2004.

Part C requires that services are coordinated with existing resources, such as Medicaid and private insurance, and with other local efforts, such as other programs for children with disabilities, maternal and child health, and Head Start (IDEA, 2004; Powell et al., 2007; Turnbull et al., 2012; Williams et al., 2013). Early intervention services are meant to address five areas of cognitive, language, physical, adaptive, and social-emotional development (IDEA, 1990). Birth-to-three services include developmental therapy (DT), occupational and/or physical therapy (OT and PT), speech therapy, nursing services, psychological or medical assessment, and social services. Services can be offered at home or in center-based programs, such as childcare or prekindergarten programs. Professionals who work in EI such as therapists, psychologists, and social workers, have educational backgrounds in healthcare and allied health sciences as well as in early education. Developmental therapists, for example, are early childhood educators with specialties in infant and toddler intervention. All service providers in EI who work with children are required to have four-year degrees or higher in a developmental field of specialty.

Under Part B of IDEA (Turnbull et al., 2012), all individuals diagnosed with disabilities from age 3 to 21 – or in some states to age 22 – are eligible to receive free and appropriate public education and special education services, such as specialized instruction, various therapies, nursing services, and technology assistance (IDEA, 1990). Assessment, diagnostic, and evaluation services are part of the eligibility determination process. Additionally, states provide funding for coordination of transition services between Part C (early intervention) and Part B (preschool) before the child's third birthday. Transition of services from Part C may be to a special education preschool or to a general or inclusive community preschool program, like Head Start, private preschool, or childcare center – when the intervention team determines that such a placement is the least restrictive option for the child's education.

Child Development and Healthcare

Essentially, children suspected of developmental delays, including those with behavioral issues, can be identified through the healthcare system. Under Part C of IDEA of 2004 (Turnbull et al., 2012), physicians are required to refer such children to the early intervention service agencies in their communities for developmental screening and identification procedures. In addition, there are three federally funded programs for low-income children that may provide screening for possible developmental and behavioral issues. These programs are Medicaid, the State Children's Health Insurance Program, and the Maternal and Child Health Block Grant Program (Powell et al., 2007; Turnbull et al., 2012; Williams et al., 2013). Children receiving services in these plans are usually entitled to receive pediatric and developmental preventive services. However, according to Williams and colleagues (2013), some families may face difficulties in identifying the correct program to contact when their child is showing signs of both potential developmental delays as well as challenging behaviors. There needs to be a clear path in place for parents and guardians to follow to inquire about early intervention services for their child. Ringwalt's (2012) compilation of qualifications for intervention by states continues to show wide variation in how states implement this programming.

Early Childhood Intervention

In general, early childhood programs that are supported via federal funding, such as Head Start and Early Head Start, as well as those funded through the state, such as state prekindergarten, are considered *early childhood intervention* programs (Turnbull et al., 2012). These programs are designed to boost the developmental and academic performance of children from low-income and minority families, and are either free to the eligible population, or may require a nominal fee. Aside from typical early education, the services offered through these programs include family support and social services.

Early Head Start and Head Start programs are required to provide developmental screening, identify children with challenging behaviors and social-emotional needs, and refer them for additional assessment and connection to mental health services (Head Start Act, 2007; Powell et al., 2007; Turnbull et al., 2012; Williams et al., 2013). State prekindergarten programs vary in their quality and standard of intervention and assessment. Not all state prekindergarten programs require developmental screening and referral, although IDEA (2004) requires family access to such services, which may be provided by healthcare providers or public schools. However, most require informal screening via observations, and recommendation for referral of those children who are suspected of having developmental issues.

In terms of professional qualifications, while some state prekindergarten programs require early childhood teachers to have four-year degrees and teaching licensure in early childhood education, other state and federally funded programs, like Head Start and Early Head Start, have not required four-year degrees for all of their teaching staff or support professionals. However, since 2013, Head Start regulations require that the head teacher have a bachelor's degree in child development or related field. While early intervention programs begin with infancy state and federal programs prior to kindergarten focus on preschool. The age span of early childhood includes the primary grades in elementary school.

Early Childhood Education

The National Association for the Education of Young Children (NAEYC) (1996; Copple & Bredekamp, 2009) defined early childhood education as any group program in a facility that serves children from birth to age eight. Accordingly, NAEYC defines the early childhood period as from birth through age eight (birth through grade three) (NAEYC, 1996). However, states may vary in their definitions of the early childhood period and associated educational grade and age levels. While in some states early childhood education programs cover from birth through third grade, others may only go up to age five or to the kindergarten level or to second grade.

Early childhood programs may include private or subsidized childcare and preschools, and private and public school through third grade. These programs offer early care and education services without necessarily providing formal screening and referral for children with challenging behaviors or other developmental issues, or any additional therapeutic or intervention programs. However, IDEA of 2004 requires universal screening of all young children served in public settings from kindergarten age and beyond.

Early childhood teachers working in public schools are required to have four-year degrees with early childhood teaching licensure. However, private preschools do not consistently require early childhood teachers to have four-year degrees in early childhood education or related fields. Teachers working in childcare programs are not necessarily required to have four-year degrees. Often states require only a high school diploma with a minimum number of post-secondary courses, although the Quality Rating and Improvement System (QRIS) – a system for improving the quality of childcare – is attempting to remedy this problem through state childcare regulations (Quality Rating and Improvement System, 2011). Yet, many families who are looking for childcare providers are unaware of the services that QRIS provides. Most rely on recommendations from friends or information they find on the Internet (Child Trends, 2014). Additionally, the early childhood field continues to struggle with providing highly qualified teachers in all childcare situations, which results in teachers possessing an uneven understanding of child development as it is manifest in the classroom. This complicates the process since teachers with minimal qualifications may not recognize symptoms that should be screened or diagnosed. For it is often the early childhood teacher who can serve as the child's and family's advocate for early intervention or mental health program referral.

Infant and Child Mental Health Programs

Mental health in children is defined as development of social–emotional competence and self-regulation in the context of family, community, and culture (Zeanah, Stafford, Nagle, & Rice, 2005; Zeanah, C. & Zeanah, P., 2001). Broadly speaking, this definition refers to any developmental issue which prevents the child from the development of healthy emotional regulation and daily socialization with peers and adults. In addition, it distinguishes mental health in early childhood from a mental illness, which indicates a psychiatric diagnosis (Zeanah et al., 2005). However, the current definition of child mental health adds to an already complex early education system; while mental illness and its treatment can be addressed through the healthcare system, it is not clear what system, early education or healthcare, addresses the mental health issues of the child (Kendall-Taylor & Mikulak, 2009). For example, under the Community Mental Health Services Block Grant program, federal funding is provided for states to support public mental health (Powell et al., 2007). However, because the funds are used for children with severe emotional disturbance, and such disturbances are often not diagnosed during or prior to preschool, little funding is actually used for children younger than six years old (Cavanaugh, Lippitt, & Moyo, 2000). Another factor affecting the access to service and its implementation is that mental health programs often serve as ancillary services rather than whole programs including education. The ancillary services include play therapy, family therapy, or family intervention services. As a result, the system of identification and intervention for children with challenging behaviors remains a fragmented one.

Child mental health professionals are developmental psychologists, pediatricians, psychiatrists, social workers, and counselors. In addition to a specialty in mental health, they are required to have highly professionalized licensure.

Issues of Debate and Controversy in Early Childhood Education

During the last two decades, the early childhood education field has faced many issues of debate and controversy, such as early childhood teacher qualifications, core curriculum and standards, universal screening and high stakes assessment, as well as focus on cognitive and academic development vs. social-emotional development. Whether directly or indirectly, these issues contribute to the current difficulties of the field of early childhood education for addressing the challenging behaviors of children. I will briefly review some of these issues in this chapter to provide the appropriate background for our discussion of children with challenging behaviors. The issues include: teacher qualifications, inclusion of young children with disabilities in early childhood programs, emphasis on cognitive and academic vs. whole child, curriculum and Common Core State Standards (CCSS), and teaching and assessment in early childhood education.

Teacher Qualification in Early Childhood Education

Professionals working in diverse early childhood programs have varying qualifications and come from numerous disciplines. Currently, there is no uniform approach to requirements for qualification of teachers in early childhood education. There are several characteristics that are similar. For example, the majority of early childhood teachers are females in their late 30s or early 40s; they usually have lower credentials when teaching infants/toddlers and preschool children as compared to those teaching the kindergarten level; and they have a high rate of turnover, mostly due to low rates of compensation (Barnett, 2011a). According to the U.S. Bureau of Labor Statistics (2013), preschool teachers, except those in special education, earn median wages of $13.04 hourly and $27,130 annually, while kindergarten teachers, except special education teachers, earn $53,090 annually. The Center for the Child Care Workforce (2011) breaks down average wages for childcare workers and preschool teachers in each state as well as the U.S. as a whole. The figures for the U.S. as a whole show an average hourly wage for childcare workers of $9.88; and for preschool teachers the average hourly wage is $16.61. Finally for those described as childcare workers, including employees in some kind of government-funded program or institution, the median wages are $9.38 hourly and $19,510 annually.

Historically, teachers working in childcare and preschool programs have not been required to have four-year degrees. The issue of early childhood teacher credential requirements directly and indirectly is linked to the rate of their salary and cost implications for the early childhood education system. For example, for each early childhood teacher having a four-year degree the costs will rise from $300 per child for a part-day program to $1500 per child for a full-day program (Barnett, 2011a).

Early childhood teachers have been among the lowest paid group in the teaching profession. The median salary for infant and toddler teachers was reported to be $19,510 in 2010 (Bureau of Labor Statistics, 2013). Teachers working in a childcare setting, including early childhood assistant teachers in preschools and kindergarten, are required to have high school diplomas or equivalent with or without some training in early childhood care and education and on-the-job training. Depending on the type of program, preschool teachers in the United States are generally required to have an associate's degree – about half of the states with prekindergarten programs require teachers to have a bachelor's degree – and have a median salary of $25,700 per year (Barnett, Friedman, Hustedt, & Stevenson-Boyd, 2009; Bureau of Labor Statistics, 2013).

Although some states require that preschool teachers be paid the salary of public school teachers, early childhood teacher salaries in general are lower compared to teachers in elementary grades and higher, the latter who have a median income of $53,090 (Barnett, 2011a; Bureau of Labor Statistics, 2013).

In the last decade, some scholars have argued that teaching young children requires a specialized training and a high degree of knowledge and cognitive abilities (Cunningham, Zibulsky, & Callahan, 2009; Gable, 2014; Zigler et al., 2011). The Federal Head Start and Early Head Start reauthorization in 2007 mandated that half of all teachers who work in preschool programs to have a bachelor's degree by 2013. Earlier, Congress required all teachers to have an associate's degree by 2011 (U.S. Department of Health and Human Services, 2008). However, today, regardless of their educational qualifications, the salary of Head Start teachers continues to be lower as compared with that of their counterparts in other early childhood settings (Barnett, 2011a).

To add to the complexity of this issue, many studies show the importance of early childhood teachers having a four-year degree. Galinsky (2006) found that teacher preparation and low turnover were important variables in achieving an economic benefit for early education. Barnett's (2011b) review of studies shows consistent results of the importance of teacher quality for child achievement outcomes.

While some scholars recommend that targeted training in child development and classroom practices rather than higher education would be sufficient for early childhood teachers (Fuller, 2011), others hold that having a bachelor's degree is necessary but actually is not sufficient (Bowman, 2011; Pianta, 2011). These scholars argue that teachers of young children should have higher and specialized education in early childhood development, psychology, early education, English language learning, and early childhood special education in addition to ongoing professional support through consultation and coaching, in order to address the diverse educational needs of children effectively (Bowman, 2011; Pianta, 2011).

From what I have discussed, it may become clear that a lack of appropriate teacher expertise and knowledge to address the mental health needs of infants and young children early on and during the most crucial time of their development is a serious issue. In addition, a teacher's limited pedagogical knowledge and skills can contribute directly to environmental and classroom factors, which may exacerbate challenging behaviors of young children both in frequency and in severity. This state of affairs increases the complexity of service delivery when the expectation is that all early childhood programs must operate with a philosophy of inclusion.

Inclusion of Children with Disabilities in Early Childhood Classrooms

The roots of the inclusion movement in education began in the 1970s in the United Kingdom. In fact, the concept of inclusion grew out of what is called a *social model of disability*, which was originally put forth by the Union of the Physically Impaired Against Segregation in the UK in 1976 (Union of the Physically Impaired Against Segregation, 1976). This movement advocated for equal rights of individuals with disabilities in the workplace. Eventually, out of this movement grew a respect for diversity and inclusion of children with disabilities in schools in educational discourse in Europe and the United States.

A dominant proportion of early childhood professionals in the United States and in Europe have come to operate from this social model of disability. The social model focuses on the child, the environment, and the interactions between the two, which may accordingly see a child as disabled or enabled (Marsala & Petretto, 2010). Based on this model, the society is collectively responsible for both the disability and the intervention for the disability (Llewellyn & Hogan, 2000). This view underscores what it means to have a disability, implies how the child with a disability may be empowered by altering the home and classroom environment, and puts appropriate support structures in place, both in school and home (Grue, 2011).

In the United States, the social model and inclusion in education is promoted by individuals with disabilities themselves and by families of children with disabilities. Such advocacy was partially responsible for the Congress of the United States signing into law the Individuals with Disabilities Education Act (IDEA) of 1990, and the Americans with Disabilities Act (ADA) of 1990. ADA is the most comprehensive law in the United States, making provisions for the rights of individuals with disabilities. Broadly speaking, the terms *Least Restrictive Environment* (LRE) and *natural environment*, which are both articulated in IDEA, imply that, to whatever degree possible, a child should be educated along with her peers in typical environments (i.e., home, childcare, preschool, school, as well as in the community).

Since the 1980s, inclusion of children with disabilities in schools and childcare settings has gradually become widespread. For example, the number of children with disabilities in inclusive classrooms more than doubled between 1985 and 2001 (Cook, Cameron, & Tankersley, 2007). The early childhood community especially embraced inclusion enthusiastically. The Division for Early Childhood (DEC) of the Council for Exceptional Children and the National Association for the Education of Young Children (NAEYC) articulated a joint position statement in 2009, in which they described early childhood education as an embodiment of values and practices that acknowledge the rights of all children to participate in early childhood education regardless of ability (DEC/NAEYC, 2009). In fact, early childhood education is described to be, in essence, an inclusive education, once it focuses on developmentally appropriate practices for all children (Copple & Bredekamp, 2009).

As a philosophy, inclusion acknowledges the equal right of all children to education along with their peers. It encourages acceptance of the child and of the place of the child in the community. In this philosophical sense, inclusion is a successful concept among educators and the public in general. In reality, however, inclusion in early childhood education, featuring best practices, is far reaching. In its practical sense, inclusion faced many challenges since its implementation. The field of early childhood education continues to see a discrepancy between teachers' attitudes toward the principles of inclusion – which are generally positive – and their willingness to work with students who have challenging behaviors, like those with Attention Deficit Hyperactivity Disorder (ADHD), and children with Autism Spectrum Disorders (ASD) (Barned, Knapp, & Neuharth-Pritchett, 2011; Gal, Schreur, & Engel-Yeger, 2010; Mikami et al., 2012; Nutbrown & Clough, 2004). Many teachers call for inclusion only if there is adequate professional training support for them, if there are sufficient auxiliary staff and resource support for the child, and if the parents are involved and collaborate with them (Nutbrown & Clough, 2004).

The current educational best practices in early childhood include differentiation of instruction and modification of structures and environments as the basic foundations of including children with disabilities in classrooms. Similarly, the law mandates designing a *behavioral intervention plan,* which would address the challenging behaviors of a child as a part of an Individualized Education Plan (IEP) (Turnbull et al., 2012). One approach to addressing challenging behaviors of children in the classroom and school is Positive Behavior Intervention Support (PBIS) (Fox & Hemmeter, 2009). PBIS focuses on fostering social competence for children. It involves designing a behavioral intervention plan to provide support and intervention for the child in the classroom and at home. Ongoing functional behavior assessment, data taking, and system change are at the heart of an individual PBIS plan.

In light of our discussion regarding early childhood teachers' qualifications, it is important to note here that special education early childhood teachers who work in public schools often hold a specialized license, whereas other early childhood educators may not necessarily have equivalent qualifications (Barnett, 2011b). This has created problems with inclusion of children in private, state, or federally funded early childhood programs in which no specialized training or special licensure is necessary for them to be qualified for teaching in early childhood classrooms.

Teaching and Assessment in Early Childhood Education

The curriculum and assessment practices of today's classroom have roots in the disparate interpretations and offerings of our past notions of the best interests of the child, beliefs that continue to shape the landscape of practice today: Childcare as women's work in the home, childcare for only the working poor, childcare and education to offer benefit to those perceived as in need of intervention due to perceived economic disadvantage (cf. Giardiello, 2014; Goffin, 2001; Morrison, 2015).

Beginning in the Great Depression and continuing through World War II, the childcare industry surged forward to serve the families with preschoolers and working mothers, a tradition with roots in practices from the times of the Industrial Revolution. Curriculum continued to be a play-based approach with teachers from varying backgrounds. A parallel system of nursery school and childcare centers continued for middle-class children, which continues today. However, a systematic nationwide approach to compensatory childcare began 50 years ago – forever changing the landscape of early childhood education through the research on curriculum effect that followed. The change came as part of President Lyndon B. Johnson's social agenda legislation.

Compensatory Education

In 1964, President Lyndon B. Johnson declared a War on Poverty, in his presidential address. For young children, "This is a very proud occasion ... for us today, because it was less than 3 months ago that we opened a new war front on poverty. We set out to make certain that poverty's children would not be forevermore poverty's captives. We called our program Project Head Start" (Johnson, 1965). Project Head Start began as did the compensatory education of young children living at economic disadvantage. Also, the Elementary and Secondary Education Act (ESEA) of 1965 provided for special assistance in the primary grades to teach reading to children in small groups. To prove the efficacy of the intervention, pre and post testing of the children in primary classrooms was required. Thus, the formal assessment of young children with standardized instruments fueled the development of ever more standardized tests. In spite of the efforts made for compensatory education, an achievement gap persists between social classes and across various ethnic groups. Efforts to cure this gap resulted in a variation of curricular approaches, largely moving toward more directed teaching, corresponding with less interest in a play-based curriculum.

Head Start Model Curricula

An exception to this move toward directed teaching in the preschool years occurred with the systematic trial of curricular models in Head Start (Head Start Information Services, 1971). One of the surviving models is the HighScope approach that is based on a Piagetian view of child development (Epstein & Hohmann, 2012; cf. Barnett, 1995). This model includes a project-based view of curriculum and a coordinated assessment system matched to the teaching approach. With HighScope and Creative Curriculum (Heroman et al., 2010; cf. Barnett, 1995) as models for preschool curriculum in Head Start, the goals of which are developmentally appropriate practice and an intentional use of a play-based, integrated holistic view of young children, large numbers of young children enjoy a professional approach to their instruction. It is in the childcare world of center-based delivery of care and education that curricular approaches vary widely, with some choosing developmentally appropriate practice and others operating from a hodge-podge mix of often inappropriate workbook and drill-based instruction. In these centers there is often little connection of method of teaching to way of testing outcome accomplishment. It is also in these centers, staffed by teachers with few professional credentials, that individuation of teaching is rarely practiced and children who do not conform or comply are punished and finally expelled. Thus, it is in the preschool years that curriculum varies widely for young children. And in infant/toddler programs, the approach to teaching and learning is even more widely varied.

Emergence of Infant/Toddler Childcare

With the exception of Early Head Start and other publicly funded infant/toddler programs – largely those serving special populations of infants and toddlers – such as those directed toward variously defined "at risk" for academic failure, infant/toddler curriculum is delivered by teachers with few professional credentials. Caregivers in these programs often see their work as "babysitting" rather than education. They practice care of babies, as they would care at home, reflecting their personal values of child-rearing techniques rather than being influenced by the theories of developmentally appropriate practice. Therefore, the curriculum in this age range is often custodial rather than educational. Teachers are frequently paid low wages and the self-esteem of the "workers" in the field is often low, which influences the way in which they interact with the babies and toddlers in their care. It is here, then, that many early signs of possible mental health issues in young children are often overlooked, behavioral issues are treated harshly, and young children begin a journey to "maladjustment." The problem of inappropriate curriculum is particularly critical since infant/toddler care is the fastest growing market in the childcare industry, since the rise of mothers in the workforce is continuing to increase (Bureau of Labor Statistics, 2010). So, in the first five years of life, when children are the most vulnerable, and the most eager to learn, early care and educational experiences are highly varied, depending on the individual center and regulated mostly by state agencies. The QRIS is an effort by many states to regulate childcare and to improve quality. With these efforts, the professionalization of childcare teachers is a key component. Turning now to the upper age range of the early childhood years (ages five to eight), the practice of teaching and learning is largely governed by the public school system.

Curriculum in the Primary Years

In these, the primary years, teachers hold professional licenses – though not always in early childhood education – more commonly in elementary education (K–8). While the early history of kindergarten, often optional in many states, focused on a curriculum of social development through play-based activities as in preschool, from the dawn of the compensatory efforts to mend the achievement gap, the public school pushed down academic curriculum to the primary years, resulting in directed teaching of academic content and a reduction of holistic, integrated, inquiry-based curriculum. Rather than learning centers and long periods for exploratory learning, the primary years have a textbook-directed, worksheet emphasis on those subjects that are tested and reported to the public as measures of educational attainment – namely reading and mathematics scores.

The emphasis on outcomes assessment of academic accomplishment was heightened in 2001 with the passage of No Child Left Behind, which dictated outcome-based testing of *all* children, beginning at third grade. States were forced to comply with this assessment practice in order to maintain eligibility for federal funds for all school programs. What had begun in the 60s with the War on Poverty (Johnson, 1965) as a testing of children at economic disadvantage, became *the* approach to push outcome-based educational goals that would once and for all "cure" the achievement gap. Some 12 years later, schools still grapple with the achievement gap and the curricular emphasis is narrowed to a focus on mathematics and literacy, leaving social studies, science, and the arts sitting beside the road and curriculum across the nation varying from district to district and state to state. Enter the National Governors Association and the Council of Chief School Officers (2010) with a solution to this dilemma and the formulation of the Common Core State Standards (CCSS).

Common Core State Standards

The CCSS or the Common Core is an approach to curriculum that will produce a critical thinking and problem-solving, college-ready, career-ready child. The hoped-for result of the Common Core is a standardization of curricular outcomes while preserving various curricular approaches across the nation. Most states have followed the Common Core with the development of state-level interpretations of the Mathematics and English Language Arts Standards, which are the two areas that will be assessed, beginning in 2014. Two contractors are developing the assessment schemes for states: PARCC and Smarter Balanced. States chose one of the two consortia or pledged to develop their own systems of assessment. While math and ELA are the early focus for assessment, science and social studies standards are in the works and will no doubt be assessed in similar outcomes-based standardized schemes. The effect on curriculum in the primary grades remains to be seen; however, at present, most schools continue to concentrate on the directed teaching of math and literacy using drill and practice as precursors of "the test" at third grade. Curriculum in the primary years is thus, varied from school to school and often, at least in the public system, teacher directed with the emphasis on "in-seat" behavior and attention to paper and pencil tasks predominating. For young children needing individualization of instruction, the teaching practices vary. This is in spite of the inclusionary practices outlined by IDEA (2004). It is the child who talks out and acts out or who sits aside without participating who creates compliance "problems" in the paper and pencil classroom of today's primary class.

Closing Remarks

In this discussion of teaching and learning, that is, curriculum, I have outlined the issues that influence teaching practices in early childhood. In the best situations, young children access a child-centered and appropriately individualized situation where challenging behaviors are treated as developmental issues to be solved and resolved. In the worst situations, young children are often humiliated, punished, and driven further into the maladaptive solutions for coping with an educational world that demands compliance to a narrowly constructed, overly interpreted outcomes-based instruction.

References

Achenbach, T. M. (1978). The child behavior profile: I. boys aged 6–11. *Journal of Consulting and Clinical Psychology, 46*(3), 478–488.

Americans with Disabilities Act, 42 U.S.C. § 12101 (1990).

Anthony, B., Anthony, L., Morrel, T., & Acosta, M. (2005). Evidence for social and behavior problems in low-income, urban preschoolers: Effects of site, classroom, and teacher. *Journal of Youth and Adolescence, 34*(1), 31–39.

Barned, N. E., Knapp, N. F., & Neuharth-Pritchett, S. (2011). Knowledge and attitudes of early childhood preservice teachers regarding the inclusion of children with Autism Spectrum Disorder. *Journal of Early Childhood Teacher Education, 32*(4), 302–321.

Barnett, W. S. (1995). Long-term effects of early childhood programs on cognitive and school outcomes. *The Future of Children, 5*(3), 25–50.

Barnett, W. S. (2011a). Minimum requirements for preschool teacher educational qualifications. In E. Zigler, W. S. Gilliam, & W. S. Barnett (Eds.), *The pre-K debates: Current controversies and issues* (pp. 48-54). Baltimore, MD: Paul H. Brookes Publishing Co.

Barnett, W. S. (2011b). Preschool education as an educational reform: Issues of effectiveness and access. National Institute for Early Education Research. Retrieved from: http://nieer.org/sites/nieer/files/NRC%20Preschool%20Report%20Rev%209%2026%2011.pdf

Barnett, W. S., Friedman, A., Hustedt, J., & Stevenson-Boyd, J. (2009). An overview of prekindergarten policy in the United States: Program governance, eligibility, standards, and finance. In R. Pianta & C. Howes (Eds.), *The promise of pre-K* (pp. 3–30). Baltimore, MD: Paul H. Brookes Publishing Co.

Beyer, T., Postert, C., Muller, J., & Furniss, T. (2012). Prognosis and continuity of child mental health problems from preschool to primary school: Results of a four-year longitudinal study. *Child Psychiatry and Human Development, 43*(4), 533–543.

Bowlby, J. (1969). *Attachment and loss, Vol. 1: Attachment.* New York: Basic Books.

Bowlby, J. (1973). *Attachment and loss, Vol. 2: Separation.* New York: Basic Books.

Bowlby, J. (1980). *Attachment and loss, Vol. 3: Loss, sadness and depression.* New York: Basic Books.

Bowman, B. T. (2011). Bachelor's degrees are necessary but not sufficient: Preparing teachers to teach young children. In E. Zigler, W. S. Gilliam, & W. S. Barnett (Eds.), *The pre-K debates: Current controversies and issues* (pp. 54–57). Baltimore, MD: Paul H. Brookes Publishing Co.

Bretherton, I. (1992). The origins of attachment theory: John Bowlby and Mary Ainsworth. *Developmental Psychology, 28*(5), 759–775.

Brown, W. H., & Conroy, M. A. (2011). Social-emotional competence in young children with developmental delays: Our reflection and vision for the future. *Journal of Early Intervention, 33*(4), 310–320.

Bureau of Labor Statistics, U.S. Department of Labor. (2010). *The Editor's Desk,* Labor force participation rates among mothers. Retrieved from: http://www.bls.gov/opub/ted/2010/ted_20100507.htm

Bureau of Labor Statistics, U.S. Department of Labor. (2013). *Occupational outlook handbook* (2012–13 ed.). Retrieved from: http://www.bls.gov/ooh/

Campbell, S. B. (1990). *Behavior problems in preschool children: Clinical and developmental issues.* New York: Guilford Press.

Campbell, S. B., Shaw, D. S., & Gilliom, M. (2000). Early externalizing behavior problems: Toddlers and preschoolers at risk for later maladjustment. *Development and Psychopathology, 12*(3), 467–488.

Carter, A. S., Briggs-Gowan, M. J., & Davis, N. O. (2004). Assessment of young children's social-emotional development and psychopathology: Recent advances and recommendations for practice. *Journal of Child Psychology and Psychiatry, 45*(1), 109–134.

Cavanaugh, D. A., Lippitt, J., & Moyo, O. (2000). *Resource guide to selected federal policies affecting children's social and emotional development and their readiness for school.* Waltham, MA: Brandeis University.

Center for the Child Care Workforce. (2011). Hourly wages for child care workers and preschool teachers. Retrieved from: http://www.ccw.org/storage/ccworkforce/documents/rankings%20side%20by%20side.pdf

Child Trends. (2014). How parents make child care decisions. Retrieved from: http://www.childtrends.org/how-parents-make-child-care-decisions/

Cicchetti, D., & Cohen, D. J. (1995). Perspectives on developmental psychopathology. In D. Cicchetti & D. J. Cohen (Eds.), *Developmental psychopathology: Vol. 1. Theory and methods* (pp. 3–20). New York: Wiley.

Cicchetti, D., & Richters, J. E. (1993). Developmental considerations in the investigation of conduct disorder. *Development and Psychopathology, 5*(1–2), 331–344.

Cook, B. G., Cameron, D. L., & Tankersley, M. (2007). Inclusive teachers' rating of their students with disabilities. *Journal of Special Education, 40*(4), 230–239.

Copple, C., & Bredekamp, S. (Eds.) (2009). *Developmentally appropriate practice in early childhood programs: Serving children from birth through age 8* (3rd ed.). Washington, DC: National Association for the Education of Young Children (NAEYC).

Cunningham, A. E., Zibulsky, J., & Callahan, M. D. (2009). Starting small: Building preschool teacher knowledge that supports early literacy development. *Reading and Writing: An Interdisciplinary Journal, 22,* 487–510.

DEC/NAEYC. (2009). *Early childhood inclusion: A joint position statement of the Division for Early Childhood (DEC) and the National Association of the Education of Young Children (NAEYC).* Chapel Hill, NC: The University of North Carolina, FPG Child Development Institute.

Dunlap, G., Strain, P. S., Fox, L., Carta, J. J., Conroy, M., Smith, B. J., ... Sowell, C. (2006). Prevention and intervention with young children's challenging behavior: Perspectives regarding current knowledge. *Behavioral Disorders, 32*(1), 29–45.

Epstein, A. S., & Hohmann, M. (2012). *The HighScope Preschool Curriculum.* Ypsilanti, MI: HighScope.

Erikson, E. H. (1968). *Identity: Youth and crisis.* New York: W.W. Norton.

Fergusson, D. M., Lynskey, M. T., & Horwood, L. J. (1996). Factors associated with continuity and changes in disruptive behavior patterns between childhood and adolescence. *Journal of Abnormal Child Psychology, 24*(5), 533–553.

Fox, L., Carta, J., Strain, P., Dunlap, G., & Hemmeter, M. L. (2010). Response to intervention and the pyramid model. *Infants & Young Children, 23*(1), 3–13.

Fox, L., & Hemmeter, M. L. (2009). A program-wide model for supporting social-emotional development and addressing challenging behavior in early childhood settings. In W. Sailor, G. Dunlap, G. Sugai, & R. Horner (Eds.), *Handbook of positive behavior support* (pp. 177–202). New York: Springer.

Fuller, B. (2011). College credentials and caring: How teacher training could lift young children. In E. Zigler, W. S. Gilliam, & W. S. Barnett (Eds.), *The pre-K debates: Current controversies and issues* (pp. 57–64). Baltimore, MD: Paul H. Brookes Publishing Co.

Gable, S. (2014). *The states of child care: Building a better system.* New York, NY: Teachers College Press.

Gal, E., Schreur, N., & Engel-Yeger, B. (2010). Inclusion of children with disabilities: Teacher's attitudes and requirements for environmental accommodations. *International Journal of Special Education, 25*(2), 89–99.

Galinsky, E. (2006). The economic benefits of high-quality early childhood programs: What makes the difference? Retrieved from: http://familiesandwork.org/site/research/reports/ced.pdf

Gardner, F., Connell, A., Trentacosta, C., Shaw, D., Dishion, T., & Wilson, M. (2009). Moderators of outcome in a brief family-centered intervention for preventing early problem behavior. *Journal of Consulting and Clinical Psychology, 77*(3), 543–553.

Gebbie, D. H., Ceglowski, D., Taylor, L. K., & Miels, J. (2012). The role of teacher efficacy in strengthening classroom support for preschool children with disabilities who exhibit challenging behaviors. *Early Childhood Education Journal, 40*(1), 35–46.

Giardiello, P. (2014). *Pioneers in early childhood education: The roots and legacies of Rachel and Margaret McMillan, Maria Montessori and Susan Isaacs.* New York: Routledge.

Gilliam, W. S. (2005). Prekindergarteners left behind: Expulsion rates in state prekindergarten programs. Foundation for Child Development: FCD policy brief series No. 3. Retrieved from: http://www.challengingbehavior.org/explore/policy_docs/prek_expulsion.pdf.

Goffin, S. G. (2001). Whither childhood care and education in the next century? In L. Cornlo (Ed.), *Education across a century: The centennial volume* (pp. 140–163). One Hundredth Yearbook of the National Society for the Study of Education Part 1. Chicago: National Society for the Study of Education.

Grue, J. (2011). Discourse analysis and disability: Some topics and issues. *Discourse and Society, 22*(5), 532–546.

Head Start Act, 42 U.S.C. §§ 635-657C (2007).

Head Start Information Services. (1971). *Head Start curriculum models: A reference list* (rev. ed.). Urbana, IL: ERIC Clearinghouse on Early Childhood Education, ED 048947.

Hemmeter, M. L., & Fox, L. (2009). The teaching pyramid: A model for the implementation of classroom practices within a program-wide approach to behavior support. *NHSA Dialog: A Research-to-Practice Journal for the Early Childhood Field, 12*(2), 133–147.

Heroman, C., Trister Dodge, D., Berke, K., Bickart, T., Colker, L., Jones, C., ... Dighe, J. (2010). *The creative curriculum for preschool* (5th ed.). Bethesda, MD: Teaching Strategies, Inc.

Individuals with Disabilities Education Act, 20 U.S.C. § 1400 (1990).

Individuals with Disabilities Education Act, 20 U.S.C. § 1400 (2004).

Johnson, L. B. (1965). Remarks on Head Start, May 18, 1965. Santa Barbara, CA: American Presidency Project Presidential Archives. Retrieved from: http://www.presidency.ucsb.edu/ws/?pid=26973

Kaiser, B., & Rasminsky, J. S. (2012). *Challenging behavior in young children: Understanding, preventing, and responding effectively* (3rd ed.). Upper Saddle River, NJ: Pearson.

Kendall-Taylor, N., & Mikulak, A. (2009). *Child mental health: A review of the scientific discourse – A FrameWorks research report.* Washington, DC: FrameWorks Institute. Retrieved from: http://www.frameworksinstitute.org/assets/files/PDF_childmentalhealth/childmentalhealthreview.pdf

Lillas, C., & Turnbull, J. (2009). *Infant/child mental health, early intervention, and relationship-based therapies: A neurorelational framework for interdisciplinary practice.* New York: W.W. Norton.

Llewellyn, A., & Hogan, K. (2000). The use and abuse of models of disability. *Disability & Society, 15*(1), 157–165.

Lyons, C. W., & O'Connor, F. (2006). Constructing an integrated model of the nature of challenging behaviour: A starting point for intervention. *Emotional and Behavioural Difficulties, 11*(3), 217–232.

Marsala, C., & Petretto, D. R. (2010). *Models of disability.* University at Buffalo, State University of New York: Center for International Rehabilitation Research Information and Exchange (CIRRIE).

Mikami, A. Y., Griggs, M. S., Lerner, M. D., Emeh, C. C., Reuland, M. M., Jack, A., & Anthony, M. R. (2012). A randomized trial of a classroom intervention to increase peers' social inclusion of children with Attention-Deficit/Hyperactivity Disorder. *Journal of Consulting and Clinical Psychology, 81*(1), 100–112.

Moffitt, T. E., Caspi, A., Dickson, N., Silva, P., & Stanton, W. (1996). Childhood-onset versus adolescent-onset antisocial conduct problems in males: Natural history from ages 3 to 18. *Development and Psychopathology, 8*(2), 399–424.

Morrison, G. S. (2015). *Early childhood education today* (13th ed.). Upper Saddle River, NJ: Pearson.

National Association for the Education of Young Children. (1996). Developmentally appropriate practice in early childhood programs serving children from birth through age 8: A position statement of the National Association for the Education of Young Children. Washington, DC: National Association for the Education of Young Children (NAEYC).

National Governors Association. (2010). *Draft K-12 Common Core state standards available for comment.* Retrieved from: http://www.nga.org/cms/home/news-room/news-releases/page_2010/col2-content/main-content-list/title_draft-k-12-common-core-state-standards-available-for-comment.html

National Scientific Council on the Developing Child. (2008). Mental health problems in early childhood can impair learning and behavior for life: Working paper #6. Retrieved from: http://www.developingchild.net

Nutbrown, C., & Clough, P. (2004). Inclusion and exclusion in the early years: Conversations with European educators. *European Journal of Special Needs Education, 19*(3), 301–315.

Pastor, P. N., Reuben, C. A., & Duran, C. R. (2012). Identifying emotional and behavioral problems in children aged 4–17 years: United States, 2001–2007. *National health statistics reports, no 48.* Hyattsville, MD: National Center for Health Statistics.

Pianta, R. C. (2011). A degree is not enough: Teachers need stronger and more individualized professional development supports to be effective in the classroom. In E. Zigler, W. S.

Gilliam, & W. S. Barnett (Eds.), *The pre-K debates: Current controversies and issues* (pp. 64–68). Baltimore, MD: Paul H. Brookes Publishing Co.

Powell, D., Fixsen, D., Dunlap, G., Smith, B., & Fox, L. (2007). A synthesis of knowledge relevant to pathways of service delivery for young children with or at risk of challenging behavior. *Journal of Early Intervention, 29*(2), 81–106.

Quality Rating and Improvement System. (2011). *A Foundation for Quality Improvement Systems: State Licensing, Preschool, and QRIS Program Quality Standards.* Retrieved from: http://qrisnetwork.org/sites/all/files/resources/gscobb/2012-03-19%2012%3A52/Report.pdf

Raver, C. C., & Knitze, J. (2002). Ready to enter: What research tells policymakers about strategies to promote social and emotional school readiness among three- and four-year-old children (NCCP Policy paper No. 3). New York: Columbia University Mailman School of Public Health.

Ringwalt, S. (2012). Summary table of states' and territories' definitions of/criteria for IDEA Part C eligibility. National Early Childhood Technical Assistance Center. Retrieved from: http://www.nectac.org/~pdfs/topics/earlyid/partc_elig_table.pdf

Sobanski, E., Banaschewski, T., Asherson, P., Buitelaar, J., Chen, W., Franke, B., ... Faraone, S. V. (2010). Emotional lability in children and adolescents with attention deficit/hyperactivity disorder (ADHD): Clinical correlates and familial prevalence. *Journal of Child Psychology and Psychiatry, 51*(8), 915–923.

Turnbull, H. R., Stowe, M., Klein, S., & Riffel, B. (2012). Matrix of key federal statutes and federal and state court decisions reflecting the core concepts of disability policy. *Beach Center on Disability.* Retrieved from: http://files.eric.ed.gov/fulltext/ED534423.pdf

Union of the Physically Impaired Against Segregation (UPIAS). (1976). *The fundamental principles of disability.* London: UPIAS.

U.S. Department of Health and Human Services. (2008). *Statutory degree and credentialing requirements for Head Start teaching staff* (ACF-IM-HS-08-12). Retrieved from: http://eclkc.ohs.acf.hhs.gov/hslc/standards/IMs_and_PIs_in_PDF/PDF_IMs/IM2011/ACF-IM-HS-11-03.pdf

Williams, M. E., Perrigo, J. L., Banda, T. Y., Matic, T., & Goldfarb, F. D. (2013). Barriers to Accessing Services for Young Children. *Journal of Early Intervention, 35*(1), 61–74.

Zeanah, P., Stafford, B., Nagle, G., & Rice, T. (2005). Addressing social-emotional development and infant mental health in early childhood systems. *Building State Early Childhood Comprehensive System Series,* no. 12. Los Angeles, CA: National Center for Infant and Early Childhood Health Policy.

Zeanah, C., & Zeanah, P. (2001). Towards a definition of infant mental health. *Zero to Three, 22,* 13–20.

Zigler, E., Gilliam, W. S., & Barnett, W. S. (Eds.). (2011). *The pre-K debates: Current controversies and issues.* Baltimore, MD: Paul H. Brookes Publishing Co.

2

EARLY RELATIONSHIPS

Foundations of Early Childhood Mental Health

In every nursery there are ghosts. They are the visitors from the unremembered past of the parents, the uninvited guests at the christening. Under all favorable circumstances the unfriendly and unbidden spirits are banished from the nursery and return to their subterranean dwelling place. The baby makes his own imperative claim upon parental love, and ... the bonds of love protect the child and his parents against the intruders, the malevolent ghosts.

(Fraiberg, Adelson, & Shapiro, 1975, p. 387)

This quote from Fraiberg's seminal and well-known work, *Ghosts in the Nursery*, began the first chapter in infant mental health. In fact, the term *infant mental health (IMH)* is attributed to Fraiberg, who along with her colleagues – a group of social workers and psychologists – established a clinical program called the Child Development Project, for parents and children from birth to age 3 in Ann Arbor, Michigan in the 1970s. Fraiberg's clinic was unique for its time, as specialists in her project worked with parents and infants together in the infant's home in order to understand the relationship dynamics between the parent and the child, and the capacities of the family (Weatherston, 2000). This kind of home visit/therapy session had never been done. Along with earlier research by Bowlby (1969) and Ainsworth (1979), Fraiberg's clinical work drew attention to two important factors: 1) an infant's development is influenced by early relationships that are formed between the primary caregiver and the child, and 2) the caregiver's behaviors toward the child (which might be influenced by the caregiver's own mental health status) is the catalyst for the quality of that relationship, which in turn shapes and influences the child's own mental health.

From the 1980s until the present, the field of IMH has attracted attention from psychoanalyst scholars and practitioners, and more recently from neuroscientists (neurobiologists and neuropsychologists in particular) – and has grown to a prominent field of research and practice with world-renowned scholars and clinicians. Core concepts and clinical practices in IMH have evolved to define infant mental health as the promotion of healthy social and emotional development of a child from conception through age 5, with their parents, families and other important caregivers (Brandt, 2014). In its most current definition of infant mental health, five ingredients are necessary for healthy mental health and development of all other domains in children: 1) a safe and healthy pregnancy; 2) opportunity and ability to "fall in love" and "be in love" with a nurturing adult; 3) support for learning and self-regulation; 4) support for learning in mutual regulation; and 5) nurturing and developmentally appropriate care (Brandt, 2014). Looking at these ingredients, the importance of the adult–child relationship and the early dyadic experiences of any infant seem quite obvious. In fact, our understanding of infancy and early childhood continues to evolve and grow with research focusing on human interactional factors and the related neurobehavioral influences – early brain architecture and mechanisms and patterns of gene expression – as the child and adults forge and maintain relationships.

In this chapter, I will look at the mechanisms of adult–child relationships and the historical and seminal research in IMH to establish an understanding of the early foundations of mental health in a child.

Who Are Primary Caregivers in the Life of an Infant?

In today's global and diverse societies, biological parents are not the only primary caregivers for children. Understanding who is family and how members relate to each other and function within a unit are complex issues and deserve examinations of pertinent topics. The concept and definition of family structure and function are fluid and changing within each culture as well as globally. For current definitions and details see Chambers, 2012; McKie and Callan, 2012; and Seymour and Walsh, 2013. Today, in most societies, there are many adults who act as primary caregivers of infants, from parents to aunts, uncles, siblings, professional caretakers, and nannies. Family members do not necessarily have to be related by blood, nor do they have to be in a typical structure, such as nuclear or extended (Chambers, 2012). Families of today are units that define themselves as such, whose members care for each other and make commitments to one another (Hanson, Lynch, & Wayman, 1990). As such, I acknowledge and respect this diversity in families' forms and structures, and although much of the traditional and contemporary infant mental health research refers to the *mother* as the primary caregiver of the child, in this and other chapters when I use the term caregiver, father, parent, or mother, I am referring to any figure (biological or non-biological) who provides the primary care for the child on a daily basis.

Attachment Theory and Its History

Bowlby (1969) developed the theory of attachment, based on a series of early studies of how the behavior of a primary caregiver toward an infant could be a direct organizer of the development of the mental health of that child. Bowlby's early research began with an empirical analysis of 44 adolescents' truancy cases in a London clinic (Bowlby, 1944). Bowlby attributed truancy and an observed lack of affection in these adolescents to be linked to shortcomings in their early relationships with their mothers. Therefore, he suggested that by helping parents early on, those shortcomings might be addressed and therefore the child could be helped. Bowlby remained interested in understanding intergenerational attachment behaviors, which formed the foundations of his attachment theory, articulated two decades later.

Bowlby's (1969) ethological attachment theory implies that for a human infant – and indeed for any other species – it is essential to survival to become attached to his primary caregiver. Accordingly, this natural attachment process begins early during the infant's life, when the primary caregiver has been consistently responsive to the infant's bids for attention – which are in addition to the infant's need to be fed or kept dry. According to Bowlby, the primary caregiver's responsiveness to the infant is the key to keeping the infant feeling safe and secure, and therefore preparing the infant for exploration, learning, and healthy development.

Bowlby (1958) described a specific set of attachment behaviors, like crying, smiling, clinging, and following, to be refined in the infant's second six months of life, to bind both the infant and the primary caregiver together. These are behaviors that serve to promote closeness to the caregiver and therefore to promote a feeling of security in the infant. According to this theory, if under some extraordinary circumstances, the caregiver is not able to positively and consistently respond to such behaviors, the infant will not be able to feel secure, and fails to form a secure attachment and establish the necessary healthy foundations for further social-emotional aspects of development. In a trilogy of his work, Bowlby (1973, 1980, 1982) summarized the theory of attachment as a natural process, which takes place when infants form emotional bonds with their primary caregiver(s), also called attachment figure(s), and use a figure as a safe haven, to return to at the times of distress, fear, or uncertainty.

Bowlby explained (1982) that infants are not born with an attachment preference. Nor do they necessarily form attachment to only one person. Rather, depending on the quality and consistency of caregiving from adults who care for the infant, infants select a number of adults to turn to in a hierarchical order: as a primary, secondary, tertiary and so on. In contemporary literature, the attachment figure or the adult primary caregiver is distinguished from ones the child interacts with daily during social engagement and play (Sroufe, Coffino, & Carlson, 2010; Zeanah, Berlin, & Boris, 2011a). Rather this figure is the one the child will turn to selectively at the times of distress to increase proximity when the child needs comfort, protection, nurturance and support (Zeanah et al., 2011a). An increase in the mobility of the toddler motivates her to seek exploration of her surrounding environment and materials. In a healthy attachment process, a toddler displays a balance between a need to explore her environment, and a need to seek proximity to her caregiver to maintain safety and feel secure (Zeanah et al., 2011a).

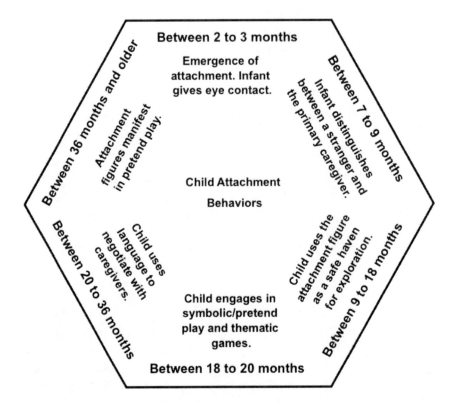

FIGURE 2.1 Attachment Behaviors and Development in Children

Though attachment is formed during the first three years of life, there are specific periods that are key in the formation of attachment. Zeanah and his colleagues (2011a) point to the following developmental periods, which mark certain attachment-related biobehavioral shifts in infants (see Figure 2.1).

Infant's Early Emotional Expressions

Based on evidence from infant brain research, we know that infants are capable of experiencing emotions such as anger and sadness, even earlier than believed by Bowlby and his contemporaries. Between two to three months after birth, infants' cortical brain activity increases drastically. The growth in the frontal lobe begins to show a remarkable activity during the second six months of life (Nakato et al., 2011). This is particularly important in infants' social emotional growth, since the frontal lobe is responsible for activation of emotion, memory and infants' general awareness of the environment. Thus, by six months of age infants are able to clearly recognize their mother's face from faces of strangers (Eliot, 1999; Nakato et al., 2011).

Infants can express simple emotions as early as three months, and begin to express a range of more complex emotions starting around six months (Steele, 2011). Crying is the first mode of the infant's expression of emotions. During the first three months of life, infants communicate their needs evoked by hunger, pain, and fatigue or discomfort through crying. After their first six months, infants are capable of expressing surprise, anger, and sadness as well. Responsiveness to early expressions of emotion, more specifically responding to infants crying during the first year of life is thought to be an important factor in the development of more complex emotions later on in childhood (Steele, 2011).

Responsiveness to crying, however, has historically been a topic of controversy in popular and academic literature. In 1928, Watson wrote *Psychological Care of Infant and Child*, in which he advised parents to feed and care for infants on a rigid schedule. Watson's behavioral approaches, which prescribed a strict adherence to a disciplined parenting, was popular until Benjamin Spock, a pediatrician, began to advocate for a different approach to parenting. In his book, *The Common Sense Book of Baby and Child Care*, Spock (1946) integrated psychoanalysis and pediatrics into a new set of recommendations. He urged parents to trust their own instincts, to respond to their babies according to their infants' needs and demands. Spock believed in the child's inherent goodness, and advocated that children needed a "gentle" and "loving" parenting as much as they needed vitamins and calories (Spock & Parker, 1998, p. 72). Spock's approach to parenting might be considered one of the most influential views of modern parenting. However, a debate regarding early parenting behaviors, such as responsiveness to the infant's cries "on demand," or on a "structured" and set schedule, continues to date. It is important to note here that recommendations which prescribe response to infants on a set schedule often ignore the developmental changes in the infant during the first year of life, or how parental responses may actually influence the infant's behaviors or development of expression of emotions further down the road (Douglas, 2012; St. James-Roberts, 2007).

In general, infants typically cry 10 percent to 20 percent of their waking hours (Steele, 2011). When infants cry longer, there is often an issue, such as sensory processing problems, gastrointestinal problems, asphyxia, or other conditions, which might be labeled as an infant's fussiness (Kheddache & Tadj, 2013). Even when special needs are involved and babies cry more frequently than typically warranted, the caregiver's response to their emotional needs in a way that does not overwhelm or lead to a feeling of neglect promotes an infant's thriving in their optimal capacities (Steele, 2011). Thus, much as Erikson (1950) contended, the caregiver's identification of the source of crying in the infant and responding to the child's needs in a consistent manner during the first three months of life will result in the development of trust.

Neurologically, from ten weeks to three months of age, the limbic system and motor networks of the infant's brain are sufficiently mature for the infants to express simple emotions, like smiling as a result of joy, or crying as a result of discomfort (Klahr, Thomas, Hopwood, Klump, & Burt, 2013). A natural progression of the caregiver's consistent responses to an infant's needs is the infant's continued maturation of emotional expressions, and development of appropriate mental representations of others and self (Steele, 2011). Bowlby (1979) referred to such a mental representation of the caregiver and self, which develops as a result of the way a caregiver responds to the infant, as an internal working model. An internal working model might be, "my parent will always be there if I need her/him and I am worthy of this love." A mental image, however, may not always be positive. For example, if the caregiver's response is sometimes positive and sometimes negative, the child's image of the adult and self may be ambiguous and inconsistent. Alternatively, if the response is completely lacking or is negative, the caregiver's as well as the complementary image of self will undoubtedly be negative.

As the infant's memory becomes refined, she will be capable of showing surprise when her expectations are not met based on her memory – for example, when the caregiver does not act as the infant predicts. In such a case, when an infant's expectation is not met, an expression of anger might follow surprise, and gradually sadness may develop (Steele, 2011). A caregiver's responses to an infant's early anger and sadness are elemental in the development of the child's regulatory system. For example, the caregiver's ability to read the infant's emotional cues and expressions and respond with appropriate body and verbal language could calm and soothe the infant. Such communicative behaviors from the caregiver will be important in establishing the mechanisms of organization and regulation of emotions in the infant (Weinberg & Tronick, 1994).

Developmentally, when infants begin to move they typically look back at the caregiver to make sure they are around to provide safety when needed. Unknown situations create fear in infants, and they often look for cues from the caregiver as to how to respond. Displaying fearful crying at the time of separation would naturally bring the caregiver back. Again, the caregiver's verbal and behavioral responses provide reassurances for the infant that she will be safe, or that the caregiver will come back soon (Steele, 2011). These consistent verbal and non-verbal messages are important not only in emotional regulation, but cognitive and language development. When the caregivers are inconsistent in their messages and behavior, or react negatively to the infant's fearful behaviors or protests, there might be long-term adverse mental effects for the infant (Steele, 2011; Zeanah, Gunnar, McCall, Kreppner, & Fox, 2011b).

Ainsworth, a close collaborator of Bowlby's, believed that the emotional availability of the caregiver and the quality and consistency of her responsiveness would result in a measurable quality of early interactions between the caregiver and the infant. She believed that it is the consistency and quality of the caregiver's responses to the infant that will lead to a *security* or *insecurity* of attachment in the infant. Ainsworth (1979) identified three main attachment styles: secure, insecure avoidant and insecure ambivalent. Ainsworth's research on classification of attachment has led to additional understanding of early healthy emotional development in infants, and to recognition of attachment disorders as a category of a mental health condition.

Classification of Attachment

In the 1950s, during her fieldwork in Kampala, Uganda, Ainsworth observed numerous interactions between infants and their mothers, which confirmed Bowlby's theory (Ainsworth, 1967). Ainsworth's observations of Ugandan babies and their mothers became the foundation for her later work, which resulted in a classification system for observing and assessing the quality of attachment between an infant and his primary caregiver (Ainsworth & Bowlby, 1991). In 1970, Ainsworth and Bell designed a 20-minute laboratory paradigm called Strange Situation Procedure (SSP). In this procedure, an infant of about 12 to 20 months old, a primary caregiver, and a female stranger are observed in a laboratory playroom. During this 20-minute episode, the infant and caregiver are separated for two very brief periods, and the infant is left with the stranger first and completely alone later.

The reaction of the infant during separation from and reunion with her caregiver is the key in determining the quality of attachment in that infant. Ainsworth, Bell, and Stayton (1974) described several characteristics to be important in sensitive caregiving. For example, a caregiver/parent should be conscious of the infant's cues and respond to them consistently. To do so, the caregiver must be able to interpret the infant's cues correctly, and respond to them accordingly. Therefore, sensitive caregiving could determine the quality of attachment that the child and caregiver will have.

Ainsworth (1979) classified attachment quality in a child into three general categories of, A: secure, B: insecure avoidant, and C: insecure resistant.

A. A child with a *secure attachment* uses his primary caregiver as a safe haven from which he explores his environment readily. He shows distress at the time of separation, and seeks comfort, resolves his distress, and resumes exploration after reunion with his caregiver.

B. A child with an *avoidant attachment* shows minimal response during separation from his caregiver, and avoids contact or ignores the caregiver at the time of reunion. In preschool, such a child may avoid conversations or group activities, or she might show inhibited affect.

C. A child with a *resistant* or *ambivalent attachment* shows intense distress during separation, and at the time of reunion he might become resistant or unable to use the caregiver to find comfort, or be rather difficult to soothe. In preschool, such a child may be passive or have immature behaviors, or display anger toward adults (Breidenstine, Bailey, Zeanah, & Larrieu, 2011).

In assessing the quality of attachment in a group of older children who had grown up in high-risk environments, Main & Soloman (1986) added a fourth category of attachment quality, a D category, *disorganized attachment*, to Ainsworth's original classification. A child categorized as having a disorganized attachment seems to have many qualities of insecurity, but also lacks an organized behavioral strategy for exploration or checking back, seeking proximity, etc. For example, this child may display a mixture of proximity seeking, avoidant and resistant, sometimes fearful, frozen behaviors, and even controlling behaviors toward the caregiver. Such behaviors usually indicate that the child is unable to seek comfort and security from the caregiver. Although many disorganized infants may go on to show organized patterns of attachment behaviors by the end of early childhood, some seem to continue to have problems even in adulthood. Thus, clinicians and scholars agree that observing disorganized attachment behaviors in a child raises concerns as a predictor of possible mental health problems in later years (Rutter, Kreppner, & Sonuga-Barke, 2009; Steele, 2011; Zeanah et al., 2011b).

Atypical Attachment Behaviors

In 1992, Cassidy, Marvin, and the MacArthur Working Group designed a modified version of Ainsworth and Bell's SSP (1970) to be used for older, preschool children. They found a category corresponding to D: disorganized attachment, and labeled it as *insecure other*. Children with insecure other attachment have many qualities of insecurity. For example, they may display some disorganized behaviors, but they would also have some behavioral qualities that are not necessarily observed in children classified in the categories of A, B, C, or D. The "insecure other" category has been found particularly helpful in studying atypical attachment behaviors, observed in children who are reared in institutions, or under severe emotional and material deprivation, such as those who grew up in Eastern European orphanages in the 1980s.

Effects of Emotional Deprivation on Infants

In 1989, after the fall of the communist government in Romania, a large number of institutionalized orphans were discovered to have lived under grave neglectful and abusive conditions. Following the dismantling of the communist regime, a great number of these orphans were adopted by families in Western Europe. Because these children showed clear signs of cognitive, physical, and social emotional delays, studying their development became a subject of interest in years to follow (for examples see Chisholm, 1998; Chisholm, Carter, Ames, & Morison, 1995). In studying Romanian adoptees, researchers observed some non-normative patterns of attachment behaviors, which did not fit in either A, B, C, or D categories (Kreppner, Rutter, Marvin, O'Connor & Sonuga-Barke, 2011). These children were unable to regulate their emotions, were hyperactive, or acted silly and sometimes disorganized (Rutter et al., 2009). Initially the category of 'insecure other' was used to refer to the patterns of attachment observed in these children. At the same time, other studies, which compared institutionalized children being raised in the UK with the Romanian adoptees, helped scholars understand atypical attachment behaviors in the

Romanian adoptees. Children who were raised in institutions in the UK and adopted did not show the same atypical attachment behaviors as the Romanian adoptees. Accordingly, serious attachment problems as those observed in the Romanian adoptees were identified as *reactive attachment disorders* (O'Connor, Rutter, & English and Romanian Adoptees Study Team, 2000).

The combination of these studies helped distinguish organized (secure/insecure) from disorganized patterns of attachment behaviors as well as the condition of attachment disorders in children. In terms of behavioral characteristics of Romanian adoptees with attachment disorders, for example, some of these children would go away with strangers, did not check back with their adoptive parents in anxiety-provoking situations even after having lived with them for more than a year, and generally showed no differentiation between a stranger and their adoptive parents (Chisholm, 1998; Chisholm et al., 1995). The implication for this observation was that for a child to be identified as securely or insecurely attached to a caregiver, the child first had to have formed some selective attachment with that caregiver. However, it is also possible that under certain circumstances, a child is not able to form any attachment to an adult. This usually occurs in highly neglectful caregiving situations. Under such conditions it is most likely that in reaction to the severe neglect, the child would fail to develop committed and intimate social relationships with an adult, which in turn would indicate an attachment disorder (Rutter et al., 2009).

In considering attachment theory, one question remains: How can one promote healthy development through early interactions and relationship building with an infant? The attachment theorists may uniformly answer that the key to the development of a healthy attachment between an infant and a caregiver is *sensitive caregiving* or *emotional availability*. Some might argue that for a caregiver to be emotionally available, it is enough to "be there" and respond consistently. However, the essence of emotional availability and sensitive caregiving is more than being simply present.

Ainsworth et al. (1974) described several characteristics important to being a sensitive caregiver. For example, a caregiver should be vigilant in answering the infant's calls. To do so, the caregiver must be able to interpret the infant's cues correctly, and respond to them accordingly and successfully. Emde, an infant mental health scholar in the U.S., has studied the dynamics of caregiver and infant interactions. In one of his early studies with a colleague (Sorce & Emde, 1981), he demonstrated that when a parent was physically present, but gave signals of being unavailable emotionally, for example was reading a paper, did not give eye contact, or did not interact physically, vocally, or affectively with the infant – the infant stopped smiling or vocalizing, and did not explore the environment. Sorce and Emde (1981) noted that the key feature of a caregiver's availability is that the caregiver is willing to respond to the infant on an emotional level. In fact, they believed that infants who had caregivers who were emotionally unavailable appeared to give up on social interactions altogether.

Thus, attachment theory can be considered as the *parent* of the current concepts and models in the field of early childhood mental health, in which the infant's *relatedness* to others, and more particularly to an adult caregiver, is at the core (Emde, 2011). Let us now turn our attention to the issue of social-emotional competence in children, and some theories of child development in which healthy relationship and neurobiology of the child are the central foci, as well as the catalyst for development in all other areas.

Importance of Social-Emotional Competence in Early Childhood

Early childhood education scholars use the concept of *social-emotional competence* to describe a set of skills that are pre-requisite to academic skills and success in early childhood classrooms (Hollingsworth, 2013; Rhoades, Warren, Domitrovich, & Greenberg, 2011; Roisman & Fraley, 2012). Social-emotional competence consists of a series of cognitive behavioral skills related to both intrapersonal and interpersonal emotional development that prompts appropriate social reactions to people and events in different environmental contexts.

Emotional competence involves the child's ability to understand the feelings of self and others, express and regulate emotions, so that the child is able to monitor, evaluate, and modify his emotions as needed and according to situations (Rose-Krasnor & Denham, 2009). Social competence involves the child's self-regulation abilities in terms of having positive engagements and effective interactions, communications, and relationships with others (Denham, 2006; Rose-Krasnor & Denham, 2009). Socially competent children are able to form and maintain friendships, are self-reliant, are assertive and have empathy, and therefore may be helpful when needed.

Social-emotional competence not only forms the foundations for school readiness in kindergarten – for example sitting, listening, cooperating and problem solving with classmates and adults, but also is a significant factor that in the long run promotes the academic success of the child (Landy, 2009; Roisman & Fraley, 2012; Rhoades et al., 2011). Social-emotional competence also plays a strong role in a child's quality of life. Without it a child will not be able to successfully navigate interactions with peers and others in social contexts, achieve personal goals, and therefore function positively and successfully in his home, school, and community (Brown & Conroy, 2011; Buysee, Goldman, West, & Hollingsworth, 2008; Landy, 2009; Guralnick, 2010). Thus, collectively, social and emotional competence involve an interconnected set of skills that enable the child to identify and regulate his own and others' emotions, interact appropriately, and form relationships within the context of the immediate environment as well as in the culture and society. Social-emotional competence is directly linked to early relationship development between a child and adult. However, the question remains: How would early dyadic relationships contribute to the developmental mechanisms that underlie learning skills that might later lead to the emotional intelligence of a child?

Relationship-Based Models of Child Development

Building on attachment theory, later models of development are also concerned with mechanisms of dyadic relationships between an infant and an adult. These models are known as *relationship-based models of child development*. There are several notable relationship-based theories, such as transactional model (Sameroff & Chandler, 1975), mutual regulation model (Tronick, 2007), and Greenspan and Thorndike's (1985) stage theory of emotional development. These models contend that a child's development takes place within an interplay between several elements including: parental/caregiving behaviors, infant's own behavior – which in turn relates to the child's neurobiological and psychobiological characteristics – and environmental factors – cultural values and practices, as well as situational risks, such as the family's socio-economic status, neighborhoods, etc.

One common element in relationship-based models of development is that they acknowledge that the child's neurobiological functioning is a determining factor in the child's emotional regulation capacities. In fact, certain neurologically related mechanisms and functions in the infant's brain form the basis of social-emotional, cognitive and behavioral development in children. Lillas and Turnbull (2009) describe four important bioneurological systems including:

1. *Regulation system*, which is responsible for various states of alertness, and infants' responses to stress and bodily signals, and energy regulation. The regulation system is fundamental to human behavioral responses.
2. *Sensory processing system*, such as sensory integration: the individual's sensitivities to sensory stimuli, such as sight, sound, taste, touch, motion, and balance, and processing of this sensory information. The sensory system is central to one's behavioral responses to information.
3. *Executive system*, which is related to attention, learning, coordination of motor action and responses, goal orientation, as well as activation and inhibition of behavior as related to emotions and thoughts. The executive function enables the individual to balance thoughts and emotions, and control her behavior as related to self and others to achieve goals.
4. *Other brain mechanisms* include those that are involved in memory and cognition, motivation, positive and negative emotions, and development of individual and shared meaning making. Besides neurological functioning issues, contemporary relationship studies consider emotional regulation and temperament.

Temperament and Emotional Regulation

Prior to the surge of infant brain studies in the 1980s, theories of temperament and personality development dominated studies of child mental health and emotional development. Temperament, the way the baby approaches the world, easily, actively, or cautiously, consists of several inherent capacities of an individual, which develop into different structures of personality and psychological outcomes (Kagan & Snidman, 1991).

In a classic longitudinal study that began in 1956 and was published in 1977, Thomas and Chess studied a group of 133 children in 84 New York families. They looked at nine different characteristics of children. These characteristics included level and extent of motor activity; regularity of different functions, such as eating, sleeping and wakefulness; responses (withdrawal or approach) to new objects or persons; adaptability to change; sensitivity to stimuli; energy level; the child's quality of mood or disposition; the child's distractibility from what he is doing; and the child's attention span and persistence.

According to their ratings of these characteristics, Thomas and Chess (1977) presented a typology of children's temperament into three distinct categories: 1) the *easy child*, who adapts to stimuli, routine, schedule, and people easily; 2) the *slow to warm-up child*, who has a relatively low activity level and tends to be slower in adapting to the new environment and stimuli as compared to the easy child; and 3) the *difficult child*, who generally has a high intensity reaction to stimuli, has a tendency to withdraw, and might have a general negativity in mood.

Thomas and Chess acknowledged that a child's temperament being either "difficult" or "easy" could be influenced by parental behaviors, which are in turn driven from cultural values and attitudinal factors. They used the term *goodness of fit* to describe the fit of parental behaviors against the child's behaviors and temperament. Thomas and Chess' (1977) study is the most seminal study in child psychology.

In later years, scholars began to look at temperament not as a trait, but rather as an emotional regulation capacity. The idea of emotional regularity drew on the results of infant brain sensory processing research ongoing during the same period. In one of the first emotional regulation/temperament studies, Goldsmith and Campos (1982) described temperament as individual differences in primary emotions, such as joy and anger. Following their lead, additional studies began to elaborate on the concept of emotional regulation and its distinction from primary emotions. For example, although the experience of an emotion and emotional regulation may both occur at the same time, the capacity for emotional regulation depends on existing neurobiological processes in the individual, like the swiftness of cortical responses to an event in the brain (Campos, Frankel, & Camras, 2004).

Rothbart and Bates (1998) developed one of the most influential modern theories of temperament and regulation, linking temperament to intentional neurobiological processes. They described temperament along two large dimensions of *reactivity* and *self-regulation*. Rothbart and Bates noted that reactivity is present at birth and is most notable through the infant's physiological reactions to sensory stimuli. On the other hand, self-regulation is related to attention and motor control. Self-regulation emerges gradually around the first year and continues through preschool and early childhood. Both reactivity and self-regulation are related to neuronal processes in affective, autonomic nervous systems, and the executive functioning of the brain – which are linked to attention and inhibitory control (Rothbart & Bates, 2006).

They noted three narrower dimensions in temperament: 1) surgency or extraversion, such as positive anticipation and sensation seeking; 2) negative affectivity, such as fear, frustration, and anger; and 3) effortful control, such as inhibition, attention, and focus.

In sum, Rothbart and Bates' model of temperament (1998) views the infant as highly reactive to stimuli. The infant's behavior gradually becomes complex and controlled during early childhood, as influenced by the regulatory process. It is important to note here that the relationship-based models of development build on this and other similar research, in which emotional experiences and regulation depend on neurobiological processes and developmental capabilities.

Transactional Model of Development

In this model, developed by Sameroff and Chandler in 1975, how a child turns out is not a function of an infant's individuality, nor is it purely based on the infant's experiences. Rather, the transactional model looks at development as a dynamic and continuous process, which depends on the interactions at multiple levels concerning the child and his experiences. A child's individuality includes any inherent neurological and biological capacities, and developmental needs or possible problems. On the other hand, the child's experiences are influenced by the child's family's individuality, cultural and societal context, and other environmental factors, such as risk elements. According to this model, even in cases of developmental special needs, any child's outcome depends on that particular child's interactions with other ongoing experiences, such as familial, cultural, material, and environmental.

For example, a child with a cognitive delay would have poor cognitive and language developmental outcomes if the child grows up in a family dealing with poverty and lack of material resources, or if the primary caregiver of the child has mental health problems such as anxiety or depression. The same child with special needs might have a different developmental outcome if she grows up in a family in which she receives regular healthy emotional and cognitive stimulations. Thus, in a transactional model, developmental achievements are not unidirectional. Development is not the function of a caregiver/family environment alone, nor is it the function of a child alone. Rather development is a bidirectional process.

To understand this model further, unlike the attachment theory in which the caregiver's sensitivity is the reason behind security or insecurity in the child, in the transactional model the child's individual developmental characteristics can influence the caregiver's behaviors and sensitivity. For example, a child's individual temperament and self-regulatory capabilities might influence how the parent responds to the child or cares for the child. This could in turn influence the development of security or insecurity in the child. For example, a parent who is anxious may have limited patience with a baby who cries constantly. The resulting neglect by the caregiver in response to the crying or the "over-response" influences the baby's subsequent behavior (Sameroff & MacKenzie, 2003).

There is some genetic evidence, which supports the transactional model of development. In 1983, Scarr and McCartney articulated a phenomenon called evocative gene-environment correlation (denoted as rGE). According to this phenomenon, although certain characteristics of a child, such as self-regulation capabilities, are influenced by genetics, it is also possible that a child's genetically influenced behaviors would elicit a specific set of responses and parenting behaviors from the caregiver. In fact, some twin studies have pointed to these rGE influences. More recently, Klahr et al. (2013) found that at any given moment, the interpersonal behavioral responses of parents could vary from one twin to another. For example, a child who is warm (e.g. smiles frequently, responds positively to and interacts well with peers and adults) is more likely to elicit warmth from the parent. In contrast, a twin who has an anxious or difficult temperament might elicit a more controlling behavior from the parent – although, this does not mean that the parent lacks warmth toward the child. It rather establishes that the parental behaviors could be influenced by the child's own behavior. These studies suggest that caregiving behaviors are not unidirectional. Rather, a child's genetics and behavioral characteristics may also play an important role in eliciting specific behaviors.

Adult/Child Mutual Regulation Model

Based on over 20 years of research studying dyadic interactions of infants and their mothers, in 2007 Tronick articulated a model of an adult/child mutual regulation. Similar to other relationship-based models, a major assumption of this view is that infants have certain inherent self-organizing and neurobehavioral capacities. These capacities organize behavioral and self-regulatory states, such as sleep and wakefulness, arousal, attention, memory, and communication. Though crucial, there are limitations to an infant's self-organizing capacities, because the infant cannot sustain these capabilities over time and on her own. A resolution occurs when the infant is viewed in a dyadic system of caregiver/child interactions, which serves to scaffold the child's limited regulatory capacities.

Earlier, in 1989, Tronick published the first of his studies of face-to-face interactions between infants and their mothers. In these studies, he closely examined the behaviors and reactions of infants to their mothers' facial expressions and verbal behaviors during guided videotaped dyadic episodes, which he called the *Face-to-Face/Still-Face* (FFSF) paradigm. Tronick noted that during typical interactions between the infant and the caregiver, a series of *mismatches* occur. For example, a mismatch could occur when an infant's expectations of the caregiver's behavior or the caregiver's expectations of the infant's behavior are not met. During a typical FFSF episode, after being engaged in a few minutes of dyadic vocal and facial reciprocal interactions with their infants, Tronick had mothers disengage from their infants by looking away, or keeping their own facial affects "still" or neutral. Tronick considered a *still face* event as a mismatch. He noted that for an infant as young as about one year old, a *mismatch* is a source of stress (Tronick, 1989).

Mismatches could be the results of differences in the communicative goals of the infant or caregiver, missing communication signals, an overload of sensory stimulations, or a lack of appropriate sensory stimulation, etc. Therefore, in any given dyadic interaction between an infant and a caregiver, there would be many mismatches and many efforts from both sides to *repair* them.

When a mismatch occurs, the infant immediately tries to repair this mismatch and get his mother to interact with him by resorting to a series of coping behaviors. Tronick's experiments, and others that replicated FFSF episodes, showed that infants' coping behaviors varied from smiling, vocalizing, arm and leg movements, looking to and from the mother's face, arching forward, etc., to drooling, crying, and showing similar signs of distress. All coping behaviors were directed toward the mother to demand the mother's attention and engagement. Tronick noted that when the infant fails to obtain the caregiver's response, he turns his body away from the caregiver, cries, and gradually begins to withdraw (Tronick, 2007). Both infants and caregivers engage in multiple mismatch and repair behaviors in a dyadic situation, which Tronick (2007) called a bidirectional and *mutual regulation* process. Ultimately, in a positive mutual regulation process, both the mother and the infant repair any mismatches successfully, which would promote healthy emotional regulation in the infant.

Tronick has acknowledged that although there are certain universal qualities to the range of affective regulatory behaviors between infants and adults, the mechanisms of this mutual regulation vary across cultures and in different societies based on values that dictate dyadic interactions (Tronick, 2007). In more recent years, Tronick has turned his attention toward studying FFSF episodes and the mutual regulation process in preterm infants, and between infants and mothers who are depressed (Tronick & Reck, 2009; Sravish, Tronick, Hollenstein, & Beeghly, 2013). Besides this ongoing research on relationship development between caregiver and infant, we need to look at research creating emotional stages of development that we have come to rely on as we interpret child behavior.

Greenspan's Emotional Stages of Development

Drawing on the developmental theories of Piaget, Erikson, and Freud in the late 1970s, Greenspan proposed a stage theory of emotional development in children (Greenspan & Thorndike Greenspan, 1985). Greenspan believed that all areas of development are interrelated with one another, and in fact the healthy emotional development in a child takes place through nurturing relationships with adults. In Greenspan's view, a healthy emotional development forms the foundations for cognitive development and intelligence, as well as language development (Greenspan, 1997). Similar to other relationship-based models of development, in Greenspan's stage theory, dyadic interactions and the formation of early relationships between infant and adult are at the core of development. According to this theory, the infant's neurobiological capacities enable or prevent the infant from being calm enough to process various stimuli from his surroundings. This will lead to a gradual lack of self-regulation that sets the child on a course of atypical development and eventually results in other complex problems as the child gets older (Greenspan & Wieder, 1998). In fact, an infant who has difficulties with processing sensory information will not be able to take an interest in the world and engage with her caregiver in the first place. Since the 1990s and up to his death in 2012, Greenspan's interest in self-regulation and sensory processing capacities led him to focus on functional emotional assessment and intervention strategies for children with special needs, specifically those with Autism Spectrum Disorders – whose core developmental deficits relate to socialization and communication (Greenspan & Wieder, 1998; Greenspan & Wieder, 2006a).

Greenspan is most known for his work in infant and early childhood mental health. The first six to seven stages of his theory are well articulated and recognized in early childhood. However, his theory includes nine stages of emotional development beginning from birth through adulthood. The first seven stages relating to early and middle childhood are as follows (Greenspan & Wieder, 2006b):

- Stage one: Security and enjoyment in the surroundings. The abilities of the infant to look, listen, and stay calm depends on the basic brain capacities to process stimulation effectively, so that the infant can experience the world.
- Stage two: Engagement with the caregiver and others. Once the basic neurological capacities are present, the infant will be able to take a special interest in the world and people in it. The infant will begin to engage and relate to others in his environment.
- Stage three: Purposeful communication. Around three months of age, the infant begins to move beyond engaging with the caregiver. A process of two-way purposeful and non-verbal communication begins between the infant and caregiver.
- Stage four: Shared social problem solving, and mood regulation. From 9 to 18 months, a continuous flow of communication takes place between the child and caregiver. The child's symbolic language and sense of self emerge. During this stage, the child's self-regulation behavior develops further based on the verbal and non-verbal cues from adults and the caregiver.
- Stage five: Creation of ideas. Between 18 and 30 months, the child's language becomes more refined, and the child begins to use language in meaningful ways. Symbolic play becomes sophisticated, and the child begins to form new ideas in play.
- Stage six: Creation of logical bridges between emotions and ideas (emotional thinking). From two and a half to five years, the child learns to combine meaningful ideas together in a cohesive narrative, and think at the symbolic level. The child begins to understand his feelings, and why he feels that way.
- Stage seven: Multi-causal thinking. From five years of age through middle childhood, the child begins to recognize multiple causations for events. Abstract

thinking becomes more complex, and the child's comparative reasoning and understanding of the different relationships and dynamics becomes refined.

Besides Greenspan's landmark work, it is important to also rely on the development of the theory of emotional intelligence.

Emotional Intelligence

The theory of *emotional intelligence (EI)* found a growing popularity in education and in the workplace since the 1990s. Specifically, the construct of emotional intelligence and the term *emotional quotient* (EQ) became an item of American popular culture since Goleman (1995), a psychologist and *New York Times* science journalist, published a book titled *Emotional Intelligence: Why It Can Matter More than IQ.* He defined emotional intelligence as the ability to understand and manage feelings, recognize feelings in others, and to motivate self and manage relationships (Goleman, 1995). Although Goleman popularized the concept of emotional intelligence, this concept was constructed and studied prior to its popularization as early as the 1960s.

In 1990, Salovey and Mayer (see also Mayer, Salovey, & Caruso, 2004) presented a theoretical model of emotional intelligence. In the next 20 years, they advanced the model and designed a test of emotional intelligence, which is used in additional research. As discussed earlier, although there were notable developmental theories that connect social emotional development to cognitive growth and development (e.g. in Greenspan's model), prior to the scientific conceptualization and definition of emotional intelligence the link between emotion and intelligence was not openly acknowledged (for details see Mayer & Salovey, 1997; Mayer et al., 2004; Salovey & Grewal, 2005). Two areas of research findings contributed to the development of the theory of emotional intelligence – in which certain social and emotional abilities are considered as a standard intelligence. First, some neurological research evidence was presented in the 1990s which explained that there is an interconnectedness between emotional processes and logical reasoning (see Damasio, 1994); and second, a theory of multiple intelligences (Gardner, 1983/1993) questioned viewing intelligence as a set of abilities related to mathematical and logical reasoning – both of these phenomena contributed to the advancement of the concept of emotional intelligence as a standard intelligence on its own merit (Brackett, Rivers, & Salovey, 2011).

Salovey and Mayer (1990) defined emotional intelligence as one's ability to "monitor one's own and others' feelings and emotions, to discriminate among them and to use this information to guide one's thinking and actions" (p. 189). Later, Mayer and Salovey (1997) broke down the definition of emotional intelligence into four distinct yet related abilities or branches that could be separated from personality: 1) perceiving emotions; 2) using emotions to facilitate thinking and reasoning; 3) understanding emotions; and 4) managing emotions (see Table 2.1).

Table 2.1 Mayer and Salovey Model of EI – Abilities of Emotionally Intelligent Individuals

Perceiving emotions: Individual can identify and understand own and others' emotions.

Using emotions to facilitate thinking and reasoning: Individual uses self's emotions and changing moods to facilitate better thinking and problem solving.

Understanding emotions: Individual understands the range of emotions in both self and others.

Managing emotions: Individual regulates emotions in self and others through change of body language, tone, and affect.

Mayer, Salovey, and Caruso (2002) developed an instrument called MSCEIT (Mayor-Salovey-Caruso Emotional Intelligence Test) to measure four branches of emotional intelligence. To date several studies have been conducted to study emotional intelligence in various groups of children and adults. These studies show children who score highly on the test of emotional intelligence report having better relationships with their peers, friends, family members, teachers, etc. In addition, those with higher emotional intelligence interact and work with other people more successfully, and view others in a more positive light (for details of these studies see Brackett, Cox, Gaines, & Salovey, 2005 as cited in Salovey and Grewal, 2005; Lopes, Salovey, & Straus, 2003). In terms of logical reasoning, children and adults scoring highly on emotional intelligence tend to have higher reasoning abilities (O'Connor & Little, 2003). In addition, emotionally intelligent students are more successful in performing academic tasks, and are less likely to engage in any deviant behaviors (Brackett, Mayer, & Warner, 2004).

The concept of emotional intelligence is clearly linked to the development of social-emotional competence and other cognitive skills required for academic success and appropriate functioning of a child in society. A strong emotional foundation is necessary for a child's success, especially once he enters early education settings. As mentioned in Chapter 1, early childhood education historically emphasized socialization experiences in preschools, and then in the 1960s began the compensatory focus on early literacy and cognitive development that dominated public school offerings of early education for all children. However, during the past two decades there has been a growing recognition of the importance of healthy emotional development as the basis for the academic success of the child (Brackett, Rivers, & Salovey, 2011).

Caregiving Behaviors Which Promote Emotional Intelligence

Each parent–infant dyad is unique with its own nuances and behavioral details from both sides. IMH research has used millions of frame-by-frame analyses of thousands of dyadic interactions between caregivers and children from a variety of socio-economic, cultural, and ethnic backgrounds around the world. As this chapter has thus far presented, this research has solidly established that positive early caregiving experiences have a direct influence on the development of the healthy social-emotional and cognitive development of the child later in life (Fraley, Roisman, & Haltigan, 2013).

However, studies that identify exact caregiving behaviors conducive to social-emotional skill learning in the child are not as abundant as those that present evidence of a lack of appropriate and sensitive parental behaviors having adverse effects on the child. For example, we seem to know more about the deleterious consequence of a caregiver's neglect, a caregiver's depression/mental health issues, or a caregiver's maltreatment of an infant/child than we know about the positive relationships formed between caregivers and young children.

Nevertheless, there are certain caregiving affective and verbal behaviors which seem to have a direct influence on the development of social-emotional competence and emotional intelligence in a child. Some of these behaviors are known to be a caregiver's emotional expressions, and the use of an interactive language that is rich with mental state narratives that describe what is or might be happening with the infant, e.g. "You feel so happy now that you have a clean diaper" (Brophy-Herb et al., 2011; Razza, Martin, & Brooks-Gunn, 2012; Rosenblum, McDonough, Sameroff, & Muzik, 2008).

A caregiver's emotional expressions seem to trigger underlying mechanisms for development of social referencing, that is: What "should I," the baby, feel? What is the response I should make. Social referencing is the beginning foundation for development of communication behavior and social relatedness (Pelaez, Virues-Ortega, Field, Amir-Kiaei, & Schnerch, 2013). Since it is this non-verbal behavior that precedes the use of words to communicate, there is strong evidence that parental expressions of emotions have a positive and strong influence, even when a child has developmental special needs (Green & Baker, 2011). Caregivers who express their emotions are more likely to reflect upon their own emotions and motivations as well. This reflection also has a positive influence on an infant's emotional competence.

A caregiver's ability to reflect upon her own emotions, motivations for actions, and those of her infant is known as *reflective function* (Fonagy & Target, 1997). Caregivers who have high reflective functions are sensitive to their infant's emotions and related behavioral cues. In addition, caregivers who are self-reflective are likely to be *mind-minded*. Mind-mindedness is the degree to which the caregiver uses self-reflective skills to engage in understanding her infant's mental states (Rosenblum et al., 2008). In other words, a mind-minded caregiver believes her infant to experience emotions, and validates these emotions regularly and frequently.

Mind-minded caregivers are able to not only reflect upon and understand their own emotions, but also those of their infant. Mind-minded caregivers frequently engage in daily verbal interactive behaviors with their infant, during which they describe their infant's mental states. A mental state or mind-minded comment may be, "You feel happy to see your big brother. You want to be just like him." Caregivers may add narratives and descriptions of their own mental states as well. For example, "Mommy is so delighted to play patty cake with you."

Mental state narration and descriptions seem to have a direct and strong relationship with development of social-emotional skills, such as development of empathy, emotion regulation and control, and prosocial behaviors, such as friendship, cooperation, and peer problem solving (Hollingsworth, 2013; Rosenblum et al., 2008). During the toddler and preschool years, caregivers' narration takes the shape of emotional coaching and socialization, and promoting a positive emotional climate by guiding the child to regulate and turn negative emotions into more positive ones (Brophy-Herb et al., 2011). For example, "I see you are angry now. Can you say, 'I am angry,' instead of screaming? Can you fist your hands and stomp your feet?"

Closing Remarks

There is enough scientific evidence to show that the first five years of life and early relational experiences promote lifelong health, healthy neural development and learning, and relationship influences (Brandt, 2014). However, there are criticisms regarding the actual role of early caregiving experience on later development (Lewis, 1998), and that subsequent experiences might indeed erase the effects of early experiences (Werner, 2013). Research on child resilience, the ability to cope in spite of developmental, social, or other impediments, for example, provides evidence that there are factors that can act as buffers for the child and mitigate the effects of adversity that would otherwise be detrimental for the child (Werner, 2013). Therefore, variations in developmental experiences of children certainly make predicting a specific outcome very difficult. Therefore, certain considerations should be taken into account when examining early adult and child relationships.

I draw upon explanations provided by Sroufe, Coffino, and Carlson (2010) that: 1) *early* is a relative concept – for example an adverse condition may have no influence on an infant during the first three months of life, whereas the same condition might have severe effects if occurring at a time during the next 11 months of life; 2) consequences of early and later events in life are cumulative, and they work in combination with other risk factors, such as genetic makeup or environmental risk factors; 3) the potential impact of any experience may be reversed by subsequent positive or negative experiences, which may differ from the earlier ones. Therefore, early experiences can create strengths or vulnerabilities as opposed to direct outcomes (Sroufe et al., 2010). In sum, regardless of what might occur later in life, early experiences remain extremely important in setting a course for certain vulnerable or strong trajectories of child mental health.

References

Ainsworth, M.D.S. (1967). *Infancy in Uganda: Infant care and the growth of love*. Baltimore, MD: The Johns Hopkins University Press.
Ainsworth, M.D.S. (1979). Infant mother attachment. *American Psychologist, 34*, 932–937.

Early Relationships **41**

Ainsworth, M.D.S., & Bell, S. M. (1970). Attachment, exploration, and separation: Illustrated by the behavior of one-year-olds in a strange situation. *Child Development, 41,* 49–67.

Ainsworth, M.D.S., Bell, S. M., & Stayton, D. J. (1974). Infant–mother attachment and social development: 'Socialization' as a product of reciprocal responsiveness to signals. In J. M. Richards (Ed.), *The integration of a child into the social world* (pp. 9–135). London and New York, NY: Cambridge University Press.

Ainsworth, M.D.S., & Bowlby, J. (1991). An ethological approach to personality development. *American Psychologist, 46*(4), 333–341.

Bowlby, J. (1944). Forty-four juvenile thieves: Their characters and home lives. *International Journal of Psychoanalysis, 25,* 19–52.

Bowlby, J. (1958). The nature of the child's tie to his mother. *International Journal of Psychoanalysis, 39,* 350–373.

Bowlby, J. (1969). *Attachment and loss, Vol. 1: Attachment.* New York, NY: Basic Books.

Bowlby, J. (1973). *Attachment and loss, Vol. 2: Separation.* New York, NY: Basic Books.

Bowlby, J. (1979). *The making and breaking of affectional bonds.* London: Tavistock Publications Limited.

Bowlby, J. (1980). *Attachment and loss, Vol. 3: Loss, sadness and depression.* New York, NY: Basic Books.

Bowlby, J. (1982). *Attachment* (2nd ed.). New York, NY: Basic Books.

Brackett, M. A., Mayer, J. D., & Warner, R. M. (2004). Emotional intelligence and its relation to everyday behavior. *Personality and Individual Differences, 36,* 1387–1402.

Brackett, M., Rivers, S. E., & Salovey, P. (2011). Emotional intelligence: Implications for personal, social, academic, and workplace success. *Social and Personality Psychology Compass, 5*(1), 88–103.

Brandt, K. (2014). Core concepts in infant family and early childhood mental health. In K. Brandt, B. D. Perry, S. Seligman, & E. Tronick (Eds.) (2014). *Infant and early childhood mental health: Core concepts and clinical practice* (pp. 1–20). Washington, DC: American Psychiatric Publishing.

Breidenstine, A. S., Bailey, L. O., Zeanah, C. H., & Larrieu, J. A. (2011). Attachment and trauma in early childhood: A review. *Journal of Child & Adolescent Trauma, 4*(4), 274–290.

Brophy-Herb, H. E., Schiffman, R. F., London Bocknek, E., Dupuis, S. B., Fitzgerald, H. E., Horodynski, M., … Hillaker, B. (2011). Toddlers' social-emotional competence in the contexts of maternal emotion socialization and contingent responsiveness in a low-income sample. *Social Development, 20*(1), 73–92.

Brown, W. H. & Conroy, M. A. (2011). Social-emotional competence in young children with developmental delays: Our reflection and vision for the future. *Journal of Early Intervention, 33*(4), 310–320.

Buysee, V., Goldman, B. D., West, T., & Hollingsworth, H. (2008). Friendships in early childhood: Implications for early education and intervention. In W. H. Brown, S. L. Odom, & S. R. McConnell (Eds.), *Social competence of young children: Risk, disability, and intervention* (pp. 77–97). Baltimore, MD: Paul H. Brookes Publishing Co.

Campos, J. J., Frankel, C. B., & Camras, L. (2004). On the nature of emotion regulation. *Child Development, 75,* 377–394.

Cassidy, J., & Marvin, R. S., with the MacArthur Working Group (1992). *Attachment organization in preschool children: Procedures and coding manual.* Unpublished manuscript, University of Virginia.

Chambers, D. (2012). *A sociology of family life: Change and diversity in intimate relations.* Cambridge: Policy Press.

Chisholm, K. (1998). A three year follow-up of attachment and indiscriminate friendliness in children adopted from Romanian orphanages. *Child Development, 69*, 1092–1106.

Chisholm, K., Carter, M. C., Ames, E. W., & Morison, S. J. (1995). Attachment security and indiscriminately friendly behavior in children adopted from Romanian orphanages. *Development and Psychopathology, 7*, 283–294.

Damasio, A. R. (1994). *Descartes' error: Emotion, reason, and the human brain.* New York, NY: Putnam Berkley Group, Inc.

Denham, S. A. (2006). Social-emotional competence as support for school readiness: What is and how do we assess it. *Early Education and Development, 17*(1), 57–89.

Douglas, P. (2012). Interdisciplinary perspectives on the management of the unsettled baby: Key strategies for improved outcome. *Australian Journal of Primary Health, 18*(4), 332–338.

Eliot, L. (1999). *What's going on in there? How the brain and mind develop in the first five years of life.* New York, NY: Bantam Books.

Emde, R. N. (2011). Potentials for infant mental health: Congress themes and moral development. *Infant Mental Health Journal, 32*(1), 5–18.

Erikson, E. H. (1950). *Childhood and society.* New York, NY: W. W. Norton.

Fonagy, P., & Target, M. (1997). Attachment and reflective-function: Their role in self-organization. *Development and Psychopathology, 9*, 679–700.

Fraiberg, S., Adelson, E., & Shapiro, V. (1975). Ghosts in the nursery: A psychoanalytic approach to the problems of impaired infant–mother relationships. *Journal of American Academy of Child Psychiatry, 14*, 387–421.

Fraley, R. C., Roisman, G. I., & Haltigan, J. D. (2013). The legacy of early experiences in development: Formalizing alternative models of how early experiences are carried forward over time. *Developmental Psychology, 49*(1), 109–126.

Gardner, H. (1983/1993). *Frames of mind: The theory of multiple intelligences* (10th anniversary edition). New York, NY: Basic Books.

Goldsmith, H. H., & Campos, J. J. (1982). Toward a theory of infant temperament. In R. N. Emde & R. Harmon (Eds.), *The development of attachment and affiliative systems* (pp. 161–193). New York, NY: Plenum Press.

Goleman, D. (1995). *Emotional intelligence: Why it can matter more than IQ.* New York, NY: Bantam Books.

Green, S., & Baker, B. (2011). Parents' emotion expression as a predictor of child's social competence: Children with or without intellectual disability. *Journal of Intellectual Disability Research, 55*(3), 324–338.

Greenspan, S. I. (with Benderly, B. L.) (1997). *The growth of the mind: And the endangered origins of intelligence.* Cambridge, MA: Perseus Books.

Greenspan, S. I., & Thorndike Greenspan, N. (1985). *First feelings: Milestones in the emotional development of your baby and child.* New York, NY: Penguin Books.

Greenspan, S. I., & Wieder, S. (with Simons, R.) (1998). *The child with special needs: Encouraging intellectual and emotional growth.* Reading, MA: Perseus Books.

Greenspan, S. I., & Wieder, S. (2006a). *Engaging autism: Using the floortime approach to help children relate, communicate, and think.* Cambridge, MA: Da Capo Lifelong Books.

Greenspan, S. I., & Wieder, S. (2006b). *Infant and early childhood mental health: A comprehensive developmental approach to assessment and intervention.* Washington, DC: American Psychiatric Publishing, Inc.

Guralnick, M. J. (2010). Early intervention approaches to enhance the peer-related social competence of young children with developmental delays: A historical perspective. *Infants & Young Children, 23*, 73–83.

Hanson, M. J., Lynch, E. W., & Wayman, K. I. (1990). Honoring the cultural diversity of families when gathering data. *Topics in Early Childhood Special Education, 10*(1), 112–131.

Hollingsworth, H. L. (2013). Teacher beliefs and practices relating to development in preschool: Importance placed on social emotional behaviors and skills. *Early Child Development and Care, 183*(12), 1758–1781.

Kagan, J., & Snidman, N. (1991). Temperamental factors in human development. *American Psychologist, 46*, 856–862.

Kheddache, Y., & Tadj, C. (2013). Acoustic measures of the cry characteristics of healthy newborns and newborns with pathologies. *Journal of Biomedical Science & Engineering, 6*, 796–804.

Klahr, A. M., Thomas, K. M., Hopwood, C. J., Klump, K. L., & Burt, S. A. (2013). Evocative gene-environment correlation in the mother–child relationship: A twin study of interpersonal processes. *Development and Psychopathology, 25*, 105–118.

Kreppner, J., Rutter, M., Marvin, R., O'Connor, T., & Sonuga-Barke, E. (2011). Assessing the concept of the 'insecure-other' category in the Cassidy-Marvin scheme: Change between 4 and 6 years in the English and Romanian adoptee study. *Social Development, 20*, 1–16.

Landy, S. (2009). *Pathways to competence: Encouraging healthy social and emotional development in young children* (2nd ed.). Baltimore, MD: Paul H. Brookes Publishing Co.

Lewis, M. (1998). *Altering fate: Why the past does not predict the future.* New York, NY: The Guilford Press.

Lillas, C., & Turnbull, J. (2009). *Infant/child mental health, early intervention, and relationship-based therapies: A neurorelational framework for interdisciplinary practice.* New York, NY: W. W. Norton.

Lopes, P. N., Salovey, P., & Straus, R. (2003). Emotional intelligence, personality, and the perceived quality of social relationships. *Personality and Individual Differences, 35*, 641–658.

Main, M., & Soloman, J. (1986). Discovery of a new, insecure-disorganized/disoriented attachment pattern. In T. B. Brazelton, & M. W. Yogman (Eds.), *Affective development in infancy* (pp. 95–124). New York, NY: Ablex Publishing.

Mayer, J. D., & Salovey, P. (1997). What is emotional intelligence? In P. Salovey & D. Sluyter (Eds.), *Emotional development and emotional intelligence: Educational implications* (pp. 3–31). New York, NY: Basic Books.

Mayer, J. D., Salovey, P., & Caruso, D. R. (2002). *The Mayer-Salovey-Caruso Emotional Intelligence Test (MSCEIT).* Toronto, Ontario: Multi-Health System.

Mayer, J. D., Salovey, P., & Caruso, D. R. (2004). Emotional intelligence: Theory, findings, and implications. *Psychological Inquiry, 15*(3), 197–215.

McKie, L., & Callan, S. (2012). *Understanding families: A global introduction.* London: Sage.

Nakato, E., Otsuka, Y., Kanazawa, S., Yamaguchi, M. K., Honda, Y., & Kakigi, R. (2011). I know this face: Neural activity during mother face perception in 7- to 8-month-old infants as investigated by near-infrared spectroscopy. *Early Human Development, 87*, 1–7.

O'Connor, R. M. Jr., & Little, I. S. (2003). Revisiting the predictive validity of emotional intelligence: Self-report versus ability-based measures. *Personality and Individual Differences, 35*, 1893–1902.

O'Connor, T. G., Rutter, M., & English and Romanian Adoptees Study Team (2000). Attachment disorder behavior following early severe deprivation: Extension and longitudinal follow-up. *Journal of the American Academy of Child and Adolescent Psychiatry, 39*, 703–712.

Pelaez, M., Virues-Ortega, J., Field, T. M., Amir-Kiaei, Y., & Schnerch, G. (2013). Social referencing in infants of mothers with symptoms of depression. *Infant Behavior and Development, 36*, 548–556.

Razza, R. A., Martin, A., & Brooks-Gunn, J. (2012). Anger and children's socioemotional development: Can parenting elicit a positive side to a negative emotion? *Journal of Child and Family Studies, 21*, 845–856.

Rhoades, B. L., Warren, H. K., Domitrovich, C. E., & Greenberg, M. T. (2011). Examining the link between preschool social-emotional competence and first grade academic achievement: The role of attention skills. *Early Childhood Research Quarterly, 26*, 182–191.

Roisman, G. I., & Fraley, R. C. (2012). A behavior-genetic study of the legacy of early caregiving experiences: Academic skills, social competence, and externalizing behavior in kindergarten. *Child Development, 83*(2), 728–742.

Rose-Krasnor, L., & Denham, S. (2009). Social-emotional competence in early childhood. In K. H. Rubin, W. M. Bukowski, & B. Laursen (Eds.), *Handbook of peer interactions, relationships, and groups* (pp. 162–179). New York, NY: The Guilford Press.

Rosenblum, K. L., McDonough, S. C., Sameroff, A. J., & Muzik, M. (2008). Reflection in thought and action: Maternal parenting reflectivity predicts mind-minded comments and interactive behavior. *Infant Mental Health Journal, 29*(4), 362–376.

Rothbart, M. K., & Bates, J. E. (1998). Temperament. In W. Damon & N. Eisenberg (Eds.), *Handbook of child psychology: Vol. 3. Social, emotional and personality development* (5th ed., pp. 105–176). New York, NY: Wiley.

Rothbart, M. K., & Bates, J. E. (2006). Temperament. In W. Damon & R. Lerner (Series Eds.), and N. Eisenberg (Vol. Ed.), *Handbook of child psychology, Vol. 3. Social, emotional, and personality development* (6th ed., pp. 99–166). New York, NY: Wiley.

Rutter, M., Kreppner, J., & Sonuga-Barke, E. (2009). Emanuel Miller lecture: Attachment insecurity, disinhibited attachment, and attachment disorders: Where do research findings leave the concepts? *Journal of Child Psychology and Psychiatry, 50*(5), 529–543.

Salovey, P., & Grewal, D. (2005). The science of emotional intelligence. *Current Directions in Psychological Science, 14*(6), 281–285.

Salovey, P., & Mayer, J. D. (1990). Emotional intelligence. *Imagination, Cognition, and Personality, 9*, 185–211.

Sameroff, A. J., & Chandler, M. J. (1975). Reproductive risk and the continuum of caretaking casualty. In F. D. Horowitz, M. Hetherington, S. Scarr Salapatek, & G. Siegal (Eds.), *Review of child development research* (Vol. 4, pp. 187–244). Chicago, IL: University of Chicago Press.

Sameroff, A. J. & MacKenzie, M. J. (2003). A quarter-century of the transactional model: How have things changed? *Zero to Three, 24*(1), 14–22.

Scarr, S., & McCartney, K. (1983). How people make their own environment: A theory of genotype environment effects. *Child Development, 54*, 424–435.

Seymour, J., & Walsh, J. (2013). Displaying families, migrant families and community connectedness: The application of an emerging concept in family life. *Journal of Comparative Family Studies, 44*(6), 689–698.

Sorce, J. F., & Emde, R. N. (1981). Mother's presence is not enough: Effect of emotional availability on infant exploration. *Developmental Psychology, 17*(6), 737–745.

Spock, B. (1946). *The common sense book of baby and child care.* New York, NY: Duell, Sloan and Pearce.

Spock, B., & Parker, S. J. (1998). *Dr. Spock's baby and child care* (7th ed.). New York, NY: Pocket Books.

Sravish, A. V., Tronick, E., Hollenstein, T., & Beeghly, M. (2013). Dyadic flexibility during the face-to-face still face paradigm: A dynamic system analysis of its temporal organization. *Infant Behavior and Development, 36*(3), 432–437.

Sroufe, L. A., Coffino, B., & Carlson, E. A. (2010). Conceptualizing the role of early experience: Lessons from the Minnesota longitudinal study. *Developmental Review, 30*, 36–51.

St. James-Roberts, I. (2007). Helping parents to manage infant crying and sleeping: A review of evidence and its implications for services. *Child Abuse Review, 16*, 47–69.

Steele, H. (2011). Early social and emotional experience matters: The first year of life. In D. Skuse, H. Bruce, L. Dowdney, and D. Mrazek (Eds.), *Child psychology and psychiatry: Frameworks for practice* (pp. 41–44). Oxford: Wiley-Blackwell.

Thomas, A., & Chess, S. (1977). *Temperament and development.* New York, NY: Brunner/Mazel.

Tronick, E. (1989). Emotion and emotional communication in infants. *American Psychologist, 44*, 112–119.

Tronick, E. (2007). *The neurobehavioral and social-emotional development of infants and children.* New York, NY: W.W. Norton.

Tronick, E., & Reck, C. (2009). Infants of depressed mothers. *Harvard Review of Psychiatry, 17*(2), 147–156.

Watson, J. B. (1928). *Psychological care of infant and child.* New York, NY: Norton.

Weatherston, D. J. (October/November 2000). The infant mental health specialist. *Zero to Three, 21*(2), 3–10.

Weinberg, M. K., & Tronick, E. Z. (1994). Beyond the face: An empirical study of infant affective configurations of facial, vocal, gestural, and regulatory behaviors. *Child Development, 65*, 1503–1515.

Werner, E. E. (2013). What can we learn about resilience from large-scale longitudinal studies? In S. Goldstein & R. B. Brooks (Eds.), *Handbook of resilience in children* (2nd ed., pp. 87–102). New York, NY: Springer.

Zeanah, C. H., Berlin, L. J., & Boris, N. W. (2011a). Practitioner review: Clinical applications of attachment theory and research for infants and young children. *Journal of Child Psychology and Psychiatry, 52*(8), 819–833.

Zeanah, C. H., Gunnar, M. R., McCall, R. B., Kreppner, J. M., & Fox, N. A. (2011b). Sensitive periods. In R. B. McCall, M. H. van IJzendoorn, F. Juffer, V. K. Groza, & C. J. Groark (Eds.), Children without permanent parental care: Research, practice and policy. *Monographs of the Society for Research in Child Development, 76*(4), 223–272.

3

CHILDHOOD TRAUMA AND ITS INFLUENCES ON PHYSICAL, MENTAL, AND BEHAVIORAL HEALTH

Young children are expected to develop and grow typically when caregivers provide physically and emotionally protective environments for them. However, sometimes this protection may be violated due to a variety of reasons and circumstances. Disruption of safe and nurturing caregiving experiences creates stressful situations for children. Repeated and prolonged stressful conditions, in which a safe and positive caregiving relationship and protection are disrupted, are traumatic for children and can corrupt the architecture of their young brains. This corruption may continue to affect their development well into the third and fourth decades of their lives (Delima & Vimpani, 2011; Ford et al., 2013). Since the widespread availability of brain imaging, we have known that traumatic experiences during early childhood may lead not only to a range of neurological problems, including such issues as problems in cogitative, emotional, behavioral, and social development, but also traumatic experiences can lead to a range of physical and health problems (Belsky & de Haan, 2011; Shonkoff, Boyce, & McEwen, 2009). Effects of exposure to trauma are different in children depending on the age when they experience the event, as well as the severity of the trauma and if the traumatic experience is chronic. Young children have an additional disadvantage of not being able to express verbally how they feel when they are threatened or feel anxious or helpless. In this chapter, I will examine sources of trauma in children, and the influence of trauma in early childhood on a child's mental health and development throughout the lifecycle.

Trauma in Childhood

Sources of trauma in childhood are varied, and can be from experiencing some personal negative emotional and physical effects, to witnessing an unusual or a violent event. Trauma can also result from experiencing a stressful situation related to self or a family member over a period of time. Trauma can happen suddenly or unexpectedly, like in an automobile accident, sudden family crisis, terrorist attack, gang shooting, earthquake or flood; or it can occur gradually by repeated exposure and experiences, like having a chronic illness, being a victim of abuse, or witnessing a parent being battered repeatedly. Aside from the severity and chronicity of trauma, children's own developmental capacity, their temperament and characteristics, and the ability of adults around them to help them cope with the trauma are important factors in determining how trauma might influence the development and functioning of a particular child (Zero to Three, 2005). *Child maltreatment* is one of the most important and common causes of traumatic experiences in children in early and middle childhood. In addition, violent acts or natural disasters witnessed or undergone by children are also important causes of severe trauma.

Child Maltreatment

Definition and classification of child maltreatment has evolved during the past four to five decades. In 1962, Kempe, a pediatrician, and his colleagues for the first time brought the issue of child maltreatment to the attention of the public with the publication of their first paper on child physical abuse, called 'The battered child syndrome' (Kempe, Silverman, Steele, Droegemueller, & Silver, 1962). In this paper, Kempe and his colleagues described detailed accounts of several cases of infants and young children whom Kempe and his team had treated in their medical practices. These injuries, which they explained, usually considered as unknown trauma, were in reality a result of physical abuse, occurring most likely at the hands of the children's care providers. The study set the parameters for recognition, diagnosis, and intervention of child physical abuse (Kempe et al., 1962). Kempe created one of the first Child Protection teams, which later operated from the Kempe Foundation for the Prevention and Treatment of Child Abuse and Neglect in Denver, Colorado. His efforts in making child maltreatment known and recognized by scholars and policy makers were the most influential in prompting the creation of U.S. mandated laws for reporting child abuse and neglect.

Before I begin discussing the definition and types of maltreatment in detail, it is important to note several factors here. First, identification of child maltreatment, which is based on a definition and measurement of this concept, has historically been challenging, because maltreatment most often takes place in the private confines of the family's home, and the perpetrators are usually parents, family members, or close friends or relatives. Second, maltreatment is an ethically sensitive and socially stigmatizing issue, because when reported, if identified and confirmed, it often results in serious or drastic consequences for the family in general, and the child in particular (Manly, 2005; Paavilainen, Lepistö, & Flinck, 2014). In terms of research, if during a research study a child is identified with maltreatment, negative consequences can result for both the researchers and research participants – for example legal and financial costs for the scholar, or physical, social, or psychological costs for the victimized child (Paavilainen et al., 2014). Finally, the standards by which Child Protection Services (CPS) define and measure maltreatment may differ from those set by scholars. For these reasons, generally, definition and dimensions of maltreatment are not very clear or straightforward.

Definitions and Types of Child Maltreatment

The Center for Disease Control (2013) defines child maltreatment to include any form of abuse and neglect of a child by a parent or caregiver, or any adult in charge of the child. In the United States, the key federal legislation addressing child maltreatment is the Child Abuse Prevention and Treatment Act (CAPTA), originally enacted in 1974. According to the most recent reauthorization of CAPTA (2010), child maltreatment is considered to be a parent or caregiver's act or failure to act, which might result in death, serious physical and emotional harm, sexual abuse or exploitation; or an act or failure to act, which might result in imminent risk or serious harm. Under CAPTA all states have statutes that require certain professionals who have frequent contact with children – such as teachers and educators, therapists, health professionals, and community service providers – to report any child maltreatment if they witness such as acts or signs of it.

In 1999, the World Health Organization (WHO) provided a definition for child maltreatment, which included all forms of physical and/or emotional ill-treatment, including "sexual abuse, neglect or negligent treatment, commercial or other exploitation, resulting in actual or potential harm to the child's health, survival, development, or dignity in the context of a relationship of responsibility, trust or power" (WHO, 1999, p. 8). The United Nations Convention on the Rights of the Child (UNCRC) of 1990, as well as a proposed convention (2012), mandate protection of the child, from all forms of maltreatment: physical or psychological, injury, neglect or negligence, including exploitation and sexual abuse while in the care of parent(s), legal guardian(s), or any other persons who care for the child (Office of the United Nations High Commissioner for Human Rights, 1990; Winrow et al., 2012).

The statistics related to children victimized by maltreatment in the United States is based on the number of incidents, which are annually reported to the Child Protection Services, which is responsible for prevention, responding to reports of, as well as, referral for intervention of child maltreatment. The most recent statistics available suggest that each year 9.2 in every 1000 children are victims of maltreatment (United States Department of Health and Human Services – DHS, 2013). The most vulnerable and maltreated children are between the ages of birth to four years, with infants having the highest rate of victimization (DHS, 2013).

All definitions of child maltreatment include different acts of *abuse*, as well as acts of *neglect*. Children may be victims of three types of abuse: *physical, sexual,* and *emotional abuse*, and five types of neglect: *medical, physical, emotional, supervisory,* and *educational neglect* (see Figure 3.1). Although these categorizations are helpful in order to understand the forms of maltreatment, it is also important to know that the

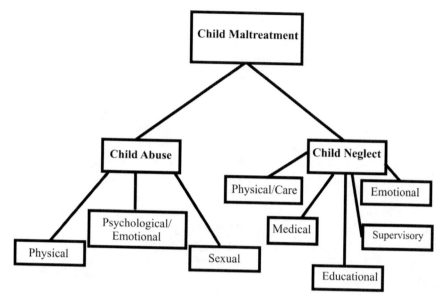

FIGURE 3.1   Categorization of Child Maltreatment

seriousness of the consequence of maltreatment depends more on the chronicity, frequency, and duration of maltreatment, or the child's repeated exposure to maltreatment, as opposed to the type of the maltreatment (Graham et al., 2010; Li & Godinet, 2014) (see Figure 3.1).

Child Abuse and Its Types

Child abuse is a form of maltreatment, which exposes the child to a traumatic experience. Children may be victimized in different ways and from different people. For example, abuse can occur in homes by family members or friends, in care institutions, such as orphanages (as in cases of those currently existing in most developing countries) and day programs by care providers, or at schools and other educational and community places by persons of authority. In regions of war and political conflict, combatants frequently abuse and exploit children. In low-resource and developing countries, poverty-stricken families might sell their children for sexual or domestic work, or children may live on the streets, where they can be exposed to violence and abuse (Southhall & MacDonald, 2013). In such situations, abuse and exploitation of children may be perpetrated not only by family members, but also by other individuals, often those who are well-off in the community or in the position of authority (Southhall & MacDonald, 2013). Early childhood is the period in which children are most likely to become victims of maltreatment. In fact, globally, young children have the highest number of victimizations, as compared to those in middle childhood and adolescence.

Physical Abuse

The most known form of child abuse is physical abuse. In economically developed countries, such as the United States, children who are physically abused are most likely to be abused by their parents or family members. The label of *battered child*, which Kempe coined in 1962, was formally used in the USA's legal system to describe children who are harmed by their caregivers (see Nelson, 2012 for details). Some definitions of physical abuse include any act that might be considered abusive, such as spanking, to more serious injuries and infanticide (Cruise, Jacobs, & Lyons, 1994). Although the caregiver's intention to harm the child is important, the current U.S. definition, which dictates the operation of Child Protective Services, does not include the intentions of the perpetrator. United States Department of Health and Human Services describes *child abuse* as "non-accidental" injury to a child, which, regardless of motive, is inflicted, or is allowed to be inflicted, on a child, which is the result of malnutrition, deprivation, or cruel punishment (U.S. Department of Health and Human Services, Administration for Children and Families, Administration on Children, Youth and Families, & Children's Bureau, 2013).

Young children are not only the most vulnerable group of children, but also they are the largest group likely to be physically abused. Infants younger than one year old have the highest rate of being physically victimized by their caregivers (Zimmerman & Mercy, 2010). The most common form of infant physical abuse is *shaken baby syndrome*. Incidents of shaking infants are commonly associated with the periods of infant's peek crying (Zimmerman & Mercy, 2010). Shaking infants may cause severe physical and intellectual impairments, and even lead to the death of the baby.

Sexual Abuse

Child sexual abuse involves engaging a child in a sexual act, including fondling of infants and children, rape, or exposing a child to any sexual activity (Center for Disease Control, 2013). Children may be sexually abused by adults or by children who are older or are developmentally more advanced – and therefore hold some authority over the younger child (Stolzenberg & Lyon, 2014). Sexual abuse is seldom identified or reported following the abusive act. Child sexual abuse is a progressive act, which is often achieved after a certain period of time (Stolzenberg & Lyon, 2014). Children of both genders are vulnerable to sexual abuse, however, girls are considered to be at higher risk (Karakurt & Silver, 2014). Estimating an exact number of children who are annually victims of sexual abuse is difficult, since the child is often sworn to secrecy by the perpetrator or the child is embarrassed to report. However, a global study estimated the prevalence of child sexual abuse around the world to be around 12 percent; with girls being victims in 18 percent of cases, and boys being victims in 7.6 percent of cases (Stoltenborgh, van IJzendoorn, Euser, & Bakermans-Kranenburg, 2011).

In most cases, the abuser is a family member or someone who has a pre-existing relationship with the child, and therefore, the perpetrator may not need to use force for the act, or for obtaining the child's silence (Stolzenberg & Lyon, 2014). Usually, the perpetrator gains the trust and compliance of the child first, before committing the abusive act (Stoltenborgh et al., 2011). Children who are victims of sexual abuse are often frightened into thinking that they will be blamed for the abusive act (Stolzenberg & Lyon, 2014). Victimized children may also fear that the disclosure may not be believed, or that some harm might come to them or others as a result of their disclosure. Like other forms of abuse, sexual abuse has severe negative consequences for children. Psychological trauma, particularly Posttraumatic Stress Disorder (PTSD), interpersonal relationship problems, depression, and substance abuse in later years are consistently associated with childhood sexual abuse (Karakurt & Silver, 2014)

Emotional/Psychological Abuse

The terms emotional and psychological abuse are used interchangeably, and there is no agreed upon definitional distinction between them. It is, understood that all forms of maltreatment, whether physical, sexual, or emotional, have an inherent embedded emotional and psychological component. For example, a child who is physically and sexually abused will automatically feel inferior or deserving of the abusive treatment (Hart & Glaser, 2011). Emotional or psychological abuse is defined as any behavior that harms a child's self-image, emotional health, and well-being (Center for Disease Control, 2013). Emotional abuse may take place as a result of repeated negative and damaging interactions between a caregiver and a child, and therefore become typical of that relationship over time. Incidence of abusive behavior may include the caregiver's terrorizing, spurning, isolating, exploiting/corrupting, or denying emotional responsiveness to the child, which in turn conveys to the child that the child is worthless, flawed, unloved, or unwanted (Hart & Glaser, 2011; Wekerle, 2011). As such, isolated incidents do not necessarily lead to or constitute emotional or psychological abuse, rather a repeated pattern of emotionally abusive behavior should occur to create harm and undermine the child's development and socialization (Hibbard, Barlow, MacMillan, Committee on Child Abuse and Neglect, & American Academy of Child and Adolescent Psychiatry, Child Maltreatment and Violence Committee, 2012). Different types of emotional abuse, such as spurning, terrorizing, isolating, and exploiting can be conveyed to the child through a variety of behaviors, such as threatening or humiliating the child, or putting the child in compromising and dangerous situations (Hibbard et al., 2012). For examples of behaviors that are emotionally abusive see Figure 3.2.

Emotional abuse is difficult to identify immediately because there are no physically observable marks on the child after the abusive act. It is also difficult to identify emotional abuse when other forms of abuse coexist with it (Hibbard et al., 2012). For this reason, psychological or emotional abuse is relatively unacknowledged and underidentified (Hart & Glaser, 2011). However, based on a review of various

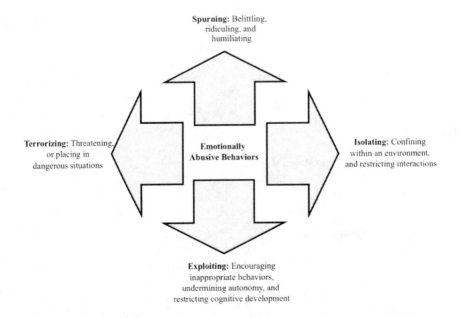

Spurning: Belittling, ridiculing, and humiliating

Terrorizing: Threatening, or placing in dangerous situations

Emotionally Abusive Behaviors

Isolating: Confining within an environment, and restricting interactions

Exploiting: Encouraging inappropriate behaviors, undermining autonomy, and restricting cognitive development

FIGURE 3.2   Types of Emotionally Abusive Behaviors

national and international self-reports, Reyome (2010) estimates that approximately 8 percent to 9 percent of women and 4 percent of men are emotionally abused substantially during childhood. Emotional abuse seems to be more prevalent in families who deal with parental mental health issues like depression, or in families with substance abuse problems (Hibbard et al., 2012; Hornor, 2012; McCullough & Shaffer, 2014).

Child Neglect and Its Types

Child neglect is the most common form of maltreatment, especially in the United States. Unlike different types of abuse, which are related to acts of commission, neglect is defined as a caregiver's acts of omission, which is the failure to meet a child's basic needs, such as safety, housing, food, clothing, and education (Center for Disease Control, 2013). Because the definition of neglect is broad, there is usually difficulty in determining whether an actual act of caregiving neglect may have taken place (Mennen, Kim, Sang, & Trickett, 2010). For this reason, scholars have designated several categories of neglect (Hibbard et al., 2012; Hornor, 2012; Mennen et al., 2010), such as:

1. *Physical or care neglect:* Failure to provide safety, food, hygiene, clothing, and shelter.
2. *Medical neglect:* Failure to provide medical care when needed, including failure to provide for mental health needs of the child.

3. *Educational neglect:* Failure to provide access to and appropriate education, including failure to engage the child in activities which would enhance development.
4. *Supervisory neglect:* Failure to provide appropriate supervision for the child.
5. *Emotional neglect:* Failure to provide expressions of emotional affection, caring, and love for the child.

Emotional neglect is particularly important to consider because it severely undermines a child's overall behavioral and emotional well-being. Caregivers who are emotionally neglectful – showing detachment and indifference, are emotionally and psychologically unavailable, or are generally unresponsive – are also likely to be emotionally abusive (McCullough & Shaffer, 2014). For example, they may be verbally hostile and rejecting. They may belittle the child or try to psychologically control the child with fear and threats.

The United States Department of Health and Human Services (DHS) reported that in 2012, over 53,000 children – 78 percent of all victims of maltreatment – suffered from neglect (DHS, 2013). Children under five years of age are at greatest risk for neglect (Bartlett, Raskin, Kotake, Nearing, & Easterbrooks, 2014). The harm, which is incurred as a result of a caregiver's neglect, is not imminently observable. Rather, effects of neglect are cumulative, and depend on the type and extent of the care omission (Graham et al., 2010; Mennen et al., 2010). Over 70 percent of children who suffer from neglect suffer from more than one type of neglect occurring together (Bartlett et al., 2014). About two-thirds of children who suffer from various forms of neglect are also victims of emotional abuse (Mennen et al., 2010). Additionally, it is also common to identify other types of abuse being incurred in children who suffer from neglect (Mennen et al., 2010).

Neglect may result not only because of a caregiver's intentional behaviors, but also may be a result of the caregiver's incapacity and inability to provide required and appropriate care. For example, neglect is common in cases of the caregiver's absence due to hospitalization or incarceration, or in cases of the caregiver's mental or physical illness or substance abuse (Mennen et al., 2010). Caregiver's depression is also a common factor, which often leads to emotional neglect and abuse. Although not all caregivers who are depressed necessarily abuse or neglect their children emotionally, research shows that parents and other caregivers who deal with depression are more likely to show hostility toward their children, or look indifferent and detached (McCullough & Shaffer, 2014).

According to available maltreatment records, there is usually an array of pervasive behaviors, which together result in a child suffering from neglect. For example, a child who suffers from care neglect usually finds no adequate food at home, or might not be fed for one or two days in a row; wears inappropriate clothing; and might not be clean or groomed (Hornor, 2012; Mennen et al., 2010). For examples of neglectful caregiving behaviors, see Figure 3.3.

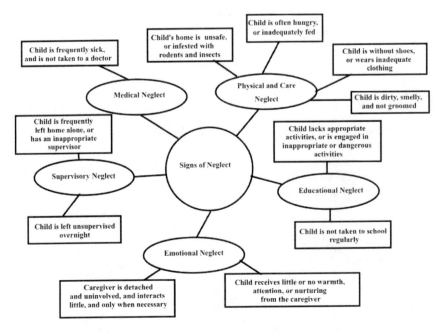

FIGURE 3.3 Some Signs of Child Neglect

Physical, Mental, and Behavioral Health Consequences of Child Maltreatment

Research consistently finds that children who are maltreated early in life are most likely to have a host of physical and mental problems – both externalizing and internalizing mental health issues, later in life (Li & Godinet, 2014; Pretty, O'Leary, Cairney, & Wade, 2013; Godinet, Li, & Berg, 2013). The most common physical health problems found in children who are maltreated during childhood include such issues as: cardiovascular problems, digestive problems, obesity, oral health issues, lung and liver disease, cancer, and unexplained pain. In terms of mental health issues, a vast array of issues such as aggression and violence, depression, anxiety, and Posttraumatic Stress Disorder have been associated with child maltreatment. In addition, research finds that children who were maltreated in childhood and suffer from physical or mental health consequences are likely to abuse drugs and alcohol as a way of alleviating their health issues (Garner, Hunter, Smith, Smith, & Godley, 2014). Table 3.4 lists various physical and health problems which may result from childhood maltreatment.

Table 3.1 Physical and Mental Health Consequences of Child Maltreatment in Later Life

Physical Issues	Emotional and Mental Health Issues
High BMI, or obesity	Posttraumatic Stress Disorder
High blood pressure	Attachment disorder, and other attachment problems
Digestive and gastrointestinal disease	
Chronic illness	Behavior problems, such as aggression
Caries disease (tooth decay)	Depression
Unexplained chest pain	Anxiety or phobias
Cancer	Relational-socialization problems
	Risk-taking or self-injurious behaviors
	Substance abuse and dependency

Physical Health Problems

Physical health depends on a complex and often interconnected web of factors, and it is often least likely that a single factor will lead to a serious health problem. However, there is strong evidence that when a child is the victim of repeated maltreatment, emotional and physical effects of maltreatment actively interact with other risk factors, and make it likely to lead to a variety of physical health issues. Most of the research on the influences of child maltreatment on later physical health is conducted on adolescents and adults during their hospital visits for health problems. Associations and links between a disease and past maltreatment are usually made after a series of analyses of patient surveys along with the examination of other health records. This leads the researchers to conclude that a strong link between child maltreatment and disease exists. For example, in an earlier study by Goodwin and Stein (2004) they found that adults who had cardiovascular disease were 3.7 times more likely to have been physically or sexually abused during their childhood. More recent studies find that children who have experienced four or more episodes of maltreatment in their childhood are likely to show signs of higher Body Mass Index (BMI), chronic illness, and unexplained chest pains as early as in adolescence (Eslick, Koloski, & Talley, 2011; Pretty et al., 2013). Thus, children who are abused or neglected earlier in their lives are more likely to develop serious health problems, such as obesity, high blood pressure, and chronic illness as adults (Pretty et al., 2013). Digestive and gastrointestinal diseases in adults, as well as Chronic Fatigue Syndrome (CFS), have also been associated with childhood maltreatment (Ålander, Heimer, Svärdsudd, & Agréus, 2008; Kempke et al., 2013). Caries disease or tooth decay, which causes the destruction of the hard tissue of the teeth, is a common condition in children who are maltreated, especially those who suffer from caregiving neglect – i.e. lack of appropriate nutrition and dental hygiene or check-ups (Lourenço, Saintrain, & Vieira, 2013).

Mental, Emotional, and Behavioral Problems

There are three research perspectives representing the outcome of adverse childhood experiences on later mental health development of the child:

1. *Neurobiological perspective*: Relying on brain studies, this perspective presents a view that adverse early childhood experiences trigger certain neurobiological response systems in the brain, which will result in a change in the brain structure and functioning. These changes will in turn influence mental, behavioral, and physical health of the individual. These studies often show specific mechanisms of brain change due to maltreatment via different techniques of brain imaging.

2. *Developmental psychopathology perspective*: In this perspective scholars present a view that development is hierarchical and each experience in development becomes a foundation for the next experience. For example, an adverse condition, such as trauma in childhood, will negatively influence later development and developmental tasks in later life. This view focuses on studying early experiences of the first five years of life, and comparing them against psychological and behavioral functioning of the same child in later stages of childhood or adolescence. Studies that use a developmental psychopathology perspective often show a link between early maltreatment and later behavioral and mental health problems, such as aggression or depression.

3. *Life course perspective*: In this perspective scholars focus on interaction of various factors on development throughout the life course. For example, an interaction of positive factors of resilience with risk factors can mitigate the influence of adverse effects of traumatic childhood experiences over time, and therefore change the course of development into a different (positive) direction. In this kind of research, the developmental picture is not as black and white to the scholar for predicting a specific outcome. Rather, dynamic changes may occur later in development, which may reverse or exacerbate the behavioral or mental health outcome for the child during adolescence. Studies that use a life course perspective often focus on behaviors of adolescents and delinquency and various risk conditions which may exist during puberty and adolescence.

Despite the differences in how these perspectives look at maltreatment and its effects, all agree on one thing: Repeated maltreatment of a child over time – as compared with a single event – has a greater impact on the mental health and behavior of that child during that period and later on (Li & Godinet, 2014).

Neurobiology of Maltreatment

Neurological research uses a variety of methods such as MRI (magnetic resonance imaging), DTI (diffusion tensor imagine), SPECT (single photon emission computed tomography), and functional MRI (for details see Delima & Vimpani, 2011). These studies indicate that repeated maltreatment of children induces both structural and functional changes in the brains of these children, which in turn confirms observations of behavioral, psychological, and cognitive problems in these children. Prolonged maltreatment activates the biological stress response, which is mediated through the hypothalamic-pituitary-adrenal axis – a regulating system that describes the brain's interactions and communication with the peripheral body via the neurons and hormones (Delima & Vimpani, 2011). Repeated activation of this biological stress response system changes the architecture of the brain. This can result in poor self-regulation, impulsivity, high or irrational emotional responses, anxiety, aggression, and tendencies to self-harm (De Bellis, Hooper, Woolley, & Shenk, 2010).

Developmental and Life Course Perspective of Maltreatment

The Longitudinal Studies of Child Abuse and Neglect (LONGSCAN), which began in early 2000, is now a consortium of five large-scale studies of over 1300 children and their families across various states. Children in this cohort were maltreated during their childhood and were identified through Childhood Protection Services. Many of the studies regarding long-term mental and behavioral effects of abuse and neglect on children draw on this ongoing source of data.

This kind of research shows that children who are exposed to repeated maltreatment commonly exhibit behavioral problems both during childhood and later in life (Proctor, Skriner, Roesch, & Litrownik, 2010; Thompson & Tabone, 2010). The most recent study by Li and Godinet (2014) using the LONGSCAN cohort confirms these results, adding that the effects of repeated maltreatment may not be as clearly obvious during early childhood. However, as time goes on, both behavioral and emotional issues become more severe in the child, such that, by age eight, most children who are exposed to repeated maltreatment before five years of age, display signs of serious emotional and behavioral problems (Li & Godinet, 2014). For example, a child who is repeatedly exposed to maltreatment at age four may only show emerging signs of behavioral or emotional problems at that age, but if the behavioral issues are not addressed appropriately, this child will have much more severe behavioral and emotional issues later on.

In another large-scale longitudinal study, in which a cohort of over 7000 mother and child pairs were studied from birth over a period of 15 years, children who had been the subject of repeated emotional abuse and/or neglect had the highest risk of developing serious mental health problems such as anxiety, depression, and Posttraumatic Stress Disorder over time (Mills, Scott, Alati, O'Callaghan, Najman, & Strathearn, 2013). These children may also resort to dangerous and risk-taking behaviors, for example self-injury or suicidal attempts in adolescence (Annerbäck, Sahlqvist, Svedin, Wingren, & Gustafsson, 2012).

Trauma and Stress-Related Psychiatric Disorders in Children

In examining the psychiatric and psychological disorders of children, I use two different systems: 1) disorders which are presented by diagnostic and statistical Manual of Mental Disorders (DSM), the most recent version of which was published in 2013 (American Psychiatric Association, 2013); and 2) early childhood disorders which are presented by DC:0-3R, Diagnostic Classification of Mental Health and Developmental Disorders of Infancy and Early Childhood, the most recent version of which was published in 2005 (Zero To Three, 2005).

Reactive Attachment Disorder

Disorders of attachment in children occur almost exclusively as a result of child abuse, emotional deprivation, and neglect. In other words, attachment disorders occur when infants and toddlers have limited opportunities to form selective attachment to a caregiver, for example, when parents or primary caregivers are unavailable and unresponsive to their infant's overtures for attention and nurturance, or when children grow up in institutions in which caregivers change frequently, or children are neglected emotionally and cognitively (Zero To Three, 2005). For example, in many developing countries, in which institutional care is more common, severe deprivation in orphanages or in other residential institutions is usually the norm and ongoing due to a lack of material and human resources (Bayat, 2014). In neglectful caregiving situations, although the capability of forming selective attachment is present in the infant, because of the limited opportunity, the child fails to develop the appropriate behavioral manifestation of selective attachment. Disorders of attachment are usually formed early during infancy, and usually manifest by nine months of age in the infants.

Reactive Attachment Disorder (RAD) is a disorder of attachment in which the child rarely turns to an attachment figure for comfort, support, protection, or nurturance, which is typical of a healthy attachment development (American Psychiatric Association, 2013). RAD develops when a child faces a lack of comforting response at times of seeking comfort. Children with this disorder may not show appropriate affect, fail to express positive emotions during interactions with their caregivers, or seem indifferent toward a caregiver. A diagnosis of RAD cannot be applied to children who have other developmental disorders with similar characteristic impairments, for example in social relatedness or emotional regulations, such as in Autism Spectrum Disorders (ASD). Unlike children with Reactive Attachment Disorders, social impairments in children with autism are directly related to inherent neurobiological causes, as opposed to neglect or abuse.

Signs of absence of or minimal attachment in children who have RAD are often present in the age range of from nine months to five years, and if caregiving neglect, deprivation, or abuse continues, these behaviors can persist to several years longer (American Psychiatric Association, 2013). Reactive Attachment Disorder is not often diagnosed in children older than five because it is not clear what the behaviors of older children with RAD may look like (American Psychiatric Association, 2013). If present, Reactive Attachment Disorder (RAD) will impair a child's ability in all areas of development, but more specifically in the area of forming and maintaining relationships, and having healthy interactions with peers and adults. Sometimes other developmental and psychological conditions may result from deprivation and neglect that may co-occur with RAD. For example, language and cognitive delays, stereotypical and repetitive behaviors, and depression may be common in some children with RAD (American Psychiatric Association, 2013).

It is important to note that not all children who grow up in neglectful caregiving situations and under severe emotional deprivation would necessarily develop Reactive Attachment Disorder. As mentioned, a variety of factors, such as a child's developmental and neurobiological capacities, play important roles in a psychiatric disorder manifestation or lack thereof.

Disinhibited Social Engagement Disorder

Another disorder of attachment, Disinhibited Social Engagement Disorder (DSED), is caused as a result of abuse and neglect. Unlike children with Reactive Attachment Disorder who are behaviorally indifferent and detached, children with DSED have patterns of culturally and socially inappropriate behaviors which are overly familiar with strangers. For example, the child does not distinguish between a parent and a complete stranger, and may go off with someone completely unfamiliar. Children with Disinhibited Social Engagement Disorder may also show signs of other developmental problems, like cognitive and language delay (American Psychiatric Association, 2013). Preschoolers with DSED, along with a lack of reticence with unfamiliar adults, usually resort to a variety of attention-seeking behaviors. In children with DSED, indiscriminate social behavior with adults may continue to occur well into middle childhood.

A diagnosis of DSED is not very common, and occurs more frequently in children who experience serious neglect from very early on (American Psychiatric Association, 2013). Some behavioral manifestation of this disorder, such as impulsive social engagement, may seem similar to impulsive behaviors in children with Attention Deficit Hyperactivity Disorder. However, in children with DSED, no attention difficulties or hyperactivity exist.

Posttraumatic Stress Disorder (PTSD)

PTSD usually presents as a pattern of symptoms in children who have experienced traumatic events, such as repeated abuse, or who have experienced or witnessed violence. In some children, such as in infants or toddlers, experiencing a single severe traumatic event can lead to symptoms of PTSD. Under DC:03R categorization, five criteria must be met for a child to be diagnosed with PTSD:

1) the child is exposed to one or a series of traumatic events; 2) the child shows signs of re-experiencing the trauma in play and outside of play; 3) the child shows signs of issues in social emotional developmental, such as in peer-related activities and socialization; 4) the child exhibits symptoms of increased arousal in sleep, attention, activities, etc.; and 5) the child's symptoms last for at least one month (Zero To Three, 2005). Behavioral and developmental signs of PTSD can include the following (Zero to Three, 2005; American Psychiatric Association, 2013):

- The child may have repeated re-enactment of aspects of the traumatic episode(s) during play.
- Outside of play, the child may experience involuntary recurrence or flashbacks of the experienced episode(s), or the memory of the episode(s).
- The child may have nightmares or dream aspects of the event(s).
- The child may ask about the experienced event(s) constantly, or seem preoccupied with aspects of the event(s).
- The child may have specific behavioral or even physiological reactions to the reminders of the event(s).
- The child may avoid emotions or stimuli associated with the traumatic event(s).
- Developmentally the child may show issues in social-emotional development, such as withdrawal, lack of appropriate affect, lack of interest, or lack of participation in typical games and activities, or relationship issues with peers and adults. The child may also have cognitive and memory issues, for example inability to remember an important aspect of the traumatic event(s).
- The child may have difficulty concentrating, be startled easily, be irritable, have anger outbursts or have temper tantrums.

Thus, early childhood teachers and other professionals should be on alert for these behaviors and consider the possibility of PTSD as a working hypothesis for investigation. PTSD is contrasted with Acute Stress Disorder, which is an immediate reaction to a traumatic experience.

Acute Stress Disorder

Symptoms of Acute Stress Disorder usually occur between three days and up to one month after a child experiences a severe traumatic experience. Symptoms of this disorder are very similar to those of Posttraumatic Stress Disorder, in that the child may have repeated flashbacks, reenact the experience or parts of the experience in and outside of play, have physiological and psychological symptoms, etc. Extreme levels of anxiety are also common in children with Acute Stress Disorder. A diagnosis of Acute Stress Disorder should take place within and up to one month after the child's exposure to the event (American Psychiatric Association, 2013). The symptoms usually resolve within or shortly after about one month passed the stressful event. However, if the symptoms persist for more than one month after the event, the diagnosis can be changed to Posttraumatic Stress Disorder (PTSD), given it meets all the related diagnostic criteria (American Psychiatric Association, 2013). Examples of this kind of traumatic experience may include such events as house fire, witnessing a shooting, or assault of a caregiver. If appropriate intervention and treatment for the child involved does not take place, then the event may lead to acute stress disorder for the child.

Other Related Disorders

Other disorders that are related to child maltreatment, stressful events, and trauma include depression or depressed mood, anxiety and fear, and uncontrolled anger (Zero To Three, 2005). In addition, children who experience and/or witness a sudden loss of a caregiver may have difficulties processing the traumatic event. It is likely that some children may experience a *Prolonged Bereavement/Grief Reaction*, which can manifest in behaviors such as repeated crying, refusing to be comforted, detachment, disrupted eating and sleeping, regression in developmental milestones already achieved, diminished range of affect, and a change in memory and cognitive functioning (Zero To Three, 2005). Parental death has also been associated with failure or low grades in school as the child gets older (Berg, Rostila, Saarela, & Hjern, 2014).

Closing Remarks

Any child may face adverse situations and events during the course of development. However, some conditions and situations may be severe enough to become traumatic for young children. Each child may react differently to a traumatic event or situation. What makes the difference is the availability of a responsive and nurturing caregiver who may help the child process and understand the traumatic event and cope with it effectively. Unfortunately, as I discussed in this chapter, there are many times that caregivers themselves can be the causes or perpetrators of the traumatic events for children – such as in cases of child abuse, neglect, and deprivation. There are also other causes of trauma, such as in cases of natural or unnatural events. No matter what kind and what the cause, the trauma does not always lead to negative consequences for the child, such as those discussed in this chapter, particularly when there is an intervention that supports the child and family in coping. There are also possible multiple sources which can act as protective factors against faced adversities, helping a child become resilient and develop in a healthy fashion despite the experienced trauma.

References

Ålander, T., Heimer, G., Svärdsudd, K., & Agréus, L. (2008). Abuse in women and men with and without functional gastrointestinal disorders. *Digestive Diseases and Sciences, 53*(7), 1856–1864.

American Psychiatric Association. (2013). *Diagnostic and statistical manual of mental disorders* (5th ed.). Arlington, VA: American Psychiatric Publishing.

Annerbäck, E. M., Sahlqvist, L., Svedin, C. G., Wingren, G., & Gustafsson, P. A. (2012). Child physical abuse and concurrence of other types of child abuse in Sweden – Associations with health and risk behaviors. *Child Abuse & Neglect, 36,* 585–595.

Bartlett, J. D., Raskin, M., Kotake, C., Nearing, K. D., & Easterbrooks, M. A. (2014). An ecological analysis of infant neglect by adolescent mothers. *Child Abuse & Neglect, 38*(4), 723–734.

Bayat, M. (2014). Understanding views of disability in the Cote d'Ivoire. *Disability & Society, 29*(1), 30–43.

Belsky, J., & de Haan, M. (2011). Annual research review: Parenting and children's brain development: The end of the beginning. *Journal of Child Psychology and Psychiatry, 52*(4), 409–428.

Berg, L., Rostila, M., Saarela, J., & Hjern, A. (2014). Parental death during childhood and subsequent school performance. *Pediatrics, 133*(4), 682–689.

CAPTA Reauthorization Act of 2010, 42 U.S.C. §5106a (2010).

Center for Disease Control. (2013). *Understanding child maltreatment.* Retrieved from: http://www.cdc.gov/violenceprevention/pdf/cm-factsheet--2013.pdf

Cruise, K. R., Jacobs, J. E., & Lyons, P. M. (1994). Definitions of physical abuse: A preliminary inquiry into children's perceptions. *Behavioral Sciences & the Law, 12*(1), 35–48.

De Bellis, M. D., Hooper, S. R., Woolley, D. P., & Shenk, C. E. (2010). Demographic, maltreatment, and neurobiological correlates of PTSD symptoms in children and adolescents. *Journal of Pediatric Psychology, 35*(5), 570–577.

Delima, J., & Vimpani, G. (2011). The neurobiological effects of childhood maltreatment: An often overlooked narrative related to the long-term effects of early childhood trauma? *Family Matters, 89,* 42–52.

Eslick, G. D., Koloski, N. A., & Talley, N. J. (2011). Sexual, physical, verbal/emotional abuse and unexplained chest pain. *Child Abuse & Neglect, 35*(8), 601–605.

Ford, J. D., Grasso, D., Greene, C., Levine, J., Spinazzola, J., & van der Kolk, B. (2013). Clinical significance of a proposed developmental trauma disorder diagnosis: Results of an international survey of clinicians. *Journal of Clinical Psychiatry, 74*(8), 841–849.

Garner, B. R., Hunter, B. D., Smith, D. C., Smith, J. E., & Godley, M. D. (2014). The relationship between child maltreatment and substance abuse treatment outcomes among emerging adults and adolescents. *Child Maltreatment, 19*(3/4), 261–269.

Godinet, M. T., Li, F., & Berg, T. (2013). Early childhood maltreatment and trajectories of behavioral problems: Exploring gender and racial differences. *Child Abuse & Neglect.* Advance online publication. doi: 10.1016/j.chiabu.2013.07.018

Goodwin, R. D., & Stein, M. B. (2004). Association between childhood trauma and physical disorders among adults in the United States. *Psychological Medicine, 34*(3), 509–520.

Graham, J. C., English, D. J., Litrownik, A. J., Thompson, R., Briggs, E. C., & Bangdiwala, S. I. (2010). Maltreatment chronicity defined with reference to development: Extension of the social adaptation outcomes findings to peer relations. *Journal of Family Violence, 25*(3), 311–324.

Hart, S. N., & Glaser, D. (2011). Psychological maltreatment: Maltreatment of the mind: A catalyst for advancing child protection toward proactive primary prevention and promotion of personal well-being. *Child Abuse & Neglect, 35*(10), 758–766.

Hibbard, R., Barlow, J., MacMillan, H, Committee on Child Abuse and Neglect, and American Academy of Child and Adolescent Psychiatry, Child Maltreatment and Violence Committee (2012). Psychological maltreatment. *Pediatrics, 130*(2), 372–378.

Hornor, G. (2012). Emotional maltreatment. *Journal of Pediatric Health Care, 26*(6), 436–442.

Karakurt, G., & Silver, K. E. (2014). Therapy for childhood sexual abuse survivors using attachment and family systems theory orientations. *American Journal of Family Therapy, 42*(1), 79–91.

Kempe, C. H., Silverman, F. N., Steele, B. F., Droegemueller, W., & Silver, H. K. (1962). The battered-child syndrome. *Journal of the American Medical Association, 181,* 17–24.

Kempke, S., Luyten, P., Claes, S., Van Wambeke, P., Bekaert, P., Goossens, L., & Van Houdenhove, B. (2013). The prevalence and impact of early childhood trauma in Chronic Fatigue Syndrome. *Journal of Psychiatric Research, 47*(5), 664–669.

Li, F., & Godinet, M. T. (2014). The impact of repeated maltreatment on behavioral trajectories from early childhood to early adolescence. *Children and Youth Services Review, 36,* 22–29.

Lourenço, C. B., Saintrain, M. V., & Vieira, A. P. (2013). Child, neglect and oral health. *BMC Pediatrics, 13*(188). doi: 10.1186/1471-2431-13-188

Manly, J. T. (2005). Advances in research definitions of child maltreatment. *Child Abuse & Neglect, 29*(5), 425–439.

McCullough, C., & Shaffer, A. (2014). Maternal depressive symptoms and child externalizing problems: Moderating effects of emotionally maltreating parenting behaviors. *Journal of Child and Family Studies, 23,* 389–398.

Mennen, F. E., Kim, K., Sang, J. & Trickett, P. K. (2010). Child neglect: Definition and identification of youth's experiences in official reports of maltreatment. *Child Abuse & Neglect, 34*(9), 647–658.

Mills, R., Scott, J., Alati, R., O'Callaghan, M., Najman, J. M., & Strathearn, L. (2013). Child maltreatment and adolescent mental health problems in a large birth cohort. *Child Abuse & Neglect, 37*(5), 292–302.

Nelson, K. (2012). The misuse of abuse: Restricting evidence of battered child syndrome. *Law and Contemporary Problems, 75,* 187–210.

Office of the United Nations High Commissioner for Human Rights. (1990). *Convention on the Rights of the Child.* New York: UNHCR. Retrieved from: http://www.ohchr.org/en/professionalinterest/pages/crc.aspx

Paavilainen, E., Lepistö, S., & Flinck, A. (2014). Ethical issues in family violence research in healthcare settings. *Nursing Ethics, 21*(1), 43–52.

Pretty, C., O'Leary, D. D., Cairney, J., & Wade, T. J. (2013). Adverse childhood experiences and the cardiovascular health of children: A cross-sectional study. *BMC Pediatrics, 13*(208). doi: 10.1186/1471-2431-13-208

Proctor, L. J., Skriner, L. C., Roesch, S., & Litrownik, A. J. (2010). Trajectories of behavioral adjustment following early placement in foster care: Predicting stability and change over 8 years. *Journal of the American Academy of Child & Adolescent Psychiatry, 49*(5), 464–473.

Reyome, N. D. (2010). Childhood emotional maltreatment and later intimate relationships: Themes from the empirical literature. *Journal of Aggression, Maltreatment, & Trauma, 19*(2), 224–242.

Shonkoff, J. P., Boyce, W. T., & McEwen, B. S. (2009). Neuroscience, molecular biology, and the childhood roots of health disparities: Building a new framework for health promotion and disease prevention. *JAMA: Journal of the American Medical Association, 301*(21), 2252–2259.

Southhall, D., & MacDonald, R. (2013). Protecting children from abuse: A neglected but crucial priority for the international child health agenda. *Pediatrics and International Child Health, 33*(4), 199–206.

Stoltenborgh, M., van Ijzendoorn, M. H., Euser, E. M., & Bakermans-Kranenburg, M. J. (2011). A global perspective on child sexual abuse: Meta-analysis of prevalence around the world. *Child Maltreatment, 16*(2), 79–101.

Stolzenberg, S. N., & Lyon, T. D. (2014). How attorneys question children about the dynamics of sexual abuse and disclosure in criminal trials. *Psychology, Public Policy, and Law, 20*(1), 19–30.

Thompson, R., & Tabone, J. K. (2010). The impact of early alleged maltreatment on behavioral trajectories. *Child Abuse & Neglect, 34*(12), 907–916.

U.S. Department of Health and Human Services, Administration for Children and Families, Administration on Children, Youth and Families, & Children's Bureau. (2013). *Child maltreatment 2012*. Retrieved from: http://www.acf.hhs.gov/programs/cb/resource/child-maltreatment-2012

Wekerle, C. (2011). Emotionally maltreated: The under-current of impairment? *Child Abuse & Neglect, 35*, 899–903.

Winrow, B., Bile, K., Hafeez, A., Davies, H., Brown, N., Zafar, S., ... Southall, D. P. (2012). A proposed new international convention supporting the rights of pregnant women and girls and their newborn infants. *Archives of Disease in Childhood, 97*, 447–451.

World Health Organization (WHO). (March 1999). *Report of the Consultation on Child Abuse Prevention*. Geneva: World Health Organization.

Zero To Three. (2005). Diagnostic classification of mental health and developmental disorders of infancy and early childhood (revised edition) (DC:0-3R). Washington, DC: Zero to Three Press.

Zimmerman, F., & Mercy, J. A. (2010). A better start: Child maltreatment prevention as a public health priority. *Zero to Three, 31*(5), 4–10.

4

CHALLENGING BEHAVIORS RELATED TO DEVELOPMENTAL AND OTHER DISORDERS IN CHILDREN

This chapter features a discussion of developmental, neurological, and social-emotional disorders that may lead to or accompany challenging behaviors, as well as the behavioral characteristics which present as challenging during early childhood. I examine diagnostic categories and classifications of such disorders and explain some basic features associated with them. My goal is to provide correct and up-to-date information about the behavioral characteristics of these disorders. I believe such knowledge may help teachers and parents understand behaviors of children with special needs and help them to identify appropriate ways of supporting social-emotional and behavioral aspects of the children's development from the onset of the appearance of the behavioral characteristics.

In learning about children who have developmental or emotional and behavioral health issues, it is important to keep several points in mind:

1. Typical development of young children, particularly from infancy through age five, undergoes a series of changes. Regardless of risks or established conditions, these changes may differ from child to child qualitatively (severity of a symptom) and quantitatively (number of presentations of the symptom). This variability is primarily due to unique differences in genetic predispositions, physical capabilities, environmental and cultural factors, and early experiences as well as child-rearing practices. Therefore, diagnoses of specific developmental disorders must be viewed in light of these dynamic phenomena. This also means that a diagnosis itself can be viewed as a tentative process, one that may change depending on the child's age, and social and emotional experiences, as well as a child's individual progression in the developmental process.

2. As discussed in previous chapters, an infant's early social experiences have direct consequences for neural and physiological development. When these

early experiences are severely distorted or traumatic, the consequences on development and behavior can indeed be grim. Therefore, understanding families and family processes must be part of the early diagnosis of every child. Working with parents and caregivers early during the development of a young child within the family's community and culture is the hallmark of intervention and education of children in early childhood.

3. Preschool-aged children may display a variety of behaviors that adults view as challenging. Although it is tempting for teachers and other educational professionals to form opinions in terms of possible diagnoses, it is important to avoid such temptations and remember:

   a. Some challenging behaviors are part of typical development.
   b. For a diagnostic assessment, clinicians use specific guidelines and rules related to the classification of disorders.
   c. Diagnostic assessments require the examination of multiple sources of data.
   d. Data sources include interviews with family members and educators, and medical records.
   e. Direct observations in both natural environments and clinical settings are an integral part of the process.

Such resources and expertise are not often at the disposal of teachers. Therefore, teachers must avoid labeling a child. Only a specialist can make a formal diagnosis.

Having considered these factors, I can now begin discussing important sources utilized for this work. Along with the most recent research literature, we make extensive use of two sources: 1) *Diagnostic and Statistical Manual of Mental Disorders: DSM-5* (American Psychiatric Association [APA], 2013), and 2) *Diagnostic Classification of Mental Health and Developmental Disorders in Infancy and Early Childhood: Revised Edition* (DC:0-3R; Zero to Three, 2005). Although a task force is in the process of revising the DC:0-3R, at the time of the writing of this book this revised diagnostic classification is not yet finalized and published (Zero to Three, 2014). The current DC:0-3R uses a complex multi-dimensional scheme that focuses on examining the infant–caregiver relationship in the context of community and culture. This approach uses information from various sources to apply to five different dimensions, called Axes: Axis I: disorders; Axis II: relationship classification; Axis III: medical and developmental disorders and conditions; Axis IV: psychosocial stressors; and Axis V: emotional and social functioning. Accordingly, information obtained from the assessment of the child based on all axes forms a comprehensive diagnosis for the child. The field of infant mental health advocates the use of the DC:0-3R along with DSM-5 to aid professionals in making a comprehensive diagnosis (Northcutt & McCarroll, 2014). It is clear that both classification sources consider various and necessary aspects of a child's development in context and enable professionals to recommend intervention and educational programs at multiple levels for young children and their families.

Therefore, in keeping with best practice recommendations, I use the DSM-5 in conjunction with the DC:0-3R to provide information and guidelines for professionals and parents. Thus, I have divided disorders, which have challenging behavioral manifestations into three general categories: 1) neurodevelopmental disorders; 2) behavior disorders; and 3) disorders of affect and emotional regulation.

Neurodevelopmental Disorders

Neurodevelopmental disorders manifest during early childhood and influence various areas of development such as cognition and learning, communication and social emotional development, adaptive and practical daily behaviors. Examples of neurodevelopmental disorders include, but are not limited to: Autism Spectrum Disorders, ADHD, intellectual disability, learning disability, global developmental delays, and communication and language disorders. In the following sections, I will describe several of these disorders. My focus will be only on disorders that are most common in early childhood along with their associated behavioral challenges.

Autism Spectrum Disorder (ASD)

The DSM-5 created a single category of Autism Spectrum Disorder (ASD) from the major diagnoses of: 1) Pervasive Developmental Disorders, Not Otherwise Specified (PDD-NOS); 2) Autistic disorder, also known as infantile autism and Kanner's disorder; and 3) Asperger's syndrome/disorder, as well as associated conditions known as high functioning autism and childhood disintegrative disorder. Accordingly, Autism Spectrum Disorder (ASD) is now a single diagnosis with three different levels of severity, from level one, representing the mildest form – such as in the previously termed Asperger's disorder – to level three, representing the most severe characteristics – such as in the previously termed autistic disorder (APA, 2013).

Children who are diagnosed with level three Autism Spectrum Disorder show severe functional, social, and communicative impairments. Such children require substantial levels of ongoing individual support in order to function successfully in both school and community (American Psychiatric Association, 2013). Children with level one and level two ASD also require support, although these levels can vary substantially and the need for ongoing individual support varies for supervisory, monitoring, and social-emotional guidance required. (For details of severity of levels of impairments, see Table 4.1.)

ASD is manifested in three major developmental and functioning areas of: 1) social-emotional/relational development; 2) communication development; and 3) the area of behavioral functioning. As related to the latter, impairments in certain neurodevelopmental areas, such as executive functioning and cognitive flexibility, influence patterns of behavior so that the child shows inflexibility and rigidity in behaviors and interests, which are often characterized as attachment issues and often as sameness and repetitive motor movements (Peters-Scheffer, Didden, Sigafoos, Green, & Korzilius, 2013).

Table 4.1 Three Levels of Impairments and Related Functional Abilities in Autism Spectrum Disorders

Impairments	Level 1 Mild impairments Supervision and monitoring support is needed.	Level 2 Moderate impairments Individual and regular monitoring and support is needed.	Level 3 Severe impairments One-on-one ongoing support is necessary.
Quality of Social Communication	• Has difficulties initiating communication • Has difficulties responding appropriately to others' social and communicative overtures.	• Has limited initiation in communication with others • Responses to other's social and communicative overtures are atypical • Has limited interest in others' interests • Has impairment in both verbal and non-verbal communication skills.	• Does not initiate communication with others • Does not respond, or seldom responds, to others' social overtures • Has no or very limited eye contact • Is usually non-verbal, or if able to verbalize may speak only in words or simple phrases.
Expressions of Emotions	• May have reduced affect • May have difficulties expressing emotions • Has difficulties understanding other's perspectives.	• Difficulties reciprocating emotions • Difficulties expressing feelings • Difficulties understanding other's perspectives.	• Does not reciprocate in verbal or non-verbal communication • Does not express emotions, or expresses feelings atypically • Does not consider/understand other's perspectives.
Quality of Social Interactions	• Has difficulties adjusting to some or all social contexts • Appears disinterested in others' interests • Has difficulties making friends, or is unsuccessful to make friends.	• Difficulties sharing imaginative or thematic play • Is not able to make friends on her own • Is not able to participate in pretend play • Is not able to share play with peers without intervention • Is unable or has severe difficulties in making friends without intervention.	• May make unusual approaches to have needs met • Does not share or seldom shares interest • Does not participate in pretend play • Does not make friends, nor seems interested to make friends • Is often isolated, or plays alone.

Behaviors	• Has narrow or single-minded interests • Has difficulties coping with change • Changing focus on something might be distressful.	• Interactions may be restricted to narrow interests • Has difficulties adjusting to change or transitions • Has difficulties shifting focus • May have repetitive behaviors • Is inflexible and adheres to specific routines	• Severe repetitive and stereotypical behaviors interfere with daily functioning • Is very rigid and inflexible and adheres to routines strictly • Is not able to cope with change and transition without support and preparation • May be anxious in social situations • May have mild to severe negative behavioral responses in reaction to change or various sources of sensory stimulations (e.g. auditory, visual, tactile, gustatory, movement, and taste) • May have aggressive behaviors toward self and others, or may have temper tantrums due to communication frustrations, anxiety, change, or in reaction to sensory stimuli
Overall Functioning	• Has good to high language abilities • Academic abilities range from average to very high • Is often unsuccessful in navigating social interactions and maintaining successful relationships • May be a loner • May be a subject of bullying.	• Is able to communicate verbally, though may speak in simple sentences or persevere in a topic of interest • Could be successful academically • Is often unsuccessful in making friends and navigating social relationship • May isolate self.	• Impairments in all areas are obvious and severe • Does not have any functional communication abilities • Usually isolates self, and is not able to make or maintain any functional and reciprocal relationships • Is not able to function in the school and community on a daily basis without a substantial ongoing and individual support • Isolates self.
Level of Support Needed	Without support, deficits could be noticeable and could cause impaired functioning.	Social deficits are obvious, and without support the child is likely to fail in social functioning.	Ongoing individual support is needed throughout life.

Source: Adapted from American Psychiatric Association. (2013). *Diagnostic and Statistical Manual of Mental Disorders: Fifth Edition*. Washington, DC: American Psychiatric Publishing.

Adaptive and daily functioning of children who are diagnosed with ASD depends on the degree and quality of the impairments in each of the three areas. For example, the degree of communication deficit determines whether or not a child has useful language, some functional language, or is completely non-verbal. The severity of impairment in social relatedness and interactions determines whether or not the child is able to share interests, make friends, expresses emotions and feelings, and understands and predicts feelings and perspectives of others – or, alternatively, seems completely indifferent to interacting with peers and adults. Finally, the level and severity of behavioral deficits determines how the child can or cannot adapt to change, and whether or not the child has repetitive patterns of behavioral and motor movements. Constant and repeated motor movements, called *stereotyped behaviors*, such as hand flapping, body rocking, finger flickering, flipping, spinning, or lining up objects and toys, often interfere with a child's daily functioning and learning (Hattlier, Matson, Macmillan, & Williams, 2013). A verbal child's repetitive behavior can manifest itself in repeated speech patterns, or echoing words, phrases, and/or sentences, called *echolalia*. Echolalia in a child can interfere with language learning (Valentino, Shillingsburg, Conine, & Powell, 2014). Furthermore, echolalia may indicate a child's need for alleviating anxiety in self, or be a result of the lack of comprehension of what is heard (Grossi, Marcone, Cinquegrana, & Gallucci, 2013).

Prevalence of ASD

In March of 2014, the Centers for Disease Control and Prevention (CDC) announced that according to its last surveillance, the prevalence of autism is currently 1 in every 68 children (these numbers vary in gender: 1 in 42 boys, and 1 in 189 girls) (Centers for Disease Control and Prevention [CDC], 2014b). The CDC surveillance system for autism is called the Autism and Developmental Disorder Monitoring (ADDM) Network, consisting of 14 communities in various states in the U.S. The ADDM uses health/medical, school, and special education records of school-aged children (eight years old) to estimate the number of children diagnosed with autism across all surveillance sites. The CDC has reported autism prevalence since 2000; at that time, the prevalence rate was 1 in 150 (CDC, 2014b). A decade earlier, this rate was reported to be 3.3 per 10,000 children (Wing, 1993).

Several factors, such as changes in the diagnostic criteria, global awareness of autism, a widespread availability of developmental screening in early childhood, and unknown environmental and genetic interplay are attributed to this rise (CDC, 2014b). For example, the 2000 version of the diagnostic classifications of psychiatric disorders, DSM-IV, which changed the diagnosis of autism from a single disorder to a spectrum of disorders, caused a decrease in diagnosis of intellectual disability and an increase in the diagnosis of ASD. This meant that children who were previously misdiagnosed with intellectual disability began to receive a diagnosis of autism since 2000. With the new and current DSM-5, which now provides more restrictive guidelines for diagnosis of ASD, some speculate that the number of children diagnosed with ASD may decrease (Maenner et al., 2014). A discussion of the possible factors contributing to the rise or fall in the incidence of autism prevalence, and the causal theories of autism is beyond the scope of this chapter. For a synthesis of causal theories of autism see Bayat (2012), and for a discussion of a rise in the prevalence of autism see Maenner et al. (2014).

Challenging Behaviors Associated with ASD

Most children with Autism Spectrum Disorder display some challenging behaviors. In fact, most parents and teachers find that addressing these challenging behaviors is one of the most stressful aspects of their daily interactions with their children and students (Hayes & Watson, 2013; Peters-Scheffer et al., 2013; Reed & Osborne, 2013). The number, quality, and severity of challenging behaviors varies from one child to the next. In general, there are several common challenging behaviors that occur in most children with ASD that can interfere with their daily functioning and learning. The most common challenging behaviors include:

- Severe overreaction or underresponsiveness (and sensory-seeking behaviors) toward one or more sensory stimuli, estimated to occur in 95 percent of children with autism and in all severity levels (Elwin, Ek, Kjellin, & Schröder, 2013; Joosten & Bundy, 2010). Examples include:
  - frequent and difficult to soothe temper tantrums
  - anxious and fearful behaviors, such as running away or lashing out
  - difficulties with change, such as transitioning from one activity to another or from one object to the next
  - hyperactivity, such as running and constant movement and/or severe stereotyped behaviors, such as repeated motoric movements
  - eating problems, such as food selectivity by type and texture, food refusal, or eating non-food items, called *pica*.
- Sleeping problems and irregularities, such as difficulties going to sleep or prolonged wakefulness during the night.
- Toileting problems, such as difficulties with being toilet trained or having specific/odd toileting habits.
- Aggression toward others, estimated in about 35 percent of children with autism (Carroll et al., 2014).
- Self-injury, such as picking skin or self-hitting.

Certain challenging behaviors seem to be more frequent than others. Many challenging behaviors can be a result of sensory problems, which is mentioned in an overwhelming majority of children with autism experiences (Chuang, Tseng, Lu, & Shieh, 2012; Joosten & Bundy, 2010). Anxious and fearful behaviors and phobias are also common in children with various functioning levels. In fact, fight or flight responses in children with autism often result from high anxiety level in combination with sensory processing difficulties.

Sleeping irregularities and toileting problems are very common during early childhood in children with all levels of autism severity. Temper tantrums are one of the highest occurring problems in children with various severity levels, particularly during early childhood (Maskey, Warnell, Parr, Le Couteur, & McConachie, 2013). Temper tantrums and aggressive behaviors are particular barriers to social skills development. Aggressive behaviors toward others or self (e.g. self-injury) are troubling and difficult to deal with, and they seem to be more common in children who have minimal expressive language abilities (Maskey et al., 2013). Furthermore, children who have limited language abilities are more likely to be placed in special schools or day programs. Figure 4.1 depicts a range of challenging behaviors in children with autism.

In the following section, I will present two case examples of children with ASD who have two different functioning levels.

Ethan: A Case Example of Level 3 ASD

As an infant, Ethan had difficulties nursing. He had and still has a very irregular sleeping cycle. He wakes up in the middle of the night and does not go to sleep for two or three hours. As an infant, Ethan did not show any interest in playing peek-a-boo or lap games with his parents or grandparents. Ethan's parents were concerned

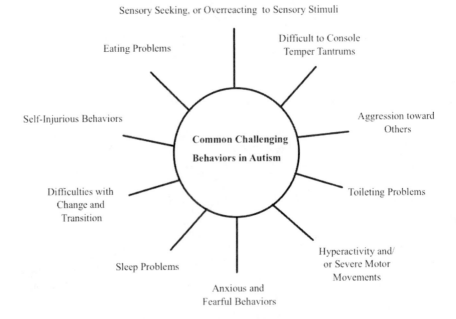

FIGURE 4.1 Range of Challenging Behaviors in Children with Autism Spectrum Disorders

about Ethan's hearing because when they called his name he seemed not to hear, that is, he did not turn his head around and seemed to be oblivious to family voices. However, a hearing test showed Ethan's hearing to be normal.

Ethan learned to walk around 11 months of age. As soon as he was able to walk, he showed an interest in carrying two hairbrushes with him around the house. When his mother took him to their backyard, Ethan went in search of little pieces of twigs and sticks, which he then picked up and carried with him around the garden. Ethan loved to run back and forth, while hanging on to his sticks or hairbrushes. Unlike other children of his age, by 14 months Ethan did not point to objects or toys of his interest or to things that he wanted. If he wanted an object, he would take his mother or father by hand to that object.

By 18 months, Ethan was able to count to three and say words like juice and several animal names, but he did not have many other words. When excited, Ethan would flap his hands in the air and make screeching noises. Ethan also made noises when he was busy playing with something. Ethan's parents consulted their pediatrician about some of Ethan's lack of language and he advised them to wait a couple of months to see whether there may be improvements with Ethan's language development.

Ethan did not imitate adults around him, nor did he show an interest in other children when his mother took him to a neighborhood playgroup. When Ethan was two years old, he showed an interest in animals. He liked to put animal figures in rows and carry small stuffed animals with him. Although Ethan did not have many words, he named several animals and could recognize various types of animal pictures in books when asked to show them.

Ethan is now two and a half years old. Despite his ability to utter some words, and although he is able to vocalize various sounds and noises, he does not use words to make his needs known. Ethan easily gets frustrated and throws temper tantrums, which are difficult to soothe. In particular, it is hard for Ethan's parents to take him to public places because of Ethan's frequent and unpredictable tantrums. Ethan seems to have a hard time with noisy places, such as restaurants and grocery stores. Going on elevators, escalators, and through sliding doors causes Ethan to act extremely frightened, which he shows by screaming and refusing to go. Ethan's parents sought help from their local Child and Family Connections, the agency through which early intervention evaluation and intervention services are provided for families. After initial developmental screening and observation, the Early Intervention Team recommended that a full evaluation for Ethan be performed as soon as possible, so that appropriate intervention can be designed and delivered.

Sophia: A Case Example of Level 1 ASD

Sophia is eight and a half years old. She is an avid reader, and is currently in third grade in a small elementary school. Her favorite books are encyclopedias and the Guinness World Records books, which she is able to read fluently. Sophia has an extraordinary memory and knows thousands of interesting facts. For example, she knows that "the inventor of Vaseline used to eat a spoonful of it every day." Sophia loves rules, and everything in her room at home has to be organized in a certain way. Having clear rules for everything makes her feel good and safe. Sophia feels anxious when she goes to crowded places. Many times, when at school and in her classroom, Sophia feels unhappy and nervous. Although Sophia likes to have many friends, she is not very good at making friends. When her teacher asks her and her classmates to work together, she tends to dominate the group time by talking about what she knows, and is impatient for others to finish their turn in the project. Sometimes, classmates show boredom when she shares facts, or they make fun of her. At such times, Sophia feels particularly vulnerable and very sad. She is extremely sensitive about what others say about her.

At certain times, when having trouble fitting in, Sophia gets so angry that she may end up screaming and lashing out at her peers. In these times, Sophia's teacher usually helps her calm down by taking her to a quiet place and suggesting a book to read. Reading books helps Sophia calm down and feel better. Sophia's teacher and the school's social worker have lately been working together with Sophia to help her talk about her feelings when she feels upset, angry, anxious, or frustrated. With their help, Sophia has learned some very useful social skills strategies. She has learned which particular words to use to ask to be included in games and groups, and how to be patient with her peers when they are speaking or expressing their own opinions. Sophia now has two good friends – Allison and Sierra – who spend much time with her in school and after school. Allison and Sierra think Sophia has a great sense of humor, and that she is very smart. They often play the *Trivial Pursuit* board game together. Sophia has learned to enjoy some games, which Allison and Sierra like as well, like the *Best Friend Sleep Over* game.

Disorders Associated with Autism

There is a growing body of evidence that suggests autism co-occurs with other neuropsychiatric disorders, and therefore challenging behaviors occur, or are exacerbated, because of these associated disorders. The presentation of one or more conditions (disorder) in addition to a primary condition is called *comorbidity*. Common comorbid conditions with autism are attention deficit hyperactive disorder (ADHD), anxiety disorders, obsessive compulsive disorder, depression, sleep and eating disorders, developmental coordination disorder, intellectual disability, and structural language disorder (APA, 2013; Joosten & Bundy, 2010; Lichtenstein, Carlström, Råstam, Gillberg, & Anckarsäter, 2010; Rommelse, Franke, Geurts, Hartman, & Buitelaar, 2010; Simonoff, Jones, Baird, Pickles, Happé, & Charman, 2013). To date, the possible genetic and environmental interplay mechanisms which may cause these disorders to overlap with autism are not known (Lichenstein et al., 2010; Rutter, 2014). However, as mentioned, there seems to be a relationship between the severity of behavioral problems and a coexistence with one or more of these disorders (Simonoff et al., 2013).

Although I will describe some of these disorders separately, it is important to acknowledge this link between the aforementioned disorders and autism to help us understand the similarities and common behavioral characteristics in children with autism with those in other children who are diagnosed with, for example, ADHD, intellectual disability, or anxiety disorders. Understanding these similarities and their causal roots and functions are essential in helping us design appropriate and effective interventions to address these challenging behaviors.

Sensory Processing Issues and Associated Challenging Behaviors

In 1972, Jane Ayers, an occupational therapist, coined the term *sensory integration* in reference to a process in which the brain receives, organizes, and processes sensory information, and, as a result, the person responds to the stimuli. Depending on the brain processing of the sensory information, the behavioral responses from the individual may vary, from aversion of one or more sensory stimuli to seeking them. According to this theory, sensory processing and the brain's ability to modulate, process, and send responses in response directly influences the regulation of emotions and behavior, as well as learning. Ayers explained that some children's difficulties in processing of sensory stimuli results in certain negative behavioral manifestations and learning difficulties (1972). For example, a child may not be able to regulate various sensory sources of information and remain calm during learning and social interactions. For this child, there are too many sources of information, such as visual, auditory, tactile or numbers of speakers, etc. The child then may become hyperactive, anxious, or aggressive as a result.

In more recent years, the term *Sensory Processing Disorder* has been used as a diagnostic term, with specific implication for treatment (Roley, Mailloux, Miller-Kuhaneck, & Glennon, 2007). Accordingly, sensory processing dysfunction is treatable through *sensory integration therapy*. In sensory integration therapy, a variety of appropriate sensory activities are designed and implemented to target processing of the information received from sensory systems. These are: *auditory*, or sound processing; *tactile*, or processing of touch; *gustatory*, processing of taste; *olfactory*, processing of smell; *visual*, processing of vision; *vestibular*, processing of movement and sense of balance; and *proprioceptive*, processing of sense of position of the body in space – adjustment of body and movement of muscles. Sensory integration therapy is implemented by an occupational therapist with specific training in this therapy.

Since the 1970s, sensory integration theory and its related sensory processing disorder are the subject of disagreement amongst clinicians and scholars. The APA (2013) does not acknowledge a separate diagnosable disorder termed as "sensory processing disorder," or a "regulatory disorder." On the contrary, the DC:0-3R (Zero to Three, 2005) does in fact use the term *Regulation Disorders of Sensory Processing* to refer to difficulties in regulating appropriate behavioral responses in reaction to sensory stimuli.

In its diagnostic categorization, DC:0-3R draws on Ayer's sensory integration theory. In fact, this theory is frequently used in scholarly literature and clinical practice throughout the field of infant mental health. One reason for the popularity of this theory is that it provides a useful explanation for behavioral and individual differences in very young children during the early years when development is subject to great variability and change (Anzalone & Ritchey, 2014). Additionally, the sensory integration theory supports a method of intervention, which utilizes adult–child engagement, interaction, and play to help infants and toddlers overcome sensory sensitivities. Currently, a sensory integration therapy designed and often delivered by an occupational therapist, or by an early childhood educator, is one of the most popular methods for young children with special needs in clinical intervention and early educational programs.

Part of the disagreement about sensory processing difficulties being a separate diagnosable disorder in child and adolescent psychiatry is that the DSM-5 describes characteristics of sensory processing difficulties, such as adverse behavioral reactions to sensory stimuli, under the behavioral symptoms of autism spectrum disorder (ASD) and Attention Deficit Hyperactivity Disorder (ADHD). The DSM-5 describes additional symptoms of sensory processing disorder, such as lack of coordination and difficulties performing sequential tasks, under *Developmental Coordination Disorder*. Thus, because there is currently not a consensus that sensory processing issues do in fact fall under a separate diagnosable condition, I refrain from taking a position on the issue here. It is important, however, to discuss specific behavioral characteristics that are related to sensory processing difficulties whether related to autism, ADHD, or Developmental Coordination Disorder, since the sensory issues are integrally related to behavioral displays.

Under the *Regulation Disorder of Sensory Processing*, the DC:0-3R, categorizes three main features: 1) sensory processing difficulties; 2) motor difficulties; and 3) specific behavioral patterns. Below is a description of categories of the common characteristics of regulation disorder, which are detailed in DC:03-R (Zero to Three, 2005) and found in current occupational therapy research (such as in Anzalone & Ritchey, 2014; Ashburner, Bennett, Rodger, & Ziviani, 2013; Chuang et al., 2012; Elwin et al., 2013; Joosten & Bundy, 2010):

1. Fear and overreaction to sensory stimuli may occur as a result of oversensitivity to various sensory stimuli, such as noise, bright lighting, specific tactile sensations and touch, smells, tastes, or movements. In such situations the child may be startled, freeze, attempt to escape, be agitated, be distracted, have angry outbursts, or cry. An overreactivity to taste and smell may result in avoiding certain foods and textures with strong smells and tastes. Children may avoid exploration of objects, activities, or refrain from interaction with others whom they perceive as being invasive sensory wise, such as being too close, too loud, or too energetic. In situations when these children feel overwhelmed or overloaded by sensory stimuli, they may react by screaming or crying for what

is perceived by others as no apparent reason. They may be difficult to soothe or calm down on their own.

2. Aggression and defiance in reaction to offensive sensory stimulation can also be common in children who are hypersensitive toward various sensory stimuli. A child may react in angry outbursts or become aggressive when overburdened by certain sensory stimuli. Some children may become distracted by the level of noise or visual clutter, and therefore be unable to focus and process the information around them. Other children may become overly attached to specific routines as a way of exerting some control or ability to predict the oncoming auditory, visual, and tactile sensory stimulation in their environment. Unpredictability of one's environment or events can be highly anxiety producing in these children, thus transition and change will be difficult for most of them.

3. Hyposensitivity toward sensory stimulation is a condition in which a child requires higher sensory input in order to appropriately process the stimuli, and therefore be able to respond to these stimuli. In this situation, the child seems passive and unresponsive to various sensory information, including social interactions that may be initiated by adults and peers around them. Poor motor coordination and clumsiness may be common, and the child may be inattentive and seem physically tired.

4. Sensory seeking may occur when a child is hyposensitive and requires a high sensory input, and therefore actively and frequently seeks sensory input to satisfy his sensory needs. Craving particular stimuli may manifest itself in highly intensive sensory movements (e.g. motor movements), high activity level, constant contact with people, disorganized behaviors, excitability, intrusiveness, and reckless and risk-taking behaviors. In addition in some children (specifically in children with autism), *pica*, or eating non-food items, is explained by sensory seeking of strong tastes or smells.

Attention Deficit Hyperactivity Disorder (ADHD)

Attention Deficit Hyperactivity Disorder (ADHD) is one of the most common childhood neurodevelopmental disorders. The number of children diagnosed with ADHD is reported to be on the rise from 7 percent in 2003 to 11 percent by 2011, in children from 4 to 17 years old (Centers for Disease Control, 2014a). The current ADHD prevalence rate of 11 percent represents over 6.4 million children in the United States, with a 6 percent average annual increase rate for the number of ADHD cases since 2003 (Visser et al., 2014). In comparing the U.S. statistics to global trends for the number of children diagnosed with ADHD the incidence level is yet unknown, which may be a factor in the availability of early intervention services. Estimates of ADHD presentation in all countries is about 5 percent of total number of children, and 2.5 percent of total number of adults (APA, 2013; Sciberras et al., 2013).

Not all children retain their diagnosis of ADHD through their adulthood (Law, Sideridis, Prock, & Sheridan, 2014). However, about 30 percent of children with ADHD do retain their diagnosis (Visser et al., 2014), and these children are the ones who are likely to show both internalizing and externalizing symptoms of mental health issues, such as depression and challenging behaviors in later years (Law et al., 2014). About 69 percent of children diagnosed with ADHD (3.5 million children in the USA) take a prescribed ADHD medication (Visser et al., 2014). A combination of medication and behavioral approaches is shown to be the most effective treatment for children with ADHD (Villodas, McBurnett, Kaiser, Rooney, & Pfifner, 2014).

We can compare the incidence of early childhood diagnoses for ADHD of 5 percent with the available statistics for the population of school-aged children (ages 7–11), which shows a somewhat higher incidence of the disorder of 11 percent. The reason for this difference is that preschool-aged and younger children with ADHD may receive a diagnosis of *Regulation Disorder of Sensory Processing* instead of ADHD. Therefore, it is likely that most children receive the new diagnosis of ADHD later on when they show problems in performing academic tasks that require more focused attention and sitting at the desk for longer periods.

There are various theories regarding specific areas of brain dysfunction in ADHD, as well as genetic-environmental interplay factors. An examination of the literature regarding these theories is beyond the scope of this chapter. (For related research syntheses see Bayat, 2012 and Schrieber, Possin, Girard, & Rey-Casserly, 2014.)

Symptoms and Behavioral Characteristics of ADHD

Although ADHD has only become popularly known during the past two decades, the disorder is documented in history since at least 1845. Heinrich Hoffman, a German physician and poet, described inattentive and hyperactive behaviors of some of his pediatric patients in his poems "Fidgety Phillip" and "The Story of Johnny Head-in-the-Air" (for details see Bayat, 2012). Since 1902, various terms have been used to refer to what we know today as ADHD, such as *restless syndrome*, *hyperactive child syndrome*, and more recently, *Attention Deficit Disorder (ADD)*.

The term Attention Deficit Disorder (ADD), which was used from the 1970s through early 1990s, emphasized the symptoms of inattention in the child, and was known to include two types, with or without hyperactivity (Barkley, 1997). In 1994 the DSM-IV formally replaced the term ADD with ADHD. The adopted ADHD terminology in the DSM-IV included the presence of three subtypes of ADHD: 1) predominantly hyperactive-impulsive type; 2) predominantly inattentive type; 3) combined type (American Psychiatric Association [APA], 2000).

The subtypes described in DSM-IV highlighted different presentations of ADHD, in that not all children who have attention problems are necessarily hyperactive, and vice versa. On the other hand, there are some children with ADHD who have attention problems, hyperactivity, and impulsivity issues.

These distinctions are not well understood by educators and parents and have created a lack of clarity in terms of symptoms, needed treatment, and educational modifications for children with ADHD in early childhood education settings and beyond. In addition, since a degree of hyperactivity and impulsivity is typical in early childhood, both parents and educators are often at a loss as to what may constitute the clinical representations of ADHD as opposed to being typical active behavior.

The DSM-5 attempts to make clarifications by doing away with subtypes of ADHD, and providing clearer explanations of the symptoms of ADHD in a unified way. As such, the criterion for diagnosis of ADHD is a pattern of inattention and/or hyperactivity and impulsivity to the extent that it interferes with developmental daily functioning, and academic performance of a child, and negatively impacts social-emotional and daily activities of a child (APA, 2013). To give the diagnosis of ADHD, the symptoms of inattention or hyperactivity and impulsivity must be present in a child prior to age 12, and should be manifested for at least six months prior to diagnosis. It is important to keep in mind that for a diagnosis of ADHD to apply, inattention and/or hyperactivity and impulsivity symptoms should be inconsistent with the developmental level of the child. Thus, the examiner or diagnostician must be thoroughly familiar with child developmental milestones and behavioral trajectory. Furthermore, none of the symptoms should be directly as a result of oppositional behaviors or failure of the child to understand the task itself (APA, 2013). The DSM-5 acknowledges that ADHD may have three different presentations of predominantly inattentive, combined, or predominantly hyperactive and impulsive.

Inattention

By virtue of their developmental characteristics, young children have a short attention span and are usually not able to sustain attention for more than 15 to 20 minutes at a time. This is primarily the reason why in preschool settings, large and small group activities and lessons are designed to take place in no longer than 10- to 20-minute periods. However, as children enter kindergarten, they are expected to be able to perform tasks that require sustained attention and focus.

Regardless of the normative tendencies of young children to be inattentive, children who have ADHD with inattention symptoms are distinguishable from their peers during preschool. These children often fail to focus during play or a lesson activity for more than a few minutes at a time. They may fail to follow all steps of a multi-step direction, or refuse to engage in cognitive lessons that require focus. Older school-aged children with ADHD with inattention symptoms frequently lose their school supplies and belongings. They may be disorganized, forgetful, or make careless mistakes in their school assignments. A lack of ability to organize thoughts in a logical sequence or having problems recalling facts in a sequential order is also common in children with ADHD (Wei, Yu, & Shaver, 2014).

Hyperactivity and Impulsivity

Hyperactivity and impulsivity are explained as a lack of motor control and emotional regulation of sensory processing. Therefore, problems of motor control, sequencing and planning, goal orientation, emotional control, and attention are linked to impairments in executive functioning in brain-connecting pathways to and from the frontal lobe, as seen through functional magnetic resonance imaging (fMRI) studies of ADHD (for details see Schrieber et al., 2014; and Skogli, Egland, Anderson, Hovik, & Øie, 2014). Additionally, in children with ADHD, there is a basic defect in the metabolism of the neurotransmitters *dopamine* and *norepinephrine* at the synaptic level. Neurotransmitters are chemicals that aid in transmission of electrical impulses (which carry sensory and other information) between neurons. Inefficiency in neurotransmitters causes a lack of or a defunct communication in the brain. This is primarily the reason why stimulant medications are effective in treatment of ADHD. Stimulants increase the amount of available dopamine and norepinephrine at the neuronal level through different cellular pathways and thus help the neurotransmitters make connections (Prasad, Brogan, Mulvaney, Grainge, Stanton, & Sayal, 2013).

In terms of symptoms, preschool-aged children with ADHD are often referred to as being "on the go." They may fidget or squirm in their seats and be unable to keep their hands and feet still or respect the space of the child sitting next to them. They often have difficulties in group and/or circle time, when they are required to be seated for a certain period. They may constantly run or climb when it is inappropriate to do so. In activities requiring cooperation and coordination of a group of children, they may fail to maintain calm, have difficulties waiting for their turn, and be unable to prevent themselves from interrupting others. A lack of emotional regulation in some children with ADHD creates difficulties in making friends and socializing with peers. Older and school-aged children with ADHD who are hyperactive and impulsive may fail to think about the consequences of their actions before resorting to a task, and therefore often have conflicts in their social interactions. In the classroom, they may fail to raise their hand when required, blurt out answers, or talk excessively and inappropriately.

A great number of children with ADHD also display oppositional and challenging behaviors. Some challenging behaviors in these children are related to a low tolerance level of others' perspectives and an inability to consider the consequences of one's action before resorting to aggressive behavior, both of which are part of symptoms of ADHD. However, in some children, patterns of externalizing behaviors, such as aggression and oppositional behaviors, as well as internalizing behaviors may also exist; these may be due to other comorbid conditions such as Oppositional Defiant Disorder, Conduct Disorder, speech, language and learning disorders, Autism Spectrum Disorder, and anxiety disorders, all of which are now known to be commonly co-morbid in a large of number of children with ADHD (Rutter, 2014; Sciberras et al., 2013; Wei et al., 2014). Children with ADHD who have another associated disorder are particularly at risk for additional mental health issues later on, as well as being likely to retain their diagnoses through their adulthood (Law et al., 2014; Sciberras et al., 2013; Wei et al., 2014).

ADHD is a serious public health concern. Children with ADHD are at risk for academic failure, and are often misunderstood by their family members and educators in that their inability to sustain attention and apply themselves to tasks is frequently misinterpreted as laziness or lack of intellectual acumen. In addition, a learning disability (LD), such as dyslexia or dyscalculia, is a common co-occurring condition with ADHD in many children, with estimations ranging from 30 percent to 80 percent of total children diagnosed with ADHD (Ashkenazi, Rubinstein, & Henik, 2009) possessing some specific learning disability as well. Retrieval and recall memory problems are common in children with ADHD (Vakil, Blachstein, Wertman-Elad, & Greenstein, 2014). Therefore, poor academic performance and school failure outcomes are likely in these children. Lack of focus on the one hand, and impulsiveness on the other hand, often result in a misinterpretation that such a child is uncooperative. Therefore, social rejection and conflicts with peers and adults are common. School-related problems together with social rejection put children with ADHD at multiple risks for future mental health problems, relationship and family issues, and social and job failure. For these reasons, it is ever more imperative that early childhood educators understand the various needs of children with ADHD and work successfully early on to reverse a possible negative developmental course for them.

Intellectual Disability (ID) or Developmental Disorder/Delay

Intellectual Disability (ID), also known as *intellectual developmental disorder*, is a deficit in major areas of intellectual functioning, such as personal, social, academic, and occupational development (APA, 2013). In the previous versions of the DSM, the term *mental retardation* was used to refer to such impairments. The term intellectual disability has been in use in the language by most special education scholars for the past two or three decades. The World Health Organization's International Classification of Diseases has also used the term intellectual developmental disorders for the past several decades. Since the 1980s, professional associations such as the American Association of Intellectual and Developmental Disabilities have advocated for a terminology change from "mental retardation" to "intellectual disability." However, the term "mental retardation," or "mental handicap," continued in psychiatric health and legal language until 2010. In 2010, President Obama signed Rosa's Law (PL 111-256). This law strikes down the term "mental retardation" replacing it with "intellectual disability" in all governmental documents related to education, health, and research. In 2014, the U.S. Supreme Court similarly struck down the term "mental retardation," replacing it with "intellectual disability" in the language of the court and all related legal processes (Mauro, 2014). With similar changes in DSM-5 terminology, the term mental retardation is now formally removed from health, science and education, and legal and governmental areas.

Currently, then, an intellectual disability is considered to be a developmental disorder marked by a delay in one or more areas of development, such as cognition, language, motor, or social-emotional. The signs of delay are usually apparent before or by age two, which is the typical period for the accomplishment of major developmental milestones. Causes of ID may be related to genetic, neurobiological, environmental, or accidental factors that can occur prenatally, or during and after birth (for a recent discussion on genetics causes of ID see Tucker et al., 2014). ID may coexist with physical and/or emotional problems, such as seizures, depression, and anxiety, and other neurodevelopmental disorders, such as autism and ADHD (APA, 2013).

An intellectual disability in children can be mild, moderate, severe, or profound, and deficits in the level of development concern three areas of functioning: 1) deficits in conceptual and intellectual functioning; 2) deficits in social and communication functioning; and 3) deficits in practical and daily living skills and functioning (APA, 2013). In a preschooler, deficits in the mentioned areas may manifest as a slow rate of processing information; difficulties with age-appropriate cognitive tasks such as putting together puzzles and block structures; delays in receptive and language development and peer interactions; and delays and difficulties with adaptive skills, such as toileting.

Assessment of ID and its severity is determined by the use of standardized measures in the three areas of deficits, i.e. adaptive functioning, social-emotional development, and intellectual functioning. Because of variation in development during early childhood, and because an accurate measure of intellectual functioning is very difficult to determine in young children, professionals in early intervention and clinical practice commonly use the term *developmental delay* or *developmental disorder*. This diagnosis may later change to ID and/or other conditions during the elementary school years. Not all children with ID have challenging behaviors; however, some children with ID may display a variety of externalizing and internalizing behavioral issues, which may be due to the child's frustrations with learning, communication, comprehension of surroundings, or difficulties with task performance and socialization.

Communication and Learning Disorders

Language and communication impairments, such as language disorder and speech disorder, in and of themselves do not necessarily have associated challenging behavioral characteristics. However, children with communication disorders are at an increased risk for challenging behaviors due to frustrations resulting from their problems with receptive and/or expressive language development. It is not uncommon for children with speech and language disorders in early childhood to have frequent temper tantrums, or to act aggressively as a result of their difficulties in comprehension (receptive language) of what is said to and around them. The same applies when these children are not able to make their needs and ideas known (expressive language). Children with language and speech impairments are likely to have other neurodevelopmental conditions such as ASD, intellectual and developmental delay, and ADHD (APA, 2013).

Children with language or speech disorders and children with LD are the largest group of children with special needs who receive special education in the USA since 1976 (U.S. Department of Education, 2014). Language and speech impairments are closely associated with LD. In fact, a number of scholars have argued that language and speech disorders are in fact the same, or that language impairments are the preliminary forms of specific learning disorders (Sun & Wallach, 2014). Therefore, children who have a communication disorder in preschool are likely to be identified with one or more kinds of learning disorders in later school years. Learning disorders are usually identified during elementary school years when children are required to perform academic tasks. Specific learning disorders can be in the areas of reading, spelling, writing, math concepts and calculation, memory and recall, and visual and auditory sequencing and processing. Challenging behavioral manifestations of learning disorders may present in the child when the child shows reluctance to participate in the learning process, or when the child displays oppositional behaviors that are likely directly or indirectly related to their frustrations with learning (APA, 2013).

Behavior Disorders

Behavior and impulse control disorders are related to situations in which a child loses emotional regulation and self-control to the extent that the behaviors violate the safety of others, e.g. through aggression, or violation of the rights of others (theft, for example). The DSM-5 lists three specific conditions under behavior disorders. These are: Oppositional Defiant Disorder (ODD), Conduct Disorder (CD), and antisocial personality disorder. Oppositional Defiant Disorder and Conduct Disorder are the most commonly diagnosed disorders, and only ODD is diagnosed during early childhood. CD is most often diagnosed after age eight, usually in adolescence. Both ODD and CD are more common in boys than girls; both disorders are marked with aggression and externalizing behaviors, and both of them are identified before adulthood (APA, 2013).

Because CD is manifested in later years, we do not focus on its features in this chapter. However, it is important to note here that ODD and CD are linked together, in that many children with ODD are later identified with CD (Rolon-Arroyo, Arnold, & Harvey, 2014). Because of this connection, the question arises as to whether or not ODD exists on a continuum, rather than being qualitatively present or not present all at once (Barry, T. D., Marcus, Barry, C. T., & Coccaro, 2013; Burke, Waldman, & Lahey, 2010). The answer is unclear. However, there is some evidence that suggests that the symptoms of CD may be in fact present during early childhood and years before a formal diagnosis (Barry et al., 2013). Such behavior as cruelty to animals, destruction of property, and violation of rules may appear as isolated or infrequent incidents in the early years, gaining in severity over time and thus making the diagnostic shift from ODD to CD.

Oppositional Defiant Disorder

Oppositional Defiant Disorder (ODD) typically is identified during the preschool years. Children with ODD display a pattern of negative behaviors from one or more of these three categories of moods and behaviors: 1) irritable, angry, or touchy mood; 2) headstrong, argumentative, defiant, antagonistic, annoying, or blaming of others; 3) hurtful, spiteful, or vindictive (APA, 2013; Ezpeleta, Granero, de la Osa, Penelo, & Domenech, 2012). Certain levels of these behaviors are typical in young children without ODD. Therefore, for a diagnosis of ODD, it is necessary that at least four behavioral symptoms from these three categories occur, at the minimum once a week and for at least six months (APA, 2013). The degree and severity of ODD varies from mild, with symptoms being present only in one setting; moderate, with symptoms being present in two settings; and severe, with symptoms being present in multiple settings (APA, 2013). The settings include home, preschool program, community, or other social situation.

ODD is a serious mental health condition and should be addressed early on. Early intervention strategies can be effective in helping young children function in social situations; the appropriate strategies for intervention will be discussed in the next chapters. Like other diagnoses, ODD may coexist with other conditions, such as ADHD, autism, and ID. There is strong evidence suggesting that children with ODD whose behaviors are dominated by irritability and headstrongness are good candidates for developing internalizing problems, such as depression, anxiety, and bipolar disorder as they get older (Tran, Beaudry, & Lajoie, 2013). On the other hand, preschoolers whose behaviors are dominated by antagonistic and defiant behaviors are candidates for CD or long-term externalizing behavior problems (Whelan, Stringaris, Maughan, & Barker, 2013).

In general, longitudinal research suggests that if not addressed early, children with ODD are likely to have a negative adult outcome trajectory, which is characterized by poor socialization and difficult interpersonal relationships, as well as poor academic outcomes and employment prospects (Burke, Rowe, & Boylan, 2014). In young adulthood, children who were diagnosed with ODD likely will have poorer romantic relationships; problems with family members and friends; poor parental relationships with their children; and difficulties in their work and job settings. Although this does not necessarily mean that a diagnosis of ODD or other similar disorders will continue to exist for these children in young adulthood, it does mean that emotional and behavioral issues may persist into adulthood, if not addressed with early intervention strategies.

Disorders of Affect and Emotional Regulation

People seldom think of young children as those who may deal with emotional problems, such as depression and anxiety. However, in the last few decades, emotional disorders have been acknowledged in early childhood as well as later in life. In DC:0-3R, emotional disorders are described under the category of *disorders of affect*, which include various conditions related to anxiety and depression (Zero to Three, 2005). The DSM-5 has a more complex and larger categorization of various forms of these disorders, such as bipolar disorders, depressive disorders, and anxiety disorders. Although possible, bipolar disorder is seldom diagnosed before age 18. Therefore, I do not consider its description appropriate here. Instead, I will focus on the conditions that are more common in early childhood.

Anxiety

Anxiety is excessive fear related to a perceived threat that may occur. In many young children between 7 to 18 months, a certain degree of displayed fear from unknown situations and people is typical and expected; this is commonly called stranger anxiety. However, anxiety disorders differ from typical fears when they persist beyond the developmental period (APA, 2013). A child may be considered to have an anxiety disorder, when 1) the distress causes the child to avoid certain settings and situations deemed threatening; 2) when the child's anxiety occurs frequently, e.g. in everyday activities; 3) when the child's anxiety is sometimes uncontrollable; 4) when it affects a child and/or family's functioning; and 4) when anxiety persists, for example for more than one month (Zero to Three, 2005; APA, 2013). Four types of anxiety disorders are described in DSM-5 (APA, 2013):

1. *Separation anxiety disorder:* Extreme fear and distress at the prospect of or as a result of separation from one or more attachment figure.
2. *Selective mutism:* Not speaking in situations where speaking is expected of the child, such as in school or in social situations, despite the child's speaking in other situations, such as with parents.
3. *Specific phobia:* Extreme anxiety and reaction to certain objects or situations, which may be expressed in freezing, tantrum, crying, or clinging.
4. *Social anxiety:* Extreme fear and anxiety about social situations, such as in school and other social settings with peers and adults where the child is required to interact with others.

As compared to the other types of anxiety disorders, stranger anxiety is the most common form of anxiety in children. As discussed in Chapter 2, a fear of strangers is expected as one of the typical attachment behaviors in infants and toddlers. However, a developmentally inappropriate anxiety that occurs as a result of separation from one or more attachment figures and cannot be explained by the presence of other conditions is considered a *separation anxiety disorder* (APA, 2013). A child with a separation anxiety disorder may display extreme distress and tantrums at times of separation from home or an attachment figure; the child may worry about being lost or kidnapped; may be afraid of going to school; may be extremely fearful of being alone; may refuse to go to bed; may have repeated nightmares; or may have physical pain, such as a stomach ache, in anticipation of a separation (Zero to Three, 2005).

Most children who have generalized anxiety show fearful behaviors, such as clinging, crying, freezing, developing somatic pain, and may have extreme tantrums related to any event that they perceive as threatening. Some children who live in poverty or those who face material and emotional deprivation may display generalized anxiety related to their life needs for food, shelter or clothes, being met. Traumatized children may also display symptoms of severe generalized anxiety. These include children whose families have lost homes, children experiencing parental loss through natural disaster, famine, war, fire, etc.

Some types of anxiety, such as selective mutism or phobia related to specific objects or events, are not as common in young children. Other types of anxiety, such as social anxiety, seem to be more common in school-aged children and are often related to a child's cognitive processing and thinking in middle and late childhood (Creswell, Murray, & Cooper, 2014). A child who has social anxiety fears being judged by peers and adults, and therefore avoids social situations. There is some evidence that young children who show preference for solitary play in preschool are more likely to develop social anxiety as they grow up, and that early negative interpersonal interactions may exacerbate a child's social anxiety later (Gazelle, 2013).

Generalized or specific anxiety is a common comorbid condition with a range of disorders such as autism, ADHD, ODD, CD, depression, ID, communication disorders, and learning disabilities. It is also common that a large number of children with various special needs, including younger children who are unable to articulate their fears verbally, will display aggressive behaviors in anticipation of the anxiety-producing event in order to ward off and defend themselves against the perceived event.

Depression

Depression and its diagnosis are more common at the outset of or after puberty (APA, 2013). However, during the last decade, identification of childhood depression has been much more prevalent than in the past (Allgaier, Krick, Opitz, Saravo, Romanos, & Schulte-Körne, 2014). Depression in children may be triggered by events in the environment. Child maltreatment and negative family environments often induce physical and chemical reactions in young children and therefore may cause childhood depression (Cutuli, Raby, Cicchetti, Englund, & Egeland, 2013).

For a diagnosis of depression, the symptoms should persist for more than two weeks and be pervasive enough that they interfere with the child's daily functioning and development (APA, 2013; Zero to Three, 2005). Symptoms of depression can be either directly observed in the child's behavior or can be apparent through verbalization. Such symptoms include: irritable mood, sadness or tearfulness; loss of or too much sleep; lack of energy and considerable fatigue; lack of interest and pleasure in food, play and other activities; failure to make expected weight gain or gaining too much weight; agitation and restlessness; and somatic physical pain (APA, 2013; Zero to Three, 2005). In children, depression can coexist with other conditions, such as ASD, ADHD, ODD, and CD.

Closing Remarks

In this chapter, I discussed a number of disorders that are common in childhood. Most disorders are caused as a result of the interplay between neurobiological, genetic risks, and environmental factors. Because I have already discussed the topic of childhood trauma and its related disorders in the previous chapter, I did not examine this issue here. However, I cannot emphasize enough the influential role of the environment, as well as adults' (families, caregivers, teachers, and community members) behaviors as effectors on the development and mental health in childhood and ultimately in later life. Problems related to family stress and child rearing, such as negative parent–child relationships, deprivation, and abuse consistently lead to a range of disorders, including anxiety disorders, depression, and emotional, behavior and intellectual disorders. Parents' relationship problems, step family issues, and negative relationships with teachers and peers also are often triggers and sources of anxiety and depression in children, which can persist through adulthood. In closing, I hope that my discussion of these factors will help teachers, parents, and caregivers understand various sources of externalizing and internalizing challenging behaviors as well as the complexity of the various ways that disorders exist, coexist, and develop during the lives of young children.

References

Allgaier, A. K., Krick, K., Opitz, A., Saravo, B., Romanos, M., & Schulte-Körne, G. (2014). Improving early detection of childhood depression in mental health care: The children's depression screener (ChilD-S). *Psychiatry Research, 217,* 248–252.

American Psychiatric Association. (2000). *Diagnostic and statistical manual of mental disorders: DSM-IV-TR* (4th ed., text rev.). Washington, DC: APA.

American Psychiatric Association. (2013). *Diagnostic and statistical manual of mental disorders* (5th ed.). Arlington, VA: American Psychiatric Publishing.

Anzalone, M. E., & Ritchey, M. (2014). Developmental and dyadic implications of challenges with sensory processing, physical functioning, and sensory-based self-regulation. In K. Brandt, B. D. Perry, S. Seligman, & E. Tronick (Eds.), *Infant and early childhood mental health: Core concepts and clinical practice* (pp. 209–222). Washington, DC: American Psychiatric Publishing.

Ashburner, J., Bennett, L., Rodger, S., & Ziviani, J. (2013). Understanding the sensory experiences of young people with autism spectrum disorder: A preliminary investigation. *Australian Occupational Therapy Journal, 60,* 171–180.

Ashkenazi, S., Rubinstein, O., & Henik, A. (2009). Attention, automaticity, and developmental dyscalculia. *Neuropsychology, 23,* 535–540.

Barkley, R. A. (1997). *ADHD and the nature of self control.* New York: Guilford Press.

Barry, T. D., Marcus, D. K., Barry, C. T., & Coccaro, E. F. (2013). The latent structure of oppositional defiant disorder in children and adults. *Journal of Psychiatric Research, 47,* 1932–1939.

Bayat, M. (2012). *Teaching Exceptional Children.* New York: McGraw Hill.

Burke, J. D., Rowe, R., & Boylan, K. (2014). Functional outcomes of child and adolescent oppositional defiant disorder symptoms in young adult men. *Journal of Child Psychology and Psychiatry, 55*(3), 264–272.

Burke, J. D., Waldman, I., & Lahey, B. B. (2010). Predictive validity of childhood oppositional defiant disorder and conduct disorder: Implication for the DSM-V. *Journal of Abnormal Psychology, 119,* 739–751.

Carroll, D., Hallett, V., McDougle, C. J., Aman, M. G., McCracken, J. T., Tierney, E., ... Scahill, L. (2014). Examination of aggression and self-injury in children with autism spectrum disorders and serious behavioral problems. *Child Adolescence Psychiatric Clinics of North America, 23,* 57–72.

Centers for Disease Control and Prevention. (2014a). *Attention Deficit Hyperactivity Disorder (ADHD): Data and statistics.* Retrieved from: http://www.cdc.gov/ncbddd/adhd/data.html

Centers for Disease Control and Prevention. (2014b). *Prevalence of Autism Spectrum Disorder among children aged 8 years – autism and developmental disabilities monitoring network, 11 sites, United States, 2010: Surveillance summaries, March 28, 2014/ 63(SS02); 1-21.* Retrieved from: http://www.cdc.gov/mmwr/preview/mmwrhtml/ss6302a1.htm?s_cid=ss6302a1_w

Chuang, I., Tseng, M., Lu, L., & Shieh, J. (2012). Sensory correlates of difficult temperament characteristics in preschool children with autism. *Research in Autism Spectrum Disorders, 6,* 988–995.

Creswell, C., Murray, L., & Cooper, P. (2014). Interpretation and expectation in childhood anxiety disorder: Age effects and social specifity. *Journal of Abnormal Child Psychology, 42,* 453–465.

Cutuli, J. J., Raby, K. L., Cicchetti, D., Englund, M. M., & Egeland, B. (2013). Contributions of maltreatment and serotonin transporter genotype to depression in childhood, adolescence, and early adulthood. *Journal of Affective Disorders, 149,* 30–37.

Elwin, M., Ek, L., Kjellin, L., & Schröder, A. (2013). Too much or too little: hyper- and hypo-reactivity in high functioning autism spectrum conditions. *Journal of Intellectual and Developmental Disability, 38*(3), 232–241.

Ezpeleta, L., Granero, R., de la Osa, N., Penelo, E., & Domenech, J. M. (2012). Dimensions of oppositional defiant disorder in 3-year old preschoolers. *Journal of Child Psychology and Psychiatry, 53*(11), 1128–1138.

Gazelle, H. (2013). Is social anxiety in the child or in the anxiety-producing nature of the child's interpersonal environment? *Child Development Perspectives, 7*(4), 221–226.

Grossi, D., Marcone, R., Cinquegrana, T., & Gallucci, M. (2013). On the differential nature of induced and incidental echolalia in autism. *Journal of Intellectual Disability Research, 57*(10), 903–912.

Hattlier, M. A., Matson, J. L., Macmillan, K., & Williams, L. (2013). Stereotyped behaviors in children with autism spectrum disorders and atypical development as measured by BPI-01. *Developmental Neurorehabilitation, 16*(5), 291–300.

Hayes, S. A., & Watson, S. L. (2013). The impact of parenting stress: A meta-analysis of studies comparing the experience of parenting stress in parents of children with and without autism spectrum disorder. *Journal of Autism and Developmental Disorders, 43*(3), 629–642.

Joosten, A. V., & Bundy, A. C. (2010). Sensory processing and stereotypical and repetitive behavior in children with autism and intellectual disability. *Australian Occupational Therapy Journal, 57,* 366–372.

Law, E. C., Sideridis, G. D., Prock, L. A., & Sheridan, M. A. (2014). Attention Deficit Hyperactivity Disorder in young children: Predictors of diagnostic stability. *Pediatrics, 133*(4), 659–667.

Lichtenstein, P., Carlström, E., Råstam, M., Gillberg, C., & Anckarsäter, H. (2010). The genetics of autism spectrum disorders and related neuropsychiatric disorders in childhood. *American Journal of Psychiatry, 167*, 1357–1363.

Maenner, M., Rice, C., Arneson, C., Cunniff, C., Schieve, L., Carpenter, L., & Van Naarden Braun, K. et al. (2014). Potential impact of DSM-5 criteria on Autism Spectrum Disorder prevalence estimates. *Journal of American Medical Association in Psychiatry, 71*(3), 292–300.

Maskey, M., Warnell, F., Parr, J. R., Le Couteur, A., & McConachie, H. (2013). Emotional and behavioral problems in children with autism spectrum disorder. *Journal of Autism and Developmental Disorders, 43*, 851–859.

Mauro, T. (2014, May). Supreme Court use of 'Intellectual Disability' wins praise. *The National Law Journal*. Retrieved from: http://www.nationallawjournal.com/id=1202657038598?slreturn=20140504121944.

Northcutt, C., & McCarroll, B. (2014). DC:0-3R: A diagnostic schema for infants and young children and their families. In K. Brandt, B. D. Perry, S. Seligman, & E. Tronick (Eds.) (2014). *Infant and early childhood mental health: Core concepts and clinical practice* (pp. 175–193). Washington, DC: American Psychiatric Publishing.

Peters-Scheffer, N., Didden, R., Sigafoos, J., Green, V. A., & Korzilius, H. (2013). Behavioral flexibility in children with autism spectrum disorder and intellectual disability. *Research in Autism Spectrum Disorders, 7*, 699–709.

Prasad, V., Brogan, E., Mulvaney, C., Grainge, M., Stanton, W., & Sayal, K. (2013). How effective are drug treatments for children with ADHD on improving on-task behaviour and academic achievement in the school classroom? A systemic review and meta-analysis. *European Child and Adolescent Psychiatry, 22*(4), 203–216.

Reed, P., & Osborne, L. (2013). The role of parenting stress in discrepancies between parent and teacher ratings of behavior problems in young children with autism spectrum disorders. *Journal of Autism and Developmental Disorders, 43*(2), 471–477.

Roley, S. S., Mailloux, Z., Miller-Kuhaneck, H., & Glennon, T. (2007). Understanding Ayers sensory integration. *OT Practice, 12*(17), Suppl. (CE1-7).

Rolon-Arroyo, B., Arnold, D. H., & Harvey, E. A. (2014). The predictive utility of conduct disorder symptoms in preschool children: A 3-year follow-up study. *Child Psychiatry and Human Development, 45*, 329–337.

Rommelse, N., Franke, B., Geurts, H., Hartman, C., & Buitelaar, J. (2010). Shared heritability of attention deficit hyperactivity disorder and autism spectrum disorder. *European Child and Adolescent Psychiatry, 19*, 281–295.

Rosa's Law Act of 2010, 20 U.S.C. § 1400 (2010).

Rutter, M. (2014). Changing concepts and findings on autism. *Journal of Autism and Developmental Disorders, 43*, 1749–1757.

Schreiber, J., Possin, K. L., Girard, J. M., & Rey-Casserly, C. (2014). Executive function in children with Attention Deficit Hyperactivity Disorder: The NIH examiner battery. *Journal of the International Neuropsychological Society, 20*(1), 41–51.

Sciberras, E., Efron, D., Schilpzand, E. J., Andeson, V., Jongelin, B., Hazell, P., ... & Nicholson, J. (2013). The children's attention project: A community based longitudinal study of children with ADHD and non-ADHD controls. *BMC Psychiatry, 13*(18). Retrieved from http://www.biomedcentral.com/1471-244X/13/18

Simonoff, E., Jones, C. R., Baird, G., Pickles, A., Happé, F., & Charman, T. (2014). The persistence and stability of psychiatric problems in adolescents with autism spectrum disorders. *Journal of Child Psychology and Psychiatry, 54*(2), 186–194.

Skogli, E. W., Egland, J., Anderson, P. N., Hovik, K. T., & Øie, M. (2014). Few differences in hot and cold executive functions in children and adolescents with combined and inattentive subtypes of ADHD. *Child Neuropsychology, 20*(2), 162–181.

Sun, L., & Wallach, G. (2014). Language disorders are learning disabilities. *Topics in Language Disorders, 34*(1), 25–38.

Tran, D. Q., Beaudry, V., & Lajoie, Y. (2013). First manic episode in an 11 year old girl. *Journal of Clinical Academy of Child and Adolescent Psychiatry, 22*(4), 324–326.

Tucker, T., Zahir, F., Malachi, G., Delaney, A., Chai, D, Tsang, E., … & Friedman, J. (2014). Single axon resolution targeted chromosomal microarray analysis of known and candidate intellectual disability genes. *European Journal of Human Genetics, 22*(6), 792–800.

U.S. Department of Education. (2014). *Fast Facts: Students with Disabilities.* Retrieved from: http://nces.ed.gov/fastfacts/display.asp?id=64

Vakil, E., Blachstein, H., Wertman-Elad, R., & Greenstein, Y. (2014). Verbal learning and memory as measured by the Rey-auditory verbal learning test: ADHD with and without learning disabilities. *Child Neuropsychology, 18*(5), 449–466.

Valentino, A. L., Shillingsburg, M. A., Conine, D. E., & Powell, N. M. (2014). Decreasing echolalia of the instruction "say" during echoic training through use of the Cues-Pause-Point procedure. *Journal of Behavioral Education, 21*(4), 315–328.

Villodas, M., McBurnett, K., Kaiser, N., Rooney, M., & Pfiffner, L. (2014). Additive effects of parent adherence on social and behavioral outcomes of a collaborative school-home behavioral intervention for ADHD. *Child Psychiatry & Human Development, 45*(3), 348–360.

Visser, S. N., Danielson, M. L., Bitsko, R. H., Holbrook, J. R., Kogan, M. D., Ghandour, R. M., … Blumberg, S. J. (2014). Trends in the parent report of health care provider diagnosed and medicated Attention Deficit Hyperactivity Disorder: United States, 2003–2011. *Journal of the American Academy of Child and Adolescent Psychiatry, 53*(1), 34–46.

Wei, X., Yu, J. W., & Shaver, D. (2014). Longitudinal effects of ADHD in children with learning disabilities and emotional disturbances. *Exceptional Children, 80*(2), 205–219.

Whelan, Y., Stringaris, A., Maughan, B., & Barker, E. (2013). Developmental continuity of oppositional defiant disorder subdimensions at ages 8, 10, and 13 years and their distinct psychiatric outcomes at age 16. *Journal of the American Academy of Child and Adolescent Psychiatry, 52*(9), 961–969.

Wing, L. (1993). The definition and prevalence of autism: A review. *European Journal of Child and Adolescent Psychiatry, 2*, 61–74.

Zero to Three. (2005). Diagnostic classification of mental health and developmental disorders of infancy and early childhood: Revised edition (DC:0-3R). Washington, DC: Zero to Three Press.

Zero to Three. (2014). *DC:0-3R.* Retrieved from: http://www.zerotothree.org/child-development/early-childhood-mental-health/diagnostic-classification-of-mental-health-and-developmental-disorders-of-infancy-and-early-childhood-revised.html

5

PREVENTION

Curricular Approaches That Promote Social-Emotional Competence and Appropriate Behaviors in Children

In this chapter I will discuss research and evidence-based strategies that are used to prevent challenging behaviors from occurring and to promote social-emotional health and competence in children. I will first describe the concepts of risk vs. resilience and the research related to these concepts. Then, I will recommend practical strategies, which are most likely to build the process of resilience in children, as well as to promote social emotional well-being and health in children.

Risks vs. Resilience Approaches in Child Development

As much as we may wish for everything to go positively in a child's life, adverse events do happen and are thought to be typical throughout every stage of a person's life cycle. Negative events that occur during early childhood undoubtedly place stress on a child, which in turn can alter the course of the child's development. Previously, I explained such risk factors as negative early relationships, maltreatment, trauma, and neurodevelopmental problems. I argued how these issues may have long-lasting effects on a child's growth and mental health development. There are, of course, multitudes of other factors that I did not discuss. These factors are environmental, familial, or situational events that serve as risks for the development of individual children. They include, but are not limited to, poverty, limited parental education, parental mental health problems, parental substance abuse, unsafe and violent communities or living conditions, and negative school and peer experiences. The constellations of factors interact with children and families in various ways and child outcomes are shaped accordingly.

Since the 1960s, research on the topic of early childhood risks ranged from effects of environmental risks on a child's overall development, to the risks as they influence a child's behavior, school and academic success or failure, and work and career outcomes in adulthood. The major influence of this literature on early education policy is found in the documentation leading to the development of Head Start and Early Head Start programs. In addition, the development of special education legislation grows from this research tradition, which resulted in the creation of early intervention and early childhood special education programs in the USA beginning in the 1970s (for a discussion of related history see Zigler & Berman, 1983).

In the 1960s and 1970s, alongside this literature, there grew a wave of research on the concept of resilience in development. Pioneer scholars in child resilience research were Norman Garmezy (1973), Michael Rutter (1979), Emmy Werner and her colleagues (Werner, Beireman, & French, 1971; Werner & Smith, 1977), and Ann Masten and her colleagues (Masten & O'Connor, 1989). Early in their works, these scholars discovered that not all children who grew up in adverse conditions turned out to have negative and unsuccessful futures, thus the tradition of documenting and describing resilience in children grew from this research. The initial research on resilience focused on developing, understanding, and measuring the phenomenon of resilience as a concept. So, what is resilience? Resilience is defined as a dynamic developmental process that enables a child to make positive adaptations, despite exposure to high environmental, social or emotional risks and threats or suffering severe trauma, all of which constitute major assaults to development and can bring about serious adverse consequences (Cicchetti, 2013; Rutter, 2006).

The body of research on resilience in developmental psychology has grown since the 1970s alongside a more recent movement called *positive psychology* (Seligman & Csikszentmihalyi, 2000). Positive psychology calls for focus on a person's positive attributes and strength, and thereby takes these factors into account for the child's health, rather than focusing on the roots of pathology through a child's maladaptive characteristics (Seligman & Csikszentmihalyi, 2000). Later, the concept of resilience was also applied to understanding and working with families. Walsh (1996, 2003) conceptualized the construct of *family resilience* to describe a family's ability to withstand adversity or a crisis, and grow out of the experience strengthened. The concept of family resilience is studied in relation to families facing crises such as poverty, disability, and chronic illness, etc. The understandings from this application of the research to families caused a major shift in mental health policy as well as in child and family clinical practice. The focus shifted from a view of negative outcomes and risks, to an emphasis on positive adaptation and resilience in child development and family processes (Rutter, 2012). Thus, an emphasis on strengthening the positive potentials of children is sorely needed in early childhood policy and practice. Much of early childhood education policy and practice continues to focus on risks and related interventions, as opposed to an emphasis on the child's positive attributes and resiliency.

My intention here is not to negate nor downplay the important role or the efficacy of early childhood intervention programs that focus on addressing and preventing risks, such as Head Start programs, particularly since Head Start has a

50-year history of focusing on whole child development and family empowerment. On the contrary, I believe that these programs are necessary and are proved as effective in providing much needed early education and care – and, in many cases, the only viable resources for some children and families.

In fact, beginning in 1974, Head Start rules mandated that 10 percent of the children served in programs must be identified as those with special needs. Most programs were easily able to identify young children with speech and language disorders and to provide clinical services for them through arrangements with public schools and other community agencies. More difficult for programs was the identification and service for young children at risk of learning disabilities and those with social/emotional support needs. The special education work in Head Start was, of course, influenced by the prevailing treatment philosophies in special education at the time of the mandate and beyond. While there are instances of the application of the latest resilience research impacting Head Start, I argue that it is still crucial to acknowledge and apply lessons learned from child resilience studies as a way to identify and implement strategies that promote social-emotional development and competencies of children.

Lessons Learned from Child Resilience Studies

In their 30-year study of children born in 1955 in the Hawaiian island of Kauai, Warner and her colleagues explained the extraordinary ability of a group of Kauai children who grew up in a variety of environmental and familial high-risk conditions (e.g. poverty, parental substance abuse, family conflict, parental mental health problems, and parental low education, etc.) to overcome the adversity of their backgrounds and to become healthy and successful adults (for details see Werner et al., 1971; Werner & Smith, 1977, 1982, 1992, 2001). Starting in the early 1970s, Garmezy found similar remarkable resilience in a group of children of parents with schizophrenia. These children faced not only stressful home environment conditions, but also genetic and neurobiological risks of psychopathology (Garmezy, 1974, 1985).

Around the same time, Rutter, who studied a group of Romanian orphans adopted in Europe following the fall of the Ceauşescu's regime, conceptualized the construct of *protective mechanisms* (Rutter, 1979; 1990; 2006). He described protective mechanisms as factors that act as buffers against high risks – including the environmental and genetic interplay – and that potentially led to resilience in a child (Rutter, 1979, 1990, 2006). Other scholars, such as Masten (2001, 2007, 2011), focused on understanding developmental processes and change as ways to promote resilience in children. Masten (2007, 2011) advocated for resilience models and approaches that can identify protective mechanisms and processes to promote competence and resilience.

In more recent years, child resilience research advanced to include examination and understanding of the neurobiological changes that may lead to resilience. In a review of their extensive work on this topic, Karatoreos and McEwen (2013) discuss the concept of *allostasis*, a term that is used to refer to a stability of an organism through change. They explain that at the time of high stress and adversity, when it detects the presence of stressors, the brain activates mediators to achieve allostasis. Allostasis is the process the body goes through to reestablish homeostasis, which is the body's natural balanced state. In the presence of a stressor (anything which takes the body out of homeostasis), the hypothalamic-pituitary adrenal axis of the brain is triggered so that the body can respond properly and eventually return allostatically, back to its balanced state.

Two of the major parts of the stress response mediator agents that the brain produces are steroid and metabolic hormones. They are produced in the hippocampus, and go beyond the hypothalamus to encompass most brain regions, such as cognitive centers. Production of these hormones leads to a plasticity in the brain's structure and function that is required for successful adaptation and coping at the time of high stress. Adverse early childhood experiences can have lasting prohibiting effects on the production of these mediators. In addition, the events physically affect neuronal architecture, such that there will be diminished gray and white matter, i.e. weaker dendritic spines. However, these potential negative effects seem to be reversible through a "top-down" cognitive and behavioral intervention approach to children (Karatoreos & McEwen, 2013).

Thus, what resilience scholars (Cicchetti, 2013; Davydon, Stewart, Ritchie, & Chaudieu, 2010; Karatoreos & McEwen, 2013; Masten, 2011; Rutter, 2012; Werner, 2012a; 2012b), concluded, influences the strategies highlighted for effective practice. The scholars agreed that what acted as protective mechanisms in children, and ultimately made the difference for resilience, were the following:

- *Adult–child positive relationships:* All the children these researchers studied had at least one positive relationship with an adult (such as a parent, a family member, or a teacher).
- *Positive school experiences:* Even when the children faced difficult circumstances in their families, positive school experiences seemed to buffer them from faced risks. A positive school experience included positive classroom environments, predictable routines, rules, supportive and high quality instruction, and a learning community that promoted friendships and positive relationships between them and their peers, and with their educators.
- *Easygoing temperament, positive emotions, and motivation for learning:* When children were easygoing, adults and peers around them seemed more responsive and caring to them. The children seemed to have positive emotions and capacity for self-regulation and mastery, and had strong motivations to learn.

It is also important to note here that resilience is an interactive and dynamic process. It is not a stable quality. The process of resilience can change based on individual differences, culture, family circumstances, timing of adverse events and experiences, the child's other experiences across the lifespan, and, most importantly, through appropriate intervention and teaching.

Strategies for Promoting Resilience and Preventing Challenging Behaviors

I use the findings presented in the last section to serve as a rationale for presenting preventive strategies that focus on building capacity for resilience in children. I suggest prevention strategies that focus on three protective mechanisms: 1) builds positive relationships; 2) teaches emotional competence and regulation in the child; and 3) uses appropriate classroom structure/routine, and instructions to guide behaviors.

Teacher–Child Relationship: A Protective Mechanism

Previously, I presented the research on the importance of caregiver–child attachment and early relationships in the lives of infants and young children. As a reminder, I explained that repeated daily interactions of children with adults and caregivers are internalized by children into representations (working models) of the self, and of self–other relationships. Thus, a child who has a secure attachment and a positive relationship with a caregiver views self as worthy of love, whereas the one who has an insecure attachment views self as unworthy or unlovable. However, I also explained that children develop attachments with multiple caregivers across different settings in their daily interactions. This process includes forming attachments with their teachers. A teacher can therefore act as a secure attachment figure for a child who may otherwise have a troubling relationship with primary caregivers.

Keeping in mind the findings I presented from resilience studies, and drawing on the attachment research and transactional model of development (Sameroff & Chandler, 1975), it is reasonable to expect that when a child enters school, a positive relationship with his teacher may act as a buffer against existing risks, compensate for the negative effects of adverse earlier experiences at home, and therefore potentially lead to reversing a negative developmental course for the child. The issue of the teacher–child relationship is examined by a number of scholars (e.g. Buyse, Verschueren, & Doumen, 2011; Pianta, Hamre, & Stuhlman, 2003; Sabol & Pianta, 2012; Verschueren, Doumen, & Buyse, 2012). In fact, in a longitudinal study, Buyse and her colleagues (2011) found that a close teacher–child relationship had buffering effects for children who had insecure attachments with their primary caregivers.

A high quality teacher–child relationship is characterized by the teacher's warmth and closeness to the child. In fact, when teachers are sensitive and responsive toward children, children with lower quality attachments to their primary caregivers are no longer at a significantly high risk for aggressive behaviors and mental health issues (Buyse et al., 2011; Sabol & Pianta, 2012).

Research also found that when teachers make the effort to form and maintain positive and close relationships with children early on, e.g. during preschool, positive pathways may open for those children toward more productive relationships with others, and lead to successful future school experiences (Verschueren et al., 2012). A teacher's close relationship with a child gives that child a positive image of self, particularly in an academic context (Verschueren et al., 2012). This positive teacher–child relationship has such a strong regulating effect on the child that even in situations when peers are not accepting of that child, the child's positive view of self via his internal working model does not waver (Verschueren et al., 2012; Sabol & Pianta, 2012). Children who grow up in uncertain, and worse, unsafe environments, with inconsistent caregivers, can then begin to trust a teacher who is available and sensitive to their needs. Such a teacher functions not only as a secure base for these children to engage in exploration and intellectual activities, but also as a presence for support and scaffolding when children need it (Ahnert, Harwardt-Heinecke, Kappler, Eckstein-Madry, & Milatz, 2012).

Thus, a teacher's emotional responsiveness toward children seems to have regulating and balancing effects on children against stressful and challenging situations faced in school and at home, and builds resilience in the child (Ahnert et al., 2012). Furthermore, research established that children who have a close relationship with their teachers seem to have better cognitive functioning and processing, and higher achievement levels on academic tasks (Ahnert, Milatz, Kappler, Schneiderwind, & Fischer, 2013).

Building Positive Relationships with Children who Have Challenging Behaviors

Forming positive relationships with children who grow up in adverse home and family conditions is neither an easy nor a smooth task. These children are usually at the center of classroom disruptions or conflicts, and display behaviors that as far as most teachers are concerned interfere with and challenge a teacher's agenda and goals for the whole class. It is important to keep in mind that many children with challenging behaviors deal with a high level of anxiety, which compels them to act with mistrust toward a world that they see as a dangerous and unpredictable place. Similarly, being highly anxious is typical of a large number of children who have neurodevelopmental special needs. Anxious children frequently react toward adult and peer interactions with hostility and aggression, or indifference or avoidance. As a result, for most teachers forming positive and productive relationships with these children is extremely difficult under the best of circumstances.

Additionally, teachers come with their personal perceptions, attitudes, and beliefs about how to best address challenging behaviors, which in turn influence their behaviors and reactions toward these children. In general, there seems to be three main relationship patterns between teachers and children in early childhood classrooms (De Kruif, McWilliam, Maher-Ridley, & Wakely, 2000; Pianta, 1994). These patterns seem to be consistent even across different cultures and educational contexts (Gregoriadis & Grammtikopoulus, 2014). These are: 1) a *positively involved* relationship; 2) a *functional/average* relationship; and 3) a *dysfunctional* relationship (Gregoriadis & Grammatikopoulos, 2014).

Teachers commonly view children's challenging behaviors as sources of stress and problems in the classroom. In such instances, teachers tend to become resentful, display hostility toward these children, and advance into having dysfunctional relationships with them (Berg-Nielsen, Solheim, Belsky, & Wichstrom, 2012). Relationships are reciprocal. It is therefore not surprising that a dysfunctional relationship with a child with challenging behaviors seems to create a vicious cycle for that child – in that the child often resorts to more challenging behaviors as a result of this negative relationship (Zhang & Sun, 2011).

This issue is particularly important for early childhood classrooms, because research consistently shows that when dysfunctional relationships between a teacher and a child begin in the preschool years, the child will develop a lack of emotional regulation, more aggressive behaviors, further conflicts with authority figures and peers, and have academic problems in future school years (Garner, Mahatmaya, Moses, & Bolt, 2014; Madill, Gest, & Rodkin, 2014; Rudasill, Neihaus, Buhs, & White, 2013). Thus, the question remains, how are teachers to help children with challenging behaviors establish positive relationships and build resilience?

The answer may be found in play-based approaches to relationship development. There are several play-based approaches that are used for children with challenging behaviors and children with neurodevelopmental disorders. Research shows that when play-based approaches are used with children who have challenging behaviors, teachers' negative attitudes toward these children begin to shift into more positive ones that are based on understanding and on an unbiased knowledge of the child. As a result, positively-involved relationships begin to flourish between these teachers and children (Driscoll, Wang, Mashburn, & Pianta, 2011; Lindo et al., 2014). Two examples of such approaches will be discussed in the following sections.

Examples of Play-Based Approaches for Children with Challenging Behaviors

Early childhood education approaches that aim to build resilience in the child must first, be developmentally appropriate; second, entice the child to interact with the teacher; third, provide a safe environment in which the child can explore and engage in play; and fourth, build trust as a foundation for a positive relationship between the child and the teacher. By necessity, these approaches must be play-based and interesting to the child.

Play therapy approaches are those that are designed as intervention for children with mental health issues and challenging behaviors (Lindo et al., 2014). In a play therapy approach, specifically trained therapists and teachers are required to implement the sessions. However, there are other play-based approaches which have been designed particularly to improve teacher–child relationships, or as a way to address special needs of children. These approaches are usually simple to implement and carry out, and no specific training is needed beyond following simple guidelines. Strategies used in these approaches are designed to promote social-emotional health in children and to create a trusting environment for children to enjoy and to learn. The *floor time* approach (Greenspan & Wieder, 1998), and *banking time* (Pianta & Hamre, 2001) are two examples of such approaches.

Floor Time

Floor time is a play-based intervention, and designed by Greenspan and Wieder in 1998 for children with neurodevelopmental disorders. As the name implies, the adult (a teacher or a caregiver) is encouraged to literally and figuratively get down "on the floor" at the child's level to interact with the child. Each playtime session is recommended to be 20 to 30 minutes, several times during the day. Floor time sessions can be carried out between the child with a teacher, therapist, or parent. The goal of floor time is to move the child through specific developmental milestones in a model of intervention called DIR (Developmental Individual-difference, Relationship based model) (Wieder & Greenspan, 2003). The essence of the DIR model is to improve the functional developmental capacities of children in the context of adult–child relationships and children's unique neurobiological processes (Wieder & Greenspan, 2003).

Through repeated floor time sessions, the adult follows the child's lead in interest, and plays with the child in affective toned interactions, in which the adult uses gestures and language to scaffold the child's development through symbolic play (Wieder & Greenspan, 2003). There are six elements to floor time: 1) self-regulation and shared attention; 2) engagement and relating; 3) two-way intentional communication; 4) purposeful complex problem-solving communication; 5) creating and elaborating symbols or ideas; 6) building bridges between ideas (Wieder & Greenspan, 2003). Although the goal of floor time play sessions is to promote a child's development, the essence of Greenspan's approach is building emotional competence through positive relationships with the child.

Banking Time

Similar to floor time, *banking time* is a play-based approach designed by Pianta and Hamre in 2001 as a part of a project to provide professional development for early childhood teachers and to assist them in improving their teaching practices. The name, banking time, emphasizes that relationships are resources for children, and teachers can invest in these resources during individual play sessions in which they establish and build on this capital – a positive relationship with the child (Pianta & Hamre, 2001).

Banking time sessions are designed to improve the quality of relationships between the teacher and the child, through giving dyadic opportunities to interact and play positively with each other (Pianta & Hamre, 2001). The teacher follows the child's interest and lead, and participates in an activity of the child's choosing for about 15 to 30 minutes from once to several times per week. During these one-on-one sessions, the teacher listens, watches, and makes positive, non-judgmental comments to the child to convey understanding and acceptance. There are four components to banking time: 1) observing the child's actions; 2) describing/narrating the child's actions; 3) labeling the child's feelings and emotions; and 4) developing relational themes by which the teacher conveys supporting messages to the child (Pianta & Hamre, 2001).

The goal of banking time is to establish and to build a positive relationship between the child and the teacher, and thereby decrease challenging behaviors in the child. Banking time is shown to be an effective method in promoting closeness and supportive relationships between teachers and children with challenging behaviors (Driscoll et al., 2011).

Recommendations for Adult–Child Play Sessions

Effective play-based approaches are child-centered and provide a safe haven for the child from which they can explore and learn. Having one-on-one play sessions is a necessary component of prevention and intervention programs for children with challenging behaviors. It provides a chance for both the child and the teacher to get to know each other in a neutral context. The following recommendations are based on principles of floor time and banking time and provide the best practice guidelines for teachers in conducting one-on-one play sessions.

Table 5.1 Rationale for Teacher's Behavior during One-on-One Play Sessions with Children

Teacher's Behavior	Reason for Teacher's Behavior
• Allow for the child to choose an activity.	• Gives the child a chance to have complete control over a situation.
• Follow the child's lead and interests.	• Empowers the child to be in charge and control. Provides a safe environment for the child.
• Do not teach.	• Gives the child a safe environment from which to play and explore, without any expectations from the adult.
• Show interest without judgment.	• Lets the child know no matter what he does, he won't be judged negatively.
• Comment or narrate what the child does.	• Shows the child that the child has the teacher's complete attention for the session.
• Accept what the child does, and get involved in play if the child asks.	• Gives the child a feeling of safety and trust.

Table 5.1 displays the rationale for the guidelines suggested below. Teachers should:

1. Allow the child to choose an activity or toys.
2. Follow the child's lead, getting involved in the child's play only when the child wishes.
3. Avoid teaching or using the play session as an opportunity to develop a concept.
4. Avoid forcing the child to communicate verbally or non-verbally during the play session.
5. Encourage and interest the child in communicating by:
    a. showing interest in the child's play repertoire
    b. playing alongside the child
    c. engaging in the same activity
    d. avoiding forced entry into the child's play
    e. making comments on, or narrating, what the child is doing
    f. waiting for the child to respond verbally or non-verbally.
6. Follow up with a comment or another question or gesture.
7. Demonstrate acceptance of the child's play repertoire.
8. Communicate that the child is safe and free to pursue his own interests and activities.
9. End the play when the child is ready to complete the play session.
10. Avoid suggesting:
    a. what the child should do
    b. teaching the child what to do
    c. making a corrective action, or
    d. making a judgment on what the child is doing, unless the child explicitly makes a request for the teacher to do so.

With these principles in mind teachers can facilitate development of children with challenging behaviors through a child-led play-based activity session.

Best Practices: Approaches in Social-Emotional Learning in Early Childhood Education

In Chapter 2 I discussed the importance of social-emotional competence in children for the foundation of healthy development and functioning. I mentioned various developmental approaches that focus on emotional development as the center of well-functioning and developmental health. In this chapter, I have argued that healthy social-emotional learning and positive relationships are also protective mechanisms against adversity and risks, which promote resilience for children.

Research on social-emotional development provides evidence that the knowledge and skills necessary to develop social-emotional competence can be taught to children (Brackett et al., 2010; Rivers & Brackett, 2011; Rivers, Brackett, Reyes, Elbertson, & Salovey, 2013). This finding has direct implications for the early education of children, in that curricula that aim at social-emotional competence and successful relationship building have a great potential for promoting resilience in children.

Studies in this area suggest that targeting skills in social and emotional learning in early childhood classrooms not only promotes emotional health in children, but also improves the overall social-emotional climate of the classroom, as well as enhancing relationships among children, and between children and teachers (Rivers et al., 2013; Hagelskamp, Brackett, Rivers, & Salovey, 2013). To date, there are a number of social-emotional learning programs designed to foster social-emotional competence and healthy emotional regulation in children. These programs are implemented as prevention for challenging behaviors and associated academic problems. Drawing on the concept of emotional intelligence (Mayer & Salovey, 1997), most of these programs aim to help the child develop *emotional literacy*. As Mayer and Salovey implied in their conceptualization of emotional intelligence, emotional literacy in a child is the child's ability to identify, understand, and respond to emotions in self and in others (Rivers & Brackett, 2011).

In the following sections, I will describe four evidence-based programs of social-emotional learning used in early childhood education settings. These programs provide examples of curricular approaches that are effective in promoting social-emotional competence, and in successfully preventing challenging behaviors in children.

Recognizing, Understanding, Labeling, Expressing, and Regulating: The RULER Approach to Social-Emotional Learning

Developed by Brackett and his colleagues (2010), the RULER approach is an evidence-based social-emotional learning program derived from the theory of emotional intelligence. Central to this approach is the premise that the understanding of emotions is necessary for successful learning and healthy development in four ways: 1) emotions affect attention and learning; 2) emotion affects decision making; 3) emotions affect relationships; and 4) emotions affect mental and physical health (Rivers & Brackett, 2011). Therefore, four important skills are emphasized by the acronym as follow: *r*ecognizing emotions, *u*nderstanding emotions, *l*abeling emotions, and *e*xpressing emotions (Brackett et al., 2010).

In the early childhood classroom, this approach focuses on using literacy-rich curricula to teach the four central skills of RULER to children. For example, children learn to recognize and identify emotions in themselves and in others using feeling words by reading and hearing stories. The goal is that, with practice, children will be able to interpret accurately feelings and motivations behind their own behaviors and behaviors of others (Rivers et al., 2013). Children also learn to understand the causes and consequences of emotions, and how emotions convey messages both intrapersonally (in self) and interpersonally (between others) (Brackett et al., 2010).

Labeling emotions in self and others through newly acquired vocabulary is another aspect of the RULER approach. The goal is that the child will explore deeper and newer meanings of different emotions, and come to understand that emotions are complex. Finally, by expressing various emotions, the child will understand and therefore predict how others may think and feel. Correct identification and expression of emotions is elemental in developing *theory of mind*, the ability to understand how others may think, feel, or believe. In the RULER approach, regulation of emotions is the final targeted skill to develop and enhance. Regulation of emotions consists of the child's ability to change thoughts and feelings, and therefore his behaviors, related to the experience of emotions (Rivers & Brackett, 2011).

Aside from the obvious benefits such an approach may have for children's social-emotional learning, relationship building, and daily functioning, the RULER approach seems to have side benefits for the classroom and school environment as well. Several studies show that when such an approach is used in early childhood and elementary classroom settings, the overall environment of the classroom flourishes. The participating classes exhibit greater emotional support and warmth among children and between children and teachers, a greater sense of community, higher engagement of children in learning tasks and activities, better classroom organization, improved teaching instruction and support, and a lower rate of challenging behaviors (Hagelskamp et al., 2013; Rivers et al., 2013).

The Incredible Years® Programs

Another approach in social-emotional learning is the *Incredible Years (IY)* program. Incredible Years is a series of curricular programs designed by Webster-Stratton in 1998 to prevent challenging behaviors in populations of at-risk children. The program is comprised of a range of developmentally based activities for children, parents, and teachers. The program focuses on strengthening positive relationships between parent, teacher, and children. The theoretical foundation for the IY program includes major principles of cognitive, social-learning, attachment, and developmental theories.

A series of parent training sessions are designed to focus on teaching strategies in three areas: 1) strengthening parent–child relationships and bonding; 2) promoting effective limit setting, nonpunitive discipline, and systematic behavior plans; and 3) strengthening parent's interpersonal skills and supportive network (Webster-Statton & Reid, 2014).

The teacher professional development program of IY focuses on the three major areas of: 1) classroom management strategies; 2) communication skills to use with families and teacher–parent partnership; 3) and ways to use ongoing consultations for implementing activities from the classroom curriculum (Ștefan & Miclea, 2013). Finally, IY has two program versions that can be delivered either to the whole class or to small groups of children. Lessons and activities that are designed for early childhood classrooms focus on strengthening social-emotional learning by understanding and communicating feelings, using effective problem-solving strategies, managing anger, practicing friendship and conversational skills, and by behaving appropriately in the classroom (Webster-Stratton & Bywater, 2014).

IY has been studied and applied to a large number of childhood education settings with at-risk children and with children with special needs, such as those with ADHD

(Webster-Stratton & Reid, 2014). Results show that early childhood programs implementing IY are successful in reducing challenging behaviors, increasing positive social behavior, improving social-emotional performance, and overall improving a positive climate in the classroom (CASEL, 2014; Ştefan & Miclea, 2013).

Promoting Alternative Thinking Strategies PATHS® Curriculum

Another evidence-based approach that focuses on enhancing the social-emotional learning and competence of children is *PATHS* (Domitrovich, Greenberg, Kusch, & Cortes, 2004; Kusch & Greenberg, 1994). The acronym PATHS represents *P*romoting *A*lternative *Th*inking *S*trategies; the curriculum is designed for use in early childhood and elementary classrooms. Domitrovich and her colleagues designed the early childhood version of PATHS in 2004. PATHS is guided by neurocognitive models of development; the curriculum aims to build the executive functioning of the brain in the developing child by targeting: 1) *vertical control:* higher-order cognitive processing exerting control over lower-level limbic impulses or actions; and 2) *horizontal control:* verbal processing of actions (Greenberg, 2006).

In preschool and kindergarten, the PATHS® lessons help children reinforce a better vertical control, or control of impulses, through practicing simple reasoning, planning, and problem solving. In higher grades, PATHS lessons help children build horizontal control, or higher verbal processing, through teaching children to verbally identify and label feelings of self and others (Hamre, Pianta, Mashburn, & Downer, 2012). An overarching goal of this program is to help children resolve conflicts peacefully, handle emotions positively, develop empathy, and make responsible decisions (Domitrovich et al., 2009).

The PATHS program is successfully used in a large number of early childhood programs. Though programs implementing PATHS do not demonstrate a decrease in challenging behaviors of children, the programs studied show improvements in the overall level of children's social-emotional competence and related skills (Hamre et al., 2012).

Teaching Pyramid Approach

The *Teaching Pyramid* is another approach that is designed both as a prevention and an intervention solution for challenging behaviors in early childhood education (Hemmeter, Ortrosky, & Fox, 2006; Fox, Dunlap, Hemmeter, Joseph, & Strain, 2003). This model was first conceptualized by Fox and her colleagues in 2003, and developed further in 2006 by Hemmeter and colleagues. The Teaching Pyramid model is a three-tiered teacher professional development program that includes teaching practices to promote social-emotional development in children, to prevent challenging behavior from occurring, and to provide support strategies for addressing children's challenging behaviors when they occur (Hemmeter, Ostrosky, & Corso, 2012).

The theoretical framework of this model builds on *function-based* behavioral approaches, *positive behavioral support* to promote healthy social–emotional development, and social learning theory. Function-based interventions are strategies for improving behaviors that focus on understanding the motivations for behaviors as well as consequences or functions shown to be associated with the behavior (Dunlap & Fox, 2011). Positive behavioral support is concerned with designing systems within the natural environments of the child that will support the child to replace challenging behaviors with new learned appropriate behaviors (Dunlap & Fox, 2011).

The tiered Teaching Pyramid has three levels of implementation:

1. A universal promotion level that consists of two foci. The first focus seeks to establish nurturing caregiving relationships between teachers and children, amongst children, and between teachers and parents. The second focus develops a positive classroom climate by establishing appropriate structure and routines, and through teaching engaging and challenging lessons.
2. The secondary prevention of the pyramid consists of the intentional teaching of social skills and emotional competence to all children via small and large group lessons.
3. The tertiary intervention level consists of intensive behavioral intervention via conducting functional behavior assessment and developing behavioral intervention plans for specific children who display challenging behaviors (Hemmeter et al., 2012). Strategies used in the Pyramid at the tertiary level include teaching new positive behaviors to the child to replace the previously challenging behaviors, and changing responses of the adults to children in ways that support maintaining new behaviors in the child (Hemmeter et al., 2012).

The Teaching Pyramid model, along with its assessment procedures, are successfully implemented and studied in a large number of early childhood settings across 15 states (Fox, Carta, Strain, Dunlap, & Hemmeter, 2010; Fox & Hemmeter, 2009; Snyder, Hemmeter, Fox, Bishop, & Miller, 2013). The program is shown to be effective in promoting social skills of all children, and in successfully addressing the challenging behaviors in targeted children (Hemmeter et al., 2012; Snyder et al., 2013).

Strategies for Establishing a Positive Climate in the Classroom

No matter which curricular approaches early childhood teachers use, there are several strategies that can be used universally to improve the classroom climate, prevent challenging behaviors from occurring, and promote resilience in children. The following guidelines help teachers implement these strategies:

•   Establish and nurture positive relationships with children by supporting children's play, responding positively to children's verbal or non-verbal communications, encouraging children with positive words and actions, and interacting with children on their own level and terms.

- Create a well-structured schedule with a balance of small and large group activities. Make available interactive individual and whole-class visual schedules for children that they can access and manipulate throughout the day. Make upcoming changes known to children in the visual schedule. Indicate transitions and new activities that may be introduced in the daily schedule.
- Set clear behavioral guidelines and rules. Teach and promote clear, simple rules for behaviors in the classroom. Rules include expectations for behaviors with clear directions, related consequences when behaviors are not appropriate. Make behavioral rules for small group and large group activities, behaviors for hallway, playground, and other areas of school, and behaviors in the home and community. Go over and repeat behavioral rules often. Post visual illustrations and reminders of the behavioral rules on the classroom wall near activity centers.
- Have transition plans and activities in place. Design well-structured transition plans and activities to use in between lessons, so as to reduce idleness, keep children engaged, and help them prepare for change.
- Engage children with appropriate instructional techniques and materials. Design activities that are meaningful and interesting to children. Be enthusiastic and keep children engaged in your interactions by using appropriate materials. When children are engaged and interested, challenging behaviors are less likely to occur.
- Use appropriate social-emotional lessons for children of all levels. Promote social-emotional competence and learning by integrating small and large group lessons that help children acquire social-emotional skills. Such learning occurs when teachers help children to: 1) identify and understand simple and complex feelings; 2) practice expressing various emotions; 3) identify and role play different ways of self-regulation; 4) learn and role play how to handle anger, disappointment and frustration; and 5) understand concepts of friendship, and practice sharing, cooperation, and collaboration in play and work with peers.
- Encourage and give appropriate feedback to all children. Be vigilant and pay positive attention to all children throughout the day. Give feedback and encouraging words to all children. When teachers provide positive attention to children consistently, children are less likely to resort to inappropriate behaviors to gain the teacher's attention.

Closing Remarks

In this chapter I drew on resilience research to provide a rationale for educational approaches that are most likely to prevent challenging behaviors and promote social-emotional health in children. Such approaches often act as protective mechanisms and buffer children against risk factors that they may face in their homes or community environments. I reiterate that establishing a warm and positive teacher–child relationship is at the core of most evidence-based and effective curricular approaches. Positive relationships that are fostered and supported within a safe and warm classroom environment nurture self-regulation as well as emotional, cognitive, and behavioral health in children.

References

Ahnert, L., Harwardt-Heinecke, E., Kappler, G., Eckstein-Madry, T., & Milatz, A. (2012). Student–teacher relationships and classroom climate in first grade: How do they relate to student's stress regulation? *Attachment & Human Development, 14*(3), 249–263.

Ahnert, L., Milatz, A., Kappler, G., Schneiderwind, J., & Fisher, R. (2013). The impact of teacher–child relationships on child cognitive performance as explored by a priming paradigm. *Developmental Psychology, 49*(3), 554–567.

Berg-Nielsen, T. S., Solheim, E., Belsky, J., & Wichstrom, L. (2012). Preschoolers' psychosocial problems: In the eyes of the beholder? Adding teacher characteristics as determinants of discrepant parent-teacher reports. *Child Psychiatry and Human Development, 43*, 393–413.

Brackett, M. A., Rivers, S. E., Maurer, M., Holzer, A. A., Shapses, S., & Elbertson, N. A. (2010). *The RULER approach: Feeling words curriculum (Grades K to 2).* New Haven, CT: Ruler Group.

Buyse, E., Verschueren, K., & Doumen, S. (2011). Preschooler's attachment to mother and risk for adjustment problems in kindergarten: Can teachers make a difference? *Social Development, 20*(1), 33–50.

CASEL. Success in Schools. Skills for Life. (2014). *Incredible Years series: Program design and implementation support.* Retrieved from: https://casel.squarespace.com/guide/programs/the-incredible-years-series

Cicchetti, D. (2013). Annual research review: Resilient functioning in maltreated children – past, present, and future perspectives. *Journal of Child Psychology and Psychiatry, 54*(4), 402–422.

Davydon, D., Stewart, R., Ritchie, K., & Chaudieu, I. (2010). Resilience and mental health. *Clinical Psychology Review, 30*, 479–495.

De Kruif, R. E. L., McWilliam, R. A., Maher-Ridley, S., & Wakely, M. B. (2000). Classification of teachers' interaction behaviors in early childhood classrooms. *Early Childhood Research Quarterly, 15*(2), 247–268.

Domitrovich, C. E., Gest, S. D., Gill, S., Bierman, K. L., Welsh, J., & Jones, D. (2009). Fostering high-quality teaching with an enriched curriculum and professional development support: The Head Start REDI program. *American Educational Research Journal, 46*, 567–597.

Domitrovich, C. E., Greenberg, M. T., Kusch, C., & Cortes, R. (2004). *The preschool PATHS curriculum.* Unpublished curriculum, Pennsylvania State University, State College.

Driscoll, K. C., Wang, L., Mashburn, A. J., & Pianta, R. C. (2011). Fostering supportive relationships: Intervention implementation in a state-funded preschool program. *Early Education and Development, 22*(4), 593–619.

Dunlap, G., & Fox, L. (2011). Function-based interventions for children with challenging behavior. *Journal of Early Intervention, 33*(4), 333–343.

Fox, L., Carta, J., Strain, P. S., Dunlap, G., & Hemmeter, M. L. (2010). Response to intervention and the pyramid model. *Infants and Young Children, 23*, 3–14.

Fox, L., Dunlap, G., Hemmeter, M. L., Joseph, G. E., & Strain, P. S. (2003). The teaching pyramid: A model for supporting social competence and preventing challenging behavior in young children. *Young Children, 58*, 48–52.

Fox, L., & Hemmeter, M. L. (2009). A program-wide model for supporting social emotional development and addressing challenging behavior in early childhood settings. In W. Sailor, G. Dunlap, G. Sugai, & R. Horner (Eds.), *Handbook of Positive Behavior Support* (pp. 177–202). New York, NY: Springer.

Garmezy, N. (1973). Competence and adaptation in adult schizophrenic patients and children at risk. In S. R. Dean (Ed.), *Schizophrenia: The first ten Dean Award lectures* (pp. 168–204). New York: M. S. S. Information Corporation.

Garmezy, N. (1974). The study of competence in children at risk for severe psychopathology. In E. J. Anthony & C. Koupernik (Eds.), *The child in his family: Children at psychiatric risk* (Vol. 3, pp. 77–97). Hoboken, NJ: Wiley.

Garmezy, N. (1985). Stress-resistant children: The search for protective factors. In A. Davids (Ed.), *Recent research in developmental psychopathology* (pp. 213–233). Elmsford, NY: Pergamon Press.

Garner, P. W., Mahatmaya, D., Moses, L. K., & Bolt, E. N. (2014). Associations of preschool type and teacher–child relational quality with young children's social-emotional competence. *Early Education and Development, 25,* 399–420.

Greenberg, M. T. (2006). Promoting resilience in children and youth: Preventive interventions and their interface with neuroscience. *Annals of the New York Academy of Science, 1094,* 139–150.

Greenspan, S. I., & Wieder, S. (1998). *The child with special needs: Encouraging intellectual and emotional growth.* Reading, MA: Perseus Books.

Gregoriadis, A., & Grammatikopoulos, V. (2014). Teacher–child relationship quality in early childhood education: The importance of relationship patterns. *Early Child Development and Care, 184*(3), 386–402.

Hagelskamp, C., Brackett, M. A., Rivers, S. E., & Salovey, P. (2013). Improving classroom quality with the RULER approach to social and emotional learning; Proximal and distal outcomes. *American Journal of Community Psychology, 52*(3–4), 530–548.

Hamre, B., Pianta, R. C., Mashburn, A. J., & Downer, J. T. (2012). Promoting young children's social competence through the preschool PATHS curriculum and My Teaching Partner professional development resources. *Early Education & Development, 23,* 809–832.

Hemmeter, M. L., Ostrosky, M. M., & Corso, R. M. (2012). Preventing and addressing challenging behaviors: Common questions and practical strategies. *Young Exceptional Children, 15*(2), 32–46.

Hemmeter, M. L., Ostrosky, M., & Fox, L. (2006). Social and emotional foundations for early learning: A conceptual model for intervention. *School Psychology Review, 35,* 583–601.

Karatoreos, I. N., & McEwen, B. S. (2013). Annual research review: The neurobiology and physiology of resilience and adaptation across the life course. *The Journal of Child Psychology and Psychiatry, 54*(4), 337–347.

Kusch, C., & Greenberg, M. T. (1994). *The PATHS curriculum.* South Eerfield, MA: Channing-Bete.

Lindo, N. A., Taylor, D. D., Meany-Walen, K. K., Purswell, K., Jayne, K., Gonzales, T., & Jones, L. (2014). Teachers as therapeutic agents: Perceptions of a school-based mental health initiative. *British Journal of Guidance & Counseling, 42*(3), 284–296.

Madill, R. A., Gest, S. D., & Rodkin, P. C. (2014). Students' perceptions of relatedness in the classroom: The role of emotionally supportive teacher–child interactions, Children's aggressive–disruptive behaviors, and peer social preference. *School Psychology Review, 43*(1), 86–105.

Masten, A. (2001). Ordinary magic: Resilience processes in development. *American Psychologist, 56,* 227–238.

Masten A. (2007). Resilience in developing systems: Progress and promise as the fourth wave rises. *Development and Psychopathology, 19,* 921–930.

Masten A. (2011). Resilience in children threatened by extreme adversity: Framework for research, practice, and translational synergy. *Development and Psychopathology, 23,* 493–506.

Masten, A. S., & O'Connor, M. J. (1989). Vulnerability, stress, and resilience in the early development of a high risk child. *Journal of the America Academy of Child & Adolescent Psychiatry, 28,* 274–278.

Mayer, J. D., & Salovey, P. (1997). What is emotional intelligence? In P. Salovey & D. Sluyter (Eds.), *Emotional development and emotional intelligence: Educational implications* (pp. 3–31). New York, NY: Basic Books.

Pianta, R. C. (1994). Patterns of relationship between children and kindergarten teachers. *Journal of School Psychology, 32*(1), 15–31.

Pianta, R. C., & Hamre, B. (2001). *Students, teachers, and relationship support (STARS).* Lutz, FL: Psychological Assessment Resources.

Pianta, R. C., Hamre, B., & Stuhlman, M. (2003). Relationships between teachers and children. In W. M. Reynolds, G. E. Miller, and I. B. Weiner (Eds.), *Handbook of Psychology: Volume 7 – educational psychology* (pp. 199–234). Hoboken, NJ: Wiley.

Rivers, S. E., & Brackett, M. A. (2011). Achieving standards in the English language arts (and more) using the RULER approach to social and emotional learning. *Reading & Writing Quarterly, 27,* 75–100.

Rivers, S. E., Brackett, M. A., Reyes, M., Elbertson, N. A., & Salovey, P. (2013). Improving the social and emotional climate of classrooms: A clustered randomized controlled trial testing the RULER approach. *Prevention Science, 14,* 77–87.

Rudasill, K. M., Neihaus, K., Buhs, E., & White, J. M. (2013). Temperament in early childhood and peer interactions in third grade: The role of teacher–child relationships in early elementary grades. *Journal of School Psychology, 51,* 703–716.

Rutter, M. (1979). Protective factors in children's responses to stress and disadvantage. In M. W. Kent & J. E. Rolf (Eds.), *Primary prevention of psychopathology: Social competence in children* (Vol. 3, pp. 49–74). Hanover, HH: University Press of New England.

Rutter, M. (1990). Psychosocial resilience and protective mechanism. In J. Rolf, A. S. Masten, D. Cicchetti, K. H. Nuechterlein, & S. Weintraub (Eds.), *Risk and protective factors in the development of psychopathology* (pp. 181–214). New York: Cambridge University Press.

Rutter, M. (2006). Implications of resilience concepts for scientific understanding. *Annals of New York Academy of Sciences, 1094,* 1–12.

Rutter, M. (2012). Resilience as a dynamic concept. *Development and Psychopathology, 24,* 335–344.

Sabol, T. J., & Pianta, R. C. (2012). Recent trends in research on teacher–child relationships. *Attachment & Human Development, 14*(3), 213–231.

Sameroff, A. J., & Chandler, M. J. (1975). Reproductive risk and the continuum of caretaking casualty. In F. D. Horowitz, M. Hetherington, S. Scarr Salapatek, & G. Siegal (Eds.), *Review of child development research* (Vol. 4, pp. 187–244). Chicago, IL: University of Chicago Press.

Seligman, M. E. P. & Csikszentmihalyi, M. (2000). Positive psychology: An introduction. *American Psychologist, 55,* 5–14.

Snyder, P. A., Hemmeter, M. L., Fox, L., Bishop, C. & Miller, M. D. (2013). Developing and gathering psychometric evidence for a fidelity instrument: The teaching pyramid observation tool – pilot version. *Journal of Early Intervention, 35*(2), 150–172.

Ştefan, C. A., & Miclea, M. (2013). Effects of multifocused prevention program on preschool children's competencies and behavior problems. *Psychology in Schools, 50*(4), 382–402.

Verschueren, K., Doumen, S., & Buyse, E. (2012). Relationships with mother, teacher, and peers: Unique and joint effects on young children's self-concept. *Attachment & Human Development, 14*(3), 233–248.

Walsh, F. (1996). The concept of family resilience: Crisis and challenge. *Family Process, 35,* 261–281.

Walsh, F. (2003). Family resilience: A framework for clinical practice. *Family Process, 42*(1), 1–18.

Webster-Stratton, C. (1998). Preventing conduct problems in Head Start children: Strengthening parenting competencies. *Journal of Consulting and Clinical Psychology, 66*(5), 715–730.

Webster-Stratton, C., & Bywater, T. (2014). Parents and teachers working together. *Better: Evidence-based Education, 6*(2), 16–17.

Webster-Stratton, C., & Reid, J. (2014). Tailoring the Incredible Years: Parent, teacher, and child interventions for young children with ADHD. In J. K. Ghuman & H. S. Ghuman (Eds.), *ADHD in preschool children: Assessment and treatment* (pp. 113–131). Oxford: Oxford University Press.

Werner, E. (2012a). Risk, resilience, and recovery. *Reclaiming Children and Youth, 21*(1), 18–22.

Werner, E. (2012b). Children and war: Risk, resilience, and recovery. *Development and Psychopathology, 24,* 553–558.

Werner, E., & Smith, R. (1977). *Kauai's children come of age.* Honolulu: University of Hawaii Press.

Werner, E., & Smith, R. (1982). *Vulnerable but invincible: A longitudinal study of resilient children and youth.* New York, NY: McGraw-Hill.

Werner, E., & Smith, R. (1992). *Overcoming the odds: High risk children from birth to adulthood.* Ithaca, NY: Cornell University Press.

Werner, E., & Smith, R. (2001). *Journey from childhood to midlife: Risk, resilience, and recovery.* Ithaca, NY: Cornell University Press.

Werner, E., Bierman, J., & French, F. (1971). *The children of Kauai.* Honolulu: University of Hawaii Press.

Wieder, S., & Greenspan, S. I. (2003). Climbing the symbolic ladder in the DIR model through floor time/interactive play. *Autism, 7*(4), 425–435.

Zhang, X., & Sun, J. (2011). The reciprocal relations between teacher's perceptions of children's behavior problems and teacher–child relationships in the first preschool year. *Journal of Genetic Psychology, 172*(2), 176–198.

Zigler, E., & Berman, W. (1983). Discerning the future of early childhood intervention. *American Psychologist, 38*(8), 894–906.

6

PLAY THERAPY

An Intervention for Addressing Challenging Behaviors and Mental Health Issues in Children

In this chapter I introduce *play therapy*, an intervention that facilitates development of children with a variety of behavioral and mental health issues. Play therapy can be employed with children as young as toddlers or preschoolers and as old as twelve-year-olds. When I refer to *play*, I am referring to the child's actions. "In order for an activity to be considered 'play,' it must be voluntary and *intrinsically motivating* to the child – that is, the child must find play enjoyable without any need for external rewards or motivation to engage in it. By watching children at play, teachers (and other professionals) can gain insight into specific developmental competencies of infants, toddlers, and young children. Play is systematically related to areas of development and learning" (Mindes & Jung, 2015, p. 124; see also Linder, 2008; Widerstrom, 2005).

Mental health professionals choose play therapy as a treatment of choice for children because play is considered as a natural mode of communication and self-expression (Kottman, 2003; Landreth, 2012). Play gives children an opportunity to playact their feelings, thoughts, events, and their emotional challenges the same way as adults can talk about their problems in therapy (Axline, 1974). In this chapter, I describe the use of play in therapy, examine the development and history of play therapy, and discuss intervention techniques.

What is Play Therapy?

Play therapy is a dynamic interpersonal relationship between a child and a therapist who provides selected toys and facilitates the development of a safe relationship in which the child explores and expresses self, thoughts, and emotions through play (Landreth, 2012). The Association for Play Therapy (Association for Play Therapy-APT, 2014) defines play therapy as the systematic use of a theoretical model to establish this interpersonal process, in which the therapist uses play to help the child prevent or resolve psychosocial difficulties, and to achieve optimal growth and development (APT, 2014). Play therapy is different from regular play because in regular play, there is no effort on the part of the adult to help the child resolve issues. Play therapy is used also with children who have special needs to promote cognitive development, such as the application of floor time (Greenspan & Weider, 1998, which is explained in Chapter 5).

Early childhood and elementary school counselors often choose play therapy because of its practicality, simplicity, and effectiveness. Play therapy approaches do not require complicated trainings since they are based in developmentally appropriate curricular practice. Thus, teachers or counselors can easily implement such approaches in their classrooms.

In contrast, historically, many child psychiatrists and psychologists have criticized play therapy as a treatment of choice due to a lack of scientific evidence to support its efficacy. However, during the past two decades a good number of research studies show the efficacy of play therapy and provide evidence that it is indeed a viable treatment option for young children (for examples see Bratton, Ray, Edwards, & Landreth, 2009; Garza, Kinsworthy, & Bennett, 2014; Meany-Walen, Bratton, & Kottman, 2014). Before providing a historical account of the development of play therapy, let us briefly describe the history of play in early childhood education to set the context for our later sections.

History of Play in Early Childhood Education

The importance of play in early childhood education is long acknowledged in the extensive research literature devoted to this topic. National and international professional and academic organizations in early childhood education disseminated a great portion of such literature to professionals on an ongoing basis (for an example see National Association for the Education of Young Children – NAEYC, 2014). The role and importance of play in early childhood education is a complex topic with a history of its own, deserving an entire book. Thus, an in-depth examination of this topic is beyond the scope of this chapter. I, therefore, provide only a cursory description of the history of play in early childhood education.

The first discussion of play in education is attributed to Plato. In *Laws*, Plato recommended that play – which he explained as a pleasurable activity – be used by teachers to teach children skills for life (Brehony, 2004). Later, John Locke (in the 17th century) and Jean-Jacques Rousseau (in the 18th century) both articulated ideas about play in early childhood education based on Plato's assertions. Locke believed that play was the natural tendency of children; therefore, they learned best by means of recreation (Gianoutsos, 2006). Rousseau, who articulated his ideas about education in *Emile*, similarly believed that play in children was instinctive and necessary for growth and development (Brehony, 2004). Rousseau encouraged teaching children through play.

In the 19th century, Friedrich Froebel, known as the father and the founder of kindergarten, articulated more comprehensive and detailed ideas about the importance of play in early childhood education. Froebel introduced the concept of learning through children's self-directed activities, games, and play, in combination with songs and music. He placed play at the center of educating young children in kindergartens and brought forward the idea of using toys, which he called *gifts*, as a way of facilitating children's learning of cultural values and vocational skills (Gutek, 1999).

Developmental theories of the 20th century emphasized the role of play in the cognitive development of children. This importance is articulated mainly through the theories of Jean Piaget and Lev Vygotsky. Piaget believed that play was for pleasure, but it was important because it demonstrated children's cognitive development and detailed how children moved from concrete to abstract thinking (Piaget, 1999). He emphasized that play was central to symbolic representation and to children's socialization (Piaget, 1999). Vygotsky described play as a facilitator of learning new skills. He believed playing to be central to learning language and promoting self-regulation (Brehony, 2004). These ideas are instrumental in the widespread use of child-centered curricula with a focus on play in early childhood education today.

History of Play Therapy: From Psychoanalysis to Child-Centered Play

The roots of play therapy are found in psychoanalytic theories. There is no agreed upon date in which play was used for the first time as a therapy or means of treatment for children, but some attribute it to Freud. In 1909, Freud treated a five-year-old child named Hans who had a phobia of horses (McLeod, 2008). Freud treated his phobia successfully through a series of correspondences with the boy's father and directing the father to work and play with the child. Later, Freud wrote a summary of his treatment of Hans (McLeod, 2008). Although the case of Hans may demonstrate the time in which children began to be considered as subjects for psychoanalytical treatment, it does not establish the creation of play therapy or the use of play as a therapy, since Freud never actually worked with Hans directly in either a play or non-play context (McLeod, 2008).

Hermine Hug-Hellmuth, a teacher and a psychoanalyst who was a contemporary to Freud, is credited with being the world's first child psychoanalyst and the first person who used toys and playful interactions as means of therapy with children (MacLean, 1986; Plastow, 2011). She first applied psychoanalysis methods of working with adults to children and soon found that such methods were inadequate (MacLean, 1986). Thereafter, bringing together her teaching experience and her psychoanalytic training, she applied systematic child observation and experimented with a form of play therapy that combined play and education together (MacLean, 1986; Plastow, 2011). However, before she was able to formulate and write down specific methods for play therapy with children, Hug-Hellmuth's life was cut short in 1924. She was killed during a physical struggle with her nephew who invaded her home at night; the same nephew on whom she had based many of her observations and earlier writings (Plastow, 2011). Hug-Hellmuth's published work prior to her death outlined the basic elements of child psychoanalysis techniques and introduced innovative methods of working with children via interactive play and utilization of toys (Plastow, 2011). These works predate Anna Freud and Melanie Klein, who are formally recognized as pioneers in play therapy for children (Landreth, 2012; MacLean, 1986; Plastow, 2011).

In the 1920s through the 1930s a number of elementary schools, which were founded on psychoanalytic principles, opened in Europe (Brehony, 2004). Notable among these schools is the Hietzing School, established in 1927 in Vienna, also known as "the Matchbox School" because of its small size (Midgley, 2008). Anna Freud, who first trained as an elementary school teacher before following in her father's footsteps in psychoanalysis, was the director for three years. One of the teachers she recruited for this school was Eric Erikson (Midgley, 2008).

Anna Freud spent a great deal of time working with early childhood teachers and professionals. She participated in several educational experiments, and engaged with some leading progressive educational ideas (Midgley, 2008). She was influenced and inspired by the ideas of John Dewy, and particularly by Maria Montessori's method of educating young children. The basic tenets of Montessori's method, which Anna Freud replicated in her school's curricula, were recognizing children's interests, providing suitable materials, and giving children the freedom to play and manipulate materials within carefully placed limits (Midgley, 2008, 2012). During World War II, after Anna Freud immigrated to Britain, she established the Hampstead War Nursery and utilized play therapy with children there (Freud Museum London, 2014). Anna Freud used play therapy mainly as a way to facilitate good feelings in children, to establish attachment between the child and the therapist, and to have children feel comfortable enough to reveal their inner thoughts (Landreth, 2012). She rarely used play therapy for children younger than seven years old (Midgley, 2012).

In 1932, Melanie Klein, a British psychoanalyst and contemporary of Anna Freud, wrote *The Technique of Early Analysis*. In this book, she described a series of play therapy techniques for children that she developed to help children express themselves through playing with toys (Melanie Klein Trust, 2014). Klein began working with young children, in some cases younger than six years old. She believed if given maximum opportunities, children could use their imaginations through spontaneous play, and therefore express their thoughts via their play (Melanie Klein Trust, 2014). Klein used simple toys for each child, such as little wooden dolls, animals, cars, houses, balls, clay, paints, paper and pencils, scissors, and glue; these she kept in a drawer belonging to each child, to represent a specific and private relationship with that child (Landreth, 2012).

Thus, in England, Anna Freud and Melanie Klein became the first psychoanalysts who promoted the use of play therapy with children. From that point forward, other professionals in the field of child psychology and psychiatry, and later, in counseling, began to use and advance play therapy and its related techniques and principles.

One of the leading figures in contemporary child-centered play therapy, Landreth (2012) describes several other influential developments in the history of play therapy that have led to the advancement of this therapy as a viable treatment for children around the world. Some of these developments are (Landreth, 2012):

- *Release play therapy*. A structured form of therapy, release play therapy was developed in the 1930s for children who experienced trauma or a specific anxiety-producing or stressful event. In this therapy, after the child spends some time engaged in free play and feels comfortable with the therapist and the environment, the therapist reenacts the stressful situation. The idea is that in the process of reenacting the experience, the child will feel in control, and be able to act out in ways that will release the experienced pain and tension. Accordingly, the therapist will help the child to regulate and come to terms with the pained experience and cope with it successfully.
- *Relationship play therapy*. This therapy, also developed in the 1930s, places a focus on building a natural relationship between the therapist and the child. A major belief in this therapy is that children are capable of changing their own behaviors constructively. There is also an emphasis placed on the child's present feelings and reactions. The goal is that through play sessions, children will realize that they can successfully form relationships and function well within a relationship with another person, and be in charge of their own behaviors (for details see Mustakas, 1997).
- *Child-centered play therapy*. Child-centered play therapy, introduced in the 1940s, is based on the belief that the child strives to learn, regulate self, and direct self. While the therapist provides a safe relationship environment for the child to play and explore, the therapist makes no effort to direct, control, or change the child. Instead, the child directs and controls the play session, using multitudes of child-chosen toys. In this therapy, there is a genuine belief that the child is resilient, and capable of successfully constructing a self-direction toward growth, maturation, and mental health. The therapist shows acceptance and validation of all thoughts, behaviors, and emotions expressed by the child by narrating the child's behaviors and/or repeating what the child says. The goal is that once the feelings of the child are identified, brought out, and accepted by the therapist, the child will learn to accept those feelings and deals with them successfully.
- *Play therapy in elementary schools*. In the 1960s and 1970s, school counselors began to use play therapy in elementary schools. Up until that time, play therapy was part of the domain of psychologists who conducted play therapy sessions in their private offices. Since the 1960s school counselors have been using play therapy in classrooms with small groups or with individual children. The goal of play therapy in schools is to help children have a positive learning experience, and maximize their opportunities to learn (for an example see Garza et al., 2014).

- *Filial therapy*. Developed in the 1960s, filial therapy focuses on improving the parent–child relationship as a way of promoting mental health in the child (Guerney, 1969). In filial therapy, therapists train parents to use basic child-centered play therapy techniques in play sessions with their children. Filial therapy techniques were modified in 2006 to form what is known today as *Child Parent Relationship Therapy (CPRT)* (Bratton, Landreth, Kellam, & Blackard, 2006).
- *Association for Play Therapy*. The Association for Play Therapy (APT) is a professional organization, established in 1982. This organization promotes research and practice in the field of play therapy primarily in the United States. The creation of APT prompted establishment of other professional organizations in play therapy in Canada and Europe. (For details see: http://www.a4pt.org/).
- *Center for Play Therapy*. In 1988, Garry Landreth established the Center for Play Therapy at the University of North Texas. Landreth was among the first scholars promoting play therapy practices in elementary schools in the 1960s. Currently, the Center for Play Therapy is recognized as the largest play therapy training program in the world, and serves as a clearing house for information regarding play therapy literature, training and research (for details see: http://cpt.unt.edu/about-us/our-history/). Today, there are over 100 universities in the United States offering play therapy professional training programs.

Other trends in play therapy, such as play therapy with hospitalized children, play therapy in response to disasters and traumatic events, and the use of filial therapy with babies and caregivers, and in preschool and early elementary schools, helped bring it to the attention of child mental health scholars and professional practitioners in the last two decades (Landreth, 2012; Urquiza & Timmer, 2012). Child Life programs implement play therapy procedures in US hospitals. The goal in the hospitals is to promote the mental and physical health in children by providing opportunities for them to express and deal with their emotions, fears, anxieties, and apprehensions (Landreth, 2012; Urquiza & Timmer, 2012).

The use of play therapy as an intervention immediately after a traumatic event or a disaster, in most cases as a single-session intervention, is designed to address the urgent need of children who may have faced a traumatic event (Homeyer & Sweeney, 2010). This kind of intervention often takes place as a disaster response approach or in the cases of deaths of family members. Finally, the adaptation of filial therapy in pre-kindergarten and early elementary school settings is rapidly gaining popularity as a prevention and early intervention for young children (Carnes-Holt & Bratton, 2014).

Theoretical Models in Play Therapy

There are different theoretical models in play therapy. Play therapy methods and techniques, such as the structure of the sessions, selection of toys, the therapist's responses and reactions to the child, and the way that the child is viewed and therefore directed to play, are all based on the specific theory of development (particularly in terms of social-emotional development). Although theoretical models vary from one another in their view of children's development and learning processes, all theoretical approaches in play therapy agree on two things: 1) children communicate their thoughts and feelings through play; and 2) play is the best and most appropriate form of intervention for children.

The most commonly practiced theoretical approaches in play therapy for younger children are child-centered nondirective play therapy (CCPT) (Axline, 1974; Mustakas, 1997; Landreth, 2002a), and child-centered Adlerian play therapy (AdPT) (Kottman, 2003). There are, of course, differences in the ways that each of these models structures and carries out play sessions. However, both models are child-centered, and there is a strong focus on establishing and maintaining a positive relationship between the child and the therapist. In the following sections I will focus on basic principles and practices of these models.

Principles of Child-Centered Play Therapy (CCPT)

The principles of CCPT are based on Carl Rogers' (1959) person-centered therapy. Rogers believed that all individuals have an inner capacity to develop in a positive direction and to solve their problems, if the provided climate allows them. The application of this view to children translates into facilitating opportunities for children to safely explore their own thoughts, feelings, and behaviors and therefore work through their issues (Landreth, 2012).

In articulating the principles of nondirective child-centered play therapy, Axline (1974), one of the founders of the nondirective approach, put forth several important principles for this model. The therapist:

- develops a warm and friendly relationship with the child
- accepts the child as the child is currently functioning
- recognizes the feelings of the child and reflects them back in a way so that the child understands his own behaviors
- respects the child as the agent of change and, assumes when given the responsibility, the child can solve problems
- follows the child and does not direct the child's actions or conversations
- establishes limits only to anchor the child to reality and to make the child aware of his responsibilities.

As these principles indicate, in a nondirective CCPT the therapist approaches the child from a place of respect, from a belief that the child is resilient and capable of coping, and from a genuine acceptance of the child the way the child is currently behaving. The child's reality and values are accepted as real, and the child's behaviors therefore reflect that reality. The non-judgmental essence of CCPT principles led into a recognition in the field that child-centered play therapy is inclusive of the child's beliefs, upbringings, values, and culture, and therefore is a culturally competent practice for children of diverse socio-economic and ethnic backgrounds (Davis & Pereira, 2014).

A theory that integrates both nondirective CCPT principles, as well as directive play techniques is Adlerian play therapy (AdPT). This model is based on Alfred Adler's individual psychology, in which the individuals are not only goal directed and creative, but also are socially embedded in that they have needs to belong in their family, environment, and cultural context (Kottman, 2001).

Using an Adlerian framework, Terry Kottman (2001, 2003) developed play therapy protocols based on this view and articulated the principles of AdPT. Although AdPT is also a child-directed approach, there are some differences between it and the nondirective CCPT model developed by Axline. While both models believe in children's capacity to change and direct their own behaviors, the therapist in the AdPT model is more active, and the role is to reeducate, orient, or direct children, so that they will gain necessary insights into solving their issues and redirecting their behaviors.

Kottman (2001) articulated four phases in Adlerian play therapy: "(a) building an egalitarian relationship with the child, (b) exploring the child's lifestyle, (c) helping the child gain insight into his or her lifestyle, and (d) providing reorientation and reeducation for the child when necessary" (p. 5). Unlike nondirective CCPT, where parents or family members are not allowed in the play sessions, the therapist in AdPT works closely with family members and parents to understand the child better to provide information for family members regarding the child's behaviors and motivations, and to collaborate or consult with them in the intervention process. Therefore, some play sessions may be structured to include parents, family members, close friends, and teachers (Kottman, 2003).

In AdPT, the therapist has a more directing role. For example, during the phase of exploring the child's lifestyle, the therapist may set up a sand tray with small figures and toys, and give the child a simple prompt, like, "Make a scene in the sand of any event you can remember with as many figures as you like" (Even & Armstrong, 2011). Then, the therapist will direct the child to recollect specific events, interpret the child's play, and reorient and reeducate the child. The reorientation and reeducation process may consist of the therapist's helping the child to reflect back and understand his own thinking and feelings and therefore regulate his behaviors. It may also consist of a process of collaboration in which the child, the therapist, and the parents or other family members work together to help the child understand his emotions and redirect his behaviors.

Toys in Play Therapy

Any space, such as a corner of a classroom or a designated room, can be used for play therapy (Axline, 1974). Toys and materials are important elements in play since they can either inhibit or encourage the child to express ideas and emotions

(Landreth, 2012). Toys should meet the following criteria (Bratton et al., 2009; Landreth, 2012):

- Make contributions to the main objective of play therapy.
- Align with the rationale for the play therapy.
- Engage children's interests.
- Represent the cultural and real life experiences of children.
- Facilitate interactions and build a positive relationship with the child.
- Allow the expression of wide range of feelings.
- Facilitate tests of limits, and limit setting.
- Encourage a positive image.
- Help the child in self-understanding.
- Provide opportunities to redirect behaviors that are unacceptable.
- Be sturdy and can be used for active play.

It is recommended that a wide range of toys be available to facilitate the therapeutic process, with a few exceptions. For example, puzzles, books, small Legos®, mechanical or computerized toys, and computer games are not recommended, because they do not encourage intrapersonal interactions and relationship building, or they may not be practical (Bratton et al., 2009; Landreth, 2012). Landreth (2012) recommended three categories of toys for play therapy: 1) real-life toys; 2) acting out toys; and 3) toys for creative expression and emotional release. Drawing on these recommendations (Landreth, 2012), I will briefly describe each category in the following sections.

Real-Life Toys

A dolls' house with puppets and figures to represent the child's family members and friends will lend itself to representing the real life, culture, and experiences of the child. Other toys in this category include cars, trucks, animals, store items, medical kits, kitchen/food items, etc. Real-life toys can help the child express feelings and play-act events that have been experienced.

Acting Out/Aggressive Toys

These are "punching toys," like Bobo dolls, dart guns and toy weapons, handcuffs, toy soldiers, aggressive puppets, rubber knives, etc. There is a controversy surrounding the use of these toys, since they may lead to the child acting out in aggression. Some have argued that the inclusion of aggressive toys invites these behaviors and can encourage and even teach children to be violent (Stone, 2000). Others, however, recommend using aggressive toys, stressing the necessity of such toys to provide children with means of symbolic expression of a wide range of emotions, such as anger and frustration, within the safety of the therapeutic play environment and in socially acceptable ways (Bratton et al., 2009; Trotter & Landreth, 2003). Aggressive play materials may symbolize several things to the same child at different times. For example, a Bobo doll can be used as a means of externalizing negative and aggressive feelings at one time, or become an object of affection and nurturing at another time (Trotter & Landreth, 2003).

Aggressive toys can be used in limit settings. For example, setting appropriate limits within the boundaries of the session can teach the child that it is not acceptable to hit his friends or adults but okay to punch the punching puppet or to pound a hammer on a pounding bench instead. Children who are aggressive seem to experience satisfaction and enhanced positive feelings when they are allowed to symbolically play-act aggression in the presence of a person who has established a relationship with the child and has set limits (Landreth, 2012).

Toys for Creative Expression and Emotional Release

Unstructured toys are materials that provide endless possibilities for use and manipulation (Landreth, 2012). Examples of these materials are sand, water, paint, blocks, papers, construction materials, etc. For example, the child can pretend that a water table is an ocean, a pool, or a bath for the baby doll. Although these materials are often messy, they allow the child to express creativity and explore both constructive and destructive feelings (Landreth, 2012). For examples of recommended toys see Table 6.1.

Table 6.1 Sample of Recommended Toys for Play Therapy

Real-Life Toys	Aggressive/Acting out Toys	Toys for Creative Expressions
Baby plastic bottle, pacifier	Bobo/punch doll, puppets	Building blocks
Balls	Dart gun	Blunt scissors
Bendable dolls/family	Dinosaur, shark	Musical instruments
Broom, dustpan	Pounding bench, hammer	Chalkboard, chalks, eraser
Doll bed, clothes, blankets	Toy guns and weapons	Crayon, pencil, paper
Doll house, furniture	Rope	Paints, easel
Dress up clothes	Rubber knife	Popsicle sticks
Hats: fireman, policeman, crown, etc.	Rubber snake, alligator	Cereal boxes
Toy kitchen items and foods	Plastic insects	Milk and egg cartons
Medical kit	Toy soldiers and army toys	Tissue
Play money, cash register		Watercolor
Puppets		
Stuffed animals		
Toy cell phones, camera, watch		
Truck, cars, airplanes, etc.		
Zoo and farm animal figure		

Source: Adapted from Landreth, G. L. (2012). *Play therapy: The art of relationship* (3rd ed.). New York: Routledge.

Relationship between the Child and the Play Therapist

Research establishes that the relationship between the therapist and the child is the essential predictor of treatment outcome for the child in the play therapy (Shirk, Kraver, & Brown, 2011; Shirk & Peterson, 2013). Clark Mustakas and his contemporaries Carl Rogers and Virginia Axline worked extensively to articulate the essence of therapeutic processes and relationships in play therapy. In Mustakas's view, the therapist's attitude and ability to be present with the child are critical to understanding the child (Mustakas, 1997). Mustakas's approach to play therapy is known as *relationship play therapy*. The philosophy forms the foundation of relationship building in child-centered play therapy approaches.

The relationship between the child and the therapist centers on a *positive and unconditional regard* for the child (Mustakas, 1997). This regard can also be thought of as an empathetic understanding of the child. During the play session, the child has the undivided attention of the therapist (Mustakas, 1997), and the caring and warm presence of the therapist remains consistent throughout (Trotter & Landreth, 2003).

The major goal of play therapy is to awaken the power of self-direction in the child, enable the child to explore freely and to understand emotions, and gradually identify and replace behaviors with acceptable ones (Mustakas, 1997). The relationship between the therapist and the child is a safe place for the child to make explorations and discoveries and alter behaviors.

The relationship between the therapist and the child begins from their very first meeting. During the introduction, the therapist clearly communicates to the child that the child is important and can be safe in the presence of the therapist. A typical statement for the first visit may be, "In this play room you can play with the toys in many of the ways you like," (Landreth, 2002b). This is an example of carefully chosen words ("many of the ways you like," instead of "any way you like"), which is used to convey freedom and self-direction and the setting of some boundaries for this freedom and relationship (Landreth, 2012). The therapist's job is to facilitate freedom with boundaries, safety, and self-control (Landreth, 2012).

The therapist needs to be genuine so that a therapeutic relationship can be established. To be genuine means to have an "openness and awareness of moment-by-moment experience and the freedom to be one's self in relationship with others" (Ray, Jayne, & Stulmaker, 2014, p. 12). Genuineness is an important characteristic, especially when a child has aggressive behaviors – i.e. hits or attempts to hurt the therapist during a session.

It is often difficult for a professional not to allow negative experiences with the child to manifest into feelings of resentment and anger. In such situations, the natural inclination of the therapist is to try to hide (or even distort) negative feelings in order to remain neutral and nonjudgmental. However, it is not beneficial for a professional to be in denial of feelings and experiences. On the contrary, being genuine means to allow for one's experiences to enter into one's awareness so that the person can reflect and practice mindfulness and openness before engaging with the child (Ray et al., 2014). The following episode provides an example to clarify this issue.

> Jane, a play therapist, had a hectic morning before leaving for work. Upon waking up that morning, Jane discovered that the furnace was not working. On top of that, her babysitter called a short while later to inform her that she was sick and could not care for the baby that day. Jane's morning progressively got worse when she got into an argument with her teenage daughter. After breakfast, Jane dropped her baby off at her parents' home 20 miles outside of the city, which prevented her from resolving the heating problem or the argument with her daughter before leaving home. She arrived at her office late, knowing that it would be a particularly long morning. She had a play session scheduled for Martin that day. Martin was an inquisitive child, who asked many questions during the play session. He was also messy, and tended to scatter blocks and toys all over the floor during play. Groaning, Jane prepared to enter the play session. Jane felt frustrated with everything: her daughter, the furnace, her babysitter, and most of all she was angry with herself for going into her play session in a bad mood. Trying to hide her anger and frustrations, Jane put on a smile with some difficulty and entered the playroom. During the play session, Jane tried hard to focus on the present, but her answers to Martin's questions were mechanical. Once during the session, when Martin repeated a question, she felt impatient and irritated, but quickly tried to hide it. However, as she was ending the session, Jane thought Martin for sure noticed her horrible mood that morning.
>
> After the session, Jane reflected on this experience. She thought she should have spent a few minutes in self-reflection before going into the session. She should have become totally mindful of the fact that she was feeling frustrated and angry and apt to becoming impatient. Had she done that, she would have been better prepared to *be present* in the moment and act genuinely.

To *be present* in the moment is called a therapeutic presence. In the therapeutic process, the act of "being" has more importance than the act of "doing" (Crenshaw & Kenney-Noziska, 2014):

> Included in the 'being' are the openness and receptiveness to the child. Also included are love for children, enjoyment of playing with children, and the ability to enter the child's world fully … 'being' is primary and what guides the therapy. The 'doing' is secondary and drives from [the therapist's] 'being.' … Rather than the dichotomy of 'being' versus 'doing,' both are of value, especially when the 'doing' emerges from the 'being.'
>
> *(Crenshaw & Kenney-Noziska, 2014, p. 35–36)*

Techniques for Relationship Building during Play Therapy

In most child-centered play therapies, three basic techniques are used to build a trusting relationship with children: 1) tracking behavior; 2) restatement or reflection of content; and 3) reflection of feeling (Axline, 1974; Kottman, 2003; Landreth, 2012).

Tracking Behavior

Tracking behavior occurs when the therapist provides a running account of the child's behavior. This occurs by physically tuning into the child's behavior: for example attentively looking at the child, turning toward the child when the child moves; and verbally, by describing or narrating what the child does, e.g. "You are looking at the yellow car." Tracking behaviors are important to convey to the child that what the child does and says is worthy and will have the therapist's undivided attention.

Restatement or Reflection of Content

Making statements that are reflections of what the child does helps the child gain validation of perceptions and experiences and therefore provides insights for the child to understand behaviors. In reflecting on content, the therapist paraphrases the verbal utterances of the child. For example, in a police play scenario, a child may say something like, "This one is a bad guy. The police will take away the bad guy. But the bad guy tells the police, 'I am a good guy.'" The therapist may reflect on the content of the child's narrative in this way: "The bad guy tells the police that he is a good guy, because he knows that the police take away the bad guys. The bad guy does not want to be taken away by the police."

Reflection of Feelings

The play therapist tries to reflect on the feelings expressed by the child through play. These feelings may be expressed verbally or through action during play. For example, the therapist may say, "You say you are sad," or the therapist may reflect on a child's action of kissing a baby doll: "You really like that baby doll, huh?" Reflection of feelings conveys to the child that the therapist understands the child. It also allows the therapist an opportunity to check the child's perception. For example, if the child kisses the doll, but replies, "No, I am punishing the doll" (or throws the doll down or in other ways demonstrates non-agreement with the therapist's interpretation), the therapist has new insight about the child's perceptions of feelings.

Setting Limits and Addressing Challenging Behaviors

As I mentioned, expression of aggressive behaviors is allowed during play therapy. Whether play is used for developmental purposes or to promote mental health, there should be a limit on how and to what extent the child can display anger during play. In some structured play therapies, such as in floor time, two specific limits are set and communicated: 1) the child will not be allowed to damage or destroy any materials and toys; and 2) the child will not be allowed to hurt self or any other person involved during floor time (Greenspan & Wieder, 1998).

Limit setting is an important component in child-centered play therapy and most theoretical models discuss limit setting as an essential component for facilitating the therapeutic process (Axline, 1974; Kottman, 2001; Landreth, 2002b; 2012; Mustakas, 1953). Limits are necessary for the child to understand the boundaries of any relationship. Additionally, having no boundaries and limits lends itself to unpredictability, and this in turn signals a lack of safety, emotional control, or security to the child. Consistent limit setting allows the child to be able to predict behavioral consequences and learn self-regulation.

The way that the play therapist chooses, establishes, and reinforces limits in the relationship determines how and to what extent the child should regulate his behaviors and thus be in control of his actions. Therefore, it is important to choose limitations that will "anchor therapy to the world of reality and make the child aware of his responsibility in the relationship" (Axline, 1974, p. 128). Limits involve specific behaviors in five areas: behaviors that 1) are harmful to the child and the therapist; 2) disrupt the therapeutic process; 3) are destructive of the materials or the space; 4) are socially unacceptable; and 5) inappropriately display affection (Landreth, 2012). In this way, limit setting provides a safe environment for the child and facilitates opportunities for the child to learn responsibility, self-regulation, and socially appropriate behaviors.

Because the therapist genuinely believes children are capable of taking responsibility to regulate and to control self, even when the child attempts to break a toy or throws objects, it is important to communicate to the child that a positive regard for the child continues to exist despite the child's unacceptable behavior (Landreth, 2002b, 2012). For children who are angry and have aggressive behaviors and who are usually criticized or rejected, it is particularly important that a message of acceptance and positive regard for their personhood is conveyed to them.

There are certain recommended steps in setting limits. In Adlerian play therapy, limit setting is a four-step process: 1) the therapist sets limits; 2) the therapist makes a guess about the child's feeling and/or the purpose of inappropriate behavior; 3) the therapist engages the child to redirect his own behavior; and 4) the therapist discusses with the child logical consequences for continued violation of the limits (Kottman, 2001).

In nondirective play therapy, a procedure is used called ACTS: Acknowledge the child's feeling, wishes, and wants; communicate the limit; target acceptable alternative behaviors; and if the child violates the limits, state the final choice (Landreth, 2012). The fourth step – of stating the final choice – is implemented only if the child violates the limits. In this case the therapist makes a statement that makes the child clearly understand that it was his choice to act in a certain way and therefore receive a certain consequence (Landreth, 2012).

Guidelines for Limit Setting during Play

I recommend the following guidelines articulated by Landreth (2012) for setting limits with children during play sessions. Limits should be:

- Set only when a situation calls for it – and not before. This will allow the child to learn to control his behavior as an opportunity presents itself.
- Stated in calm, matter-of-fact, and firm way.
- Absolute and clearly stated, instead of being tentative, for example instead of saying, "You can tap the door, but not kick it hard," say, "The door is not for kicking."

When stating limits, the therapist should:

- Create a message with a focus and an emphasis on the child, not others.
  - For example, instead of saying, "In here, we do not break toys," say, "Toys are not for breaking."
- Give the responsibility of choosing an alternative behavior and resulting consequences directly to the child.
  - For example, the statement, "If you choose to throw the car again, you will choose not to play with this car today," puts the responsibility squarely on the child's shoulder. If the child chooses to repeat the violation, then the consequence of removing the car should follow immediately.
- Develop an alternative replacement behavior for the child.
  - For example: "I am not for hitting. You can choose to hit the Bobo doll or hit the punching pillow instead."

Play Therapy in Early Childhood Programs and Elementary Schools

Although some school counselors use play therapy as an intervention of choice for preschool, kindergarten, and elementary grade children with challenging behaviors, the use of play therapy is not widespread or common in schools. One reason may be that play therapy requires specific professional training; the other reason may be due to national and local educational policies that continue to downplay the value of play in the education of children.

Play therapy is used effectively in early childhood and elementary education settings with individual children and with small groups of children. In one study, teachers from 10 prekindergarten programs were taught basic child-centered play therapy techniques to use in their classrooms (Lindo et al., 2014). The professional training for the teachers included simple play therapy techniques, such as tracking, reflecting on child's feelings and behaviors, and limit settings. These teachers were able to successfully conduct individual play sessions with children who had challenging behaviors, and in return to reduce challenging behaviors and to build children's social-emotional skills (Lindo et al., 2014).

Early childhood and elementary teachers can also implement group therapy techniques with carefully selected small groups of children in their classrooms. During group playtime, the focus of the trained teacher or therapist is on observing and promoting what are called the *crucial Cs* of children's interactions (Garza et al., 2014). Children's crucial Cs are the ability to *connect*, feel *capable*, to *count*, and to have *courage*. A teacher can achieve this goal by understanding the child's ability to: 1) connect, by observing each child's skills in cooperation; 2) feel capable, by observing each child's initiatives; 3) count, by observing each child's contributions; and 4) have courage, by observing the child's resilience (Garza et al., 2014). In group therapy, the teacher then takes steps to promote the crucial Cs by building relationships, promoting expression of emotions, and setting appropriate limits. Techniques such as tracking, reflecting, and setting specific limits are all directed toward the group instead of the individual child and implemented during the small group interactions and play.

Closing Remarks

In this chapter I described play therapy as one of the most natural and effective ways of working with children. Historically, play and its role both in education and in clinical intervention is downplayed at the policy level and in practice. However, research in this area is providing increasing evidence that play therapy is a viable and effective method of working with children with behavioral and mental health problems. In my opinion, this natural approach should be one of the first methods utilized with children in all school programs, assuming appropriate professional development for the teachers and counselors implementing the approach is provided.

References

Association for Play Therapy. (2014). *Play therapy makes a difference*. Retrieved from: http://www.a4pt.org/?page=PTMakesADifference

Axline, V. M. (1974). *Play therapy*. New York: Ballantine Books.

Bratton, S., Landreth, G., Kellam, T., & Blackard, S. (2006). *Child parent relationship therapy (CPRT) treatment manual* [includes CD-ROM]. New York, NY: Brunner-Routledge.

Bratton, S. C., Ray, D. C., Edwards, N. A., & Landreth, G. (2009). Child-centered play therapy (CCPT): Theory, research, and practice. *Person-Centered and Experiential Psychotherapies, 8*(4), 266–281.

Brehony, K. E. (2004). Theories of play. In P. S. Fass (Ed.). *Encyclopedia of children and childhood: In history and society*. New York and London: Macmillan Reference USA. Retrieved from: http://www.faqs.org/childhood/Th-W/Theories-of-Play.html

Carnes-Holt, K., & Bratton, S. C. (2014). The efficacy of child parent relationship therapy for adopted children with attachment disruptions. *Journal of Counseling and Development, 92*, 328–337.

Crenshaw, D. A., & Kenney-Noziska, S. (2014). Therapeutic presence in play therapy. *International Journal of Play Therapy, 23*(1), 31–43.

Davis, E. S., & Pereira, J. K. (2014). Child-centered play therapy: A creative approach to culturally competent counseling. *Journal of Creativity in Mental Health, 9*, 262–274.

Even, T. A., & Armstrong, S. A. (2011). Sandtray for early recollections with children in Adlerian play therapy. *Journal of Individual Psychology, 67*(4), 391–407.

Freud Museum London. (2014). *Anna Freud: Life and work of Anna Freud.* Retrieved from: http://www.freud.org.uk/education/topic/40053/anna-freud/

Garza, Y., Kinsworthy, S., & Bennett, M. (2014). Supervision in group play therapy: A skills checklist. *The Journal of Individual Psychology, 70*(1), 31–44.

Gianoutsos, J. (2006). Locke and Rousseau: Early childhood education. *The Pulse, 4*(1), 1–23.

Greenspan, S. I., & Wieder, S. (1998). *The child with special needs: Encouraging intellectual and emotional growth.* Reading, MA: Perseus Books.

Guerney, B. (1969). Filial therapy: Description and rationale. *Journal of Consulting Psychology, 28*, 304–310.

Gutek, G. L. (1999). *Friedrich Froebel (1782–1852) – Biography, Froebel's kindergarten philosophy: The kindergarten curriculum, diffusion of the kindergarten.* Retrieved from: http://education.stateuniversity.com/pages/1999/Froebel-Friedrich-1782-1852.html

Homeyer, L., & Sweeney, D. (2010). *Sandtray therapy: A practical manual* (2nd ed.). New York: Routledge.

Kottman, T. (2001). Adlerian play therapy. *International Journal of Play Therapy, 10*(2), 1–12.

Kottman, T. (2003). *Partners in play: An Adlerian approach to play therapy* (2nd ed.). Alexandria, VA: American Counseling Association.

Landreth, G. L. (2002a). *Play therapy: The art of relationship* (2nd ed.). New York: Routledge.

Landreth, G. L. (2002b). Therapeutic limit setting in the play therapy relationship. *Professional Psychology: Research and Practice, 33*(6), 529–535.

Landreth, G. L. (2012). *Play therapy: The art of relationship* (3rd ed.). New York: Routledge.

Linder, T. (2008). *Transdisciplinary play-based assessment: A functional approach to working with young children.* Baltimore, MD: Paul H. Brookes.

Lindo, N. A., Taylor, D. D., Meany-Walen, K. K., Purswell, K., Jayne, K., Gonzales, T., & Jones, L. (2014). Teachers as therapeutic agents: Perceptions of a school-based mental health initiative. *British Journal of Guidance & Counseling, 42*(3), 284–296.

MacLean, G. R. (1986). A brief story about Dr. Hermine Hug-Helmuth. *Canadian Journal of Psychiatry, 31*, 586–589.

McLeod, S. A. (2008). *Little Hans – Freud (1909).* Retrieved from: http://www.simplypsychology.org/little-hans.html

Meany-Walen, K., Bratton, S. C., & Kottman, T. (2014). Effects of Adlerian play therapy on reducing students' disruptive behaviors. *Journal of Counseling and Development, 92*, 47–56.

Melanie Klein Trust. (2014). *Furthering the psychoanalytic theory and technique of Melanie Klein.* Retrieved from: http://www.melanie-klein-trust.org.uk/child-analysis

Midgley, N. (2008). The 'Matchbox School' (1927–1932): Anna Freud and the idea of a 'psychoanalytically informed education.' *Journal of Child Psychotherapy, 34*(1), 23–42.

Midgley, N. (2012). Peter Heller's 'A child analysis with Anna Freud': The significance of the case for the history of child psychoanalysis. *Journal of the American Psychoanalytic Association, 60*(45), 45–69.

Mindes, G., & Jung, L. A. (2015). *Assessing young children* (5th ed.). Upper Saddle River, NJ: Pearson.

Mustakas, C. (1953). *Children in play therapy: A key to understanding normal and disturbed emotions.* New York: McGraw-Hill.

Mustakas, C. E. (1997). *Relationship play therapy.* Northvale, NJ: Jason Aronson.

National Association for the Education of Young Children – NAEYC. (2014). *Play and Children's Learning.* Retrieved from: http://www.naeyc.org/play

Piaget, J. (1999). *Play, dreams and imitation in childhood*. London: Routledge.

Plastow, M. (2011). Hermine Hug-Hellmuth, the first child psychoanalyst: Legacy and dilemmas. *Australian Psychiatry, 19*(3), 206–210.

Ray, D. C., Jayne, K. M., & Stulmaker, H. L. (2014). A way of being in the playroom: Experience-expression congruence model (EECM). *International Journal of Play Therapy, 23*(1), 18–30.

Rogers, C. (1959). A theory of therapy, personality, and interpersonal relationships as developed in the client-centered framework. In S. Koch (Ed.), *Psychology: A study of a science: Vol. III. Formulations of the person and the social context* (pp. 184–256). New York: McGraw-Hill.

Shirk, S. R., Kraver, M. S., & Brown, R. (2011). The alliance in child and adolescent psychotherapy. *Psychotherapy, 48*, 17–24.

Shirk, S. R., & Peterson, E. (2013). Gaps, bridges, and the bumpy road to improving clinic-based therapy for youth. *Clinical Psychology: Science and Practice, 20*, 107–113.

Stone, B. (2000, September). Bop-bags: To use or not to use? *APT Newsletter, 19*, 11–12.

Trotter, D. E., & Landreth, G. (2003). A place for Bobo in play therapy. *International Journal of Play Therapy, 12*(1), 117–139.

Urquiza, A. J., & Timmer, S. (2012). Parent–child interaction therapy: Enhancing parent–child relationships. *Psychosocial Intervention, 21*(2), 145–156.

Widerstrom, A. H. (2005). *Achieving learning goals through play: Teaching young children with special needs* (2nd ed.). Baltimore, MD: Paul H. Brookes.

7

ADDRESSING CHALLENGING BEHAVIORS VIA POSITIVE BEHAVIOR SUPPORT (PBS)

Positive behavior support (PBS), also known as positive behavioral interventions and supports (PBIS), emerged in the late 1980s as a reaction against the use of aversive behavior management (punishment procedures), which existed in applied behavior analysis (ABA) approaches. ABA is a behavioral analytical approach established in the 1960s as a treatment method for children and youths with various forms of neurodevelopmental disorders. A body of research on ABA and its efficacy with children with Autism Spectrum Disorder led to the popularity of ABA use, and establishing it as an effective intervention treatment for childhood (or children with) autism and those with challenging and self-injurious behaviors. However, some of the techniques used in ABA, such as the use of aversives (a term used by behaviorists to describe a punishing stimulus) came under heavy criticism from scholars and educators. Therefore, at the beginning of the 1990s, PBS was proposed as an alternative and effective behavioral approach to challenging behaviors, leading to PBS as the focus of attention in the education of children and those with special needs and challenging behavior.

In this chapter, I will describe the development of PBS through an examination of the history of ABA, since ABA principles form the foundations of a PBS framework. I will then describe central concepts in both approaches and point to the distinguishing features of each.

The Origins of Behavioral Approaches in the Education of Children with Special Needs

Over 100 years' worth of empirical research anchors behaviorism in general, and over 50 years of research on behavioral analytic interventions for children with various forms of special needs exists. Behavioral analysis and intervention methods are solidly rooted in experimental research psychology methods and design.

As we have seen in the previous chapters, in the early 1900s psychoanalytic traditions dominated the field of psychology until Pavlov introduced his idea of classical conditioning. In 1913, John Watson in his classic article, "Psychology as the Behaviorist Views it," asserted that Pavlov's classical conditioning can explain all human behaviors from language to emotional responses. According to Watson, people's behavioral responses were based on their reactions to stimuli they received from their environments. This is known as *stimulus-response* (SR). Watson believed that it was important to study the relationship between the environment and behavior, the same way that one studies biology or physics (Watson, 1913).

In the 1930s, B. F. Skinner proposed what is now known as the "experimental analysis of behavior," (Dixon, Vogel, and Tarbox, 2012). Skinner did not think that the stimulus–response idea explained all behaviors, particularly those behaviors that seemed to have no apparent reasons (Dixon et al., 2012). Skinner noticed that it was not only the stimulus that occurred prior to the behavior (*antecedents*) that determined reoccurrence of a behavior, but what followed or occurred as a result of the behavior (*consequences*). In his opinion, however, consequences not only influenced the behavior, but also had a more dominant role in causing the behavior to reoccur (Skinner, 1938). In this way, Skinner proposed a model of contingency, as *stimulus-response-stimulus*, a version of which we know today as an ABC model – *Antecedent, Behavior,* and *Consequence* (Sturmey & Bernstein, 2004). This method focused on studying behaviors by observing and manipulating variables in the environment that occurred prior to and after the behavior. Skinnerian methods of analyzing behaviors and related variables, however, were only implemented in the laboratory with animals in the early years of Skinner's research.

In the 1950s, methods for analyzing behaviors were applied to human behavior, mainly to adults with neurodevelopmental and mental disorders. The first published clinical analytical behavioral study was by Allyon and Michael (1959), two psychologists who trained a group of nurses in a mental hospital to use behavioral principles with a group of mental patients in order to modify the patients' challenging and self-injurious behaviors. Their simple method of analyzing components influencing patients' behaviors and using simple reinforcement and aversives proved to be successful in reducing self-injurious behaviors in these patients. Because of the success of Allyon and Michael's study (1959), these approaches were tried with other groups of individuals with self-injurious and challenging behaviors.

Even though behavioral principles were considered and applied to the education of typically developing children (for examples see Skinner, 1965, 2001), prior to the work of Allyon and Michael, behaviorists did not consider that children with developmental disabilities were educable. Thus, Allyon and Michael's work sparked research on applications of behavioral methods for the education of children with special needs.

Birth of Applied Behavior Analysis (ABA)

Applied behavior analysis (ABA) derives its components from Skinnerian behavioral principles. Unlike popular belief, ABA is not just a treatment for autism. In fact, ABA is successfully applied to populations of children and adults with different kinds of neurodevelopmental disorders and severity levels. The use of this technique in the treatment of Autism Spectrum Disorder, however, is key in popularizing ABA, and making it considered one of the most effective treatments for children with autism.

It is the work of Baer, Wolf, and Risley (1968) using the base of the Skinnerian approach that coined the term applied behavior analysis and described its basic components. A major difference in ABA as presented by Baer and his colleagues was that ABA was to be applied as a single subject design, one that bases research conclusions on one individual, as opposed to an experimental group design, which utilizes multiple individuals in the research. As described by them (1968), in an ABA it was essential that the components responsible for behavioral change in a single individual be *analyzed*, and exactly or *technologically* described. In this way, it will become obvious what directly contributed to a change in a specific behavior (for example, in reducing the frequency and/or severity of a behavior). This was important to address effectively and *extinguish* or eliminate said behavior (Baer et al., 1968). Baer et al. focused attention on studying ABA as a way of eliminating or moderating self-injurious behavior and other behaviors difficult to tolerate in social settings.

ABA and Treatment of Children with Autism

In the 1960s, Ivar Lovaas pioneered the use of ABA first with children with communication disorders and then with those showing self-injurious behaviors; and later with children with autism. Lovaas's groundbreaking work with children with autism and their families spanned over 50 years, until his death in 2010. Lovaas received his training in learning and clinical psychology from the University of Washington in 1958 (Larsson & Wright, 2011). After receiving his PhD, he joined the faculty of the University of Washington, where he met and was mentored by the major proponent of ABA, Don Baer (Smith & Eikeseth, 2011).

Lovaas joined the faculty of the University of California in Los Angeles in 1961, where he conducted research and worked with children with autism. Lovaas was a firm believer in using *positive reinforcers* with children above all other things (Smith & Eikeseth, 2011). However, during his early studies, he used aversive techniques to eliminate self-injurious behaviors (Bowman & Baker, 2014). These aversive techniques consisted of low doses of electric shock for life-threatening self-injurious behaviors, and slaps on the thigh for less urgent behaviors (Bowman & Baker, 2014; Smith & Eikeseth, 2011). In 1965, a photographic article published in *Life* magazine titled "Screams, Slaps, and Love" showed Lovaas administrating an electric shock to a nine-year-old girl with autism (Grant, 1965). Grant, the author and photographer of that essay, described the ABA method (which was to be known as the Lovaas method at that time) as a combination of punishment along with patience and tenderness: "Even more than punishment, patience and tenderness are lavished on the child. Every hour of lesson time has a 10-minute break for affectionate play" (Grant, 1965, p. 93). The *Life* magazine article, with its shocking photographs, began a controversy about the use of aversive procedures, which I mentioned initiated the birth of the positive behavior support (PBS) movement a decade later.

When conducting a series of studies on interventions for children with autism, Lovaas's ABA method with a strong focus on positive reinforcers became so successful that he abandoned using any form of aversives altogether by the end of the 1980s. The staple ABA approach recommended for use with children with ASD based on Lovaas's method is an individual task-learning format, also known as *discrete trial*. The ABA therapist uses positive reinforcements in reaction to each successful learned response of the child, while ignoring the child's unsuccessful or inappropriate responses. The therapist also provides various levels of physical and verbal *prompts* to scaffold the child's unsuccessful attempts. Lovaas proposed that intervention with children with autism should be started earlier than was then customary – namely to begin as early as toddler or preschool age and in the family's home instead of in hospitals or institutions. The result was his seminal breakthrough study, showing the successful result of his two-year intensive therapy with a group of 19 children with autism (1987).

In his 1987 study, Lovaas and his team of graduate students provided intensive ABA therapy in discrete trial formats to 19 preschool-aged children individually and in their homes for eight hours per day for each child. Lovaas and his team trained the parents of their subjects to carry out ABA techniques through their interactions with their children even after therapy hours had formally ended. In this way, children received ABA around the clock (Lovaas, 1987). The results of this study indicated that 9 out of 19 children had achieved "normal functioning" – had recovered in such a way that they were no longer distinguishable from their typically developing peers (Lovaas, 1987). These children were thereafter integrated fully into regular classrooms, while teachers and administrators of their schools were unaware of, nor ever suspected, their autism diagnoses (Lovaas, 1987). Thus, Lovaas challenged many prevailing ideas of the time that children with autism can only learn little and will always remain socially isolated (Smith & Eikeseth, 2011).

Lovaas strongly believed that children with autism should have at least 40 hours of therapy during the week if they were to have the same learning opportunities that were available to typically developing children who learn all day, every day (Smith & Eikeseth, 2011). In the decades that followed, Lovaas received federal grants and successfully replicated his study in other centers and locations (Larsson & Wright, 2011). In 1994, he established the Lovaas Institute for Early Intervention and continued to publish papers until his retirement in his late seventies. Lovaas's ABA and subsequent published studies on ABA established this method as evidence-based and one of the most effective treatment and educational models for children with autism.

The Advent of Positive Behavior Support (PBS)

In the mid-1980s, concerns were raised about the use of aversive procedures (for examples see Lavigna & Donnellan, 1986; Meyer & Evans, 1989) with children or youth with neurodevelopmental disorders in order to reduce their self-injurious and aggressive behaviors. Horner and his colleagues coined the term *positive behavior support* in 1990 as an alternative behavioral intervention approach which did not use punishment procedures. The framework had its roots in ABA, but differed in some features. For example, Horner et al. (1990) believed that to address challenging behaviors in children, the appropriate approach should emphasize child-centered planning, meaningful outcomes, and respect for the child's dignity and life within the child's culture and community.

Although Horner et al. (1990) did not detail a specific positive behavioral support framework at that time, they emphasized several distinguishing components that should be central to any PBS approach. These components, which differed from an ABA approach, included taking into account influences of the behavioral and developmental context and other people in the child's environment. Horner et al. (1990) also recommended teaching specific appropriate behaviors, *replacement behaviors*, in place of inappropriate ones – instead of simply extinguishing the inappropriate behavior. In this way, the child's development will not only be supported, but it will be relevant to the child's and family's needs and community/cultural context. They articulated the following features as necessary components for any positive behavioral support approach (Horner et al., 1990):

- Understanding an emphasis on lifestyle changes of the child across time.
- Using a functional behavior analysis.
- Manipulating environmental setting events.
- Manipulating antecedents.
- Teaching adaptive behaviors.
- Building effective environments and consequences.
- Minimizing use of punishers.
- Distinguishing emergency procedures from proactive programming.
- Using social validity standards with a priority for the role of human dignity.
- Prohibiting or restricting use of specific classes of behavioral intervention (e.g. procedures that involve pain or harm).

Since the original proposal by Horner and his colleagues, several definitions of positive behavior support have emerged (for examples see Dunlap, Carr, Horner,

Zarcone, & Schwartz, 2008; Sugai & Simonson, 2012; Wacker & Berg, 2002). Thus, various applications of PBS emerged throughout the 1990s in schools at programmatic and classroom levels, as well as with individual children in classrooms. Added emphasis on the evolution for using these tools came with the reauthorization of the Individuals with Disabilities Education Act, which mandated the creation of a behavioral intervention plan (BIP) as a part of the Individualized Education Plan (IEP) for any child showing a challenging behavior (IDEA, 1997). The Act legislated a federal grant to create a national Center on Positive Behavioral Interventions and Supports (www.pbis.org), which was established through a consortium of several universities.

This center is currently in Year 16 and provides direct professional development and technical assistance to establish School-Wide Positive Behavior Interventions and Supports (SWPBIS) systems. At the first international conference on positive behavior support held in Orlando, Florida in 2003 the Association for Positive Behavior Support (APBS) was founded (http://www.apbs.org). PBS is currently a highly visible approach in education, with widespread applications in many public and private schools across the nation.

Given the variability of definitions of positive behavior support, I offer an interpretation of PBS that includes elements of most of the existing definitions: A positive behavior support (PBS) framework is not a single intervention. Rather, PBS is a multilevel behavioral approach that uses positive behavioral technologies, which respect the dignity of the child and aim to improve the quality of life for the child and family within their community and culture. A PBS framework is a tiered system based on behavioral analytic principles to address challenging behaviors of children at three distinct levels:

1. School-Wide: At this level, PBS creates a positive and safe school environment by preventing challenging behaviors from occurring. The preventive school-wide PBS includes a behavioral support system that includes behavioral guidelines for students as well as clear, consistent, and unified consequences implemented by well-trained school professionals and support staff. The approach relies on positive reinforcement of appropriate behaviors, teaching replacement behaviors, and consistent consequences for inappropriate and challenging behaviors.
2. Classroom: At this level, PBS creates a positive classroom environment and implements a behavioral support system. The classroom PBS includes effective social-emotional individualized and group instruction, supportive classroom structures and consistent routines, and clear, specific, and consistent behavioral guidelines with articulated consequences for deviation from the rules. Similar to the school-wide approach, the classroom PBS relies on positive reinforcement of appropriate behaviors and teaching replacement behaviors.
3. Individual: At this level, PBS requires conducting a functional behavioral assessment of the child who exhibits challenging behaviors and designing and

implementing a behavioral intervention plan (BIP) to address the child's challenging behaviors effectively.

After the reauthorization of IDEA in 1997, *Functional Behavior Assessment* was proposed as a part of a PBS approach in order to develop a behavioral intervention plan (BIP) for a child who exhibits challenging behaviors. A functional behavior assessment consists of a variety of assessment protocols to obtain information related to a child's behaviors and development in order to design an effective behavioral intervention plan for that child. An assessment protocol can include interviews (of the family members and teachers), questionnaires, and behavior rating scales. A functional assessment may or may not include conducing a functional behavior analysis (FBA), which I will describe later. An FBA is considered the gold standard for a function-based behavioral intervention for a child with challenging behaviors (Dunlap & Fox, 2011). For the sake of clarity, when I use the acronym FBA, I refer to a functional behavior analysis. When I describe the entire assessment process and procedures within a positive behavior support framework, I will use the term functional behavior assessment.

Function-Based Interventions

To begin to understand the elements of function-based intervention, let's review the components. A *behavior* is commonly described as what a person does. A behaviorist believes that all behaviors whether adaptive or not adaptive are learned. Description of a behavior, or what a behavior is, is called the *topography* of a behavior. For example, when a child bites her own hands, or hits her head on the wall, the child's behavior topography is described as self-injurious. Furthermore, every behavior occurs for a reason. In particular, any behavior that is repeated usually has one or more purposes, called the *function* of that behavior. Thus, a function of a behavior describes *why* a behavior occurs as opposed to its topography, or *what* the behavior is. In other words, the function of a behavior is the motivation for a behavior in order to obtain one or more specific consequences.

Conceptualization of this view of the function of a behavior took place in the late 1970s. Up to that time, a challenging behavior, regardless of its causes, was understood simply as an unwanted learned behavior that needed to be extinguished (Dunlap & Fox, 2011). However, the natural implication of investigating and understanding the function(s) of a behavior is that solutions will address the purpose of the behavior and therefore be more effective than simply getting rid of the behavior without addressing its causes or function of it for the individual. This approach is known as a *function-based* intervention. Conducting an FBA is the way one or more functions can be identified. The implication is that an appropriate (replacement) behavior will serve the same function as the original maladaptive behaviors. Therefore, an FBA is necessary to inform the design of an intervention plan, as well as to address the necessary teaching skills to replace the behavioral function (Dunlap & Fox, 2011).

The Origins of Functional Behavior Analysis (FBA)

A *functional behavior analysis (FBA)*, also known as a *functional analysis*, is a data-driven behavioral method of isolating different variables related to a behavior so as to understand its function(s) for the purpose of designing a behavior intervention plan. The first published study on functional behavior analysis is attributed to Lovaas, who used a rough form of FBA in a study of a child with self-injurious behaviors (Dixon et al., 2012; Larsson & Wright, 2011). In this study, Lovaas and his colleagues systematically described and outlined how antecedents and consequences maintained a series of self-injurious behaviors in that child (Lovaas, Freitag, Gold, and Kassorla, 1965). Accordingly, by manipulating consequences related to the child's behavior, they were able to successfully decrease self-injury.

In 1977, Edward Carr formally conceptualized the function-based approaches to analyzing challenging behavior. Carr (1977) explained that all challenging behaviors are functional in that they are related to a set of predictable consequences (e.g. to either gain attention or avoid demanding tasks). He proposed that the interventionist should first form a hypothesis about the function of a challenging behavior based on the data on the behavior variables, and then should accordingly devise an appropriate intervention plan with articulated strategies. He described three categories of consequences that might logically lead to most forms of challenging behaviors: 1) *positive reinforcement*; 2) *negative reinforcement*; and 3) *sensory or automatic reinforcement* (Carr, 1977). Accordingly, by understanding these consequences, the interventionist can design a more precise and effective plan of intervention.

In the 1980s, Iwata and his colleagues designed the first comprehensive experimental FBA and evaluated Carr's hypothesized categories. In their seminal study, which was republished and became popular in 1994, Iwata and his colleagues tested Carr's hypothesized categories (of positive, negative, and automatic reinforcements) under four different experimental conditions. They confirmed that these categories indeed represented all possible functions for different challenging behaviors in the subjects they had studied (Iwata, Dorsey, Slifer, Bauman, & Richman, 1994). Gradually, a format called the ABC (Antecedent, Behavior, Consequence) model for conducting an FBA emerged. This model is used in most ABA and PBS approaches today (Dixon et al., 2012; Dunlap & Fox, 2011; Hagopian, Rooker, Jessel, & Deleon, 2013; Schlinger & Normand, 2013).

The ABC Observation Model and Data Collection

As a reminder, in FBA the three variables that are related to behaviors are Antecedents (A), Behavior (B), and Consequences (C). The variables are the same in the ABC model, which is shown in Figure 7.1.

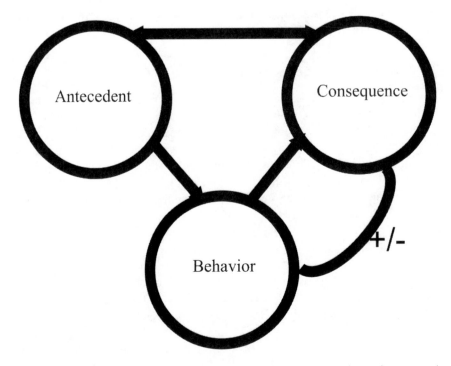

FIGURE 7.1   The ABC Behavior Model: Antecedents Trigger the Behavior, and Consequences Maintain and Reinforce the Behavior

Figure 7.1 shows that antecedents and consequences are both factors that contribute to the occurrence of a behavior. Antecedents trigger a behavior; and consequences maintain, strengthen, or decrease a behavior. Antecedents and consequences also influence each other. Let us consider an example to show how to apply the ABC model:

Emily, a preschooler, has frequent temper tantrums in her classroom, which are difficult to soothe. Her temper tantrums seem to occur at different times of day, and appear to be related to different events, such as disliking an activity. However, her tantrums do occur more regularly in the mornings during the arrival times. It seems to Ms. Smith and Ms. Brown, the classroom teacher and teacher's assistant, that Emily's temper tantrums are a habit and a pattern that is now difficult to break. It sometimes takes Ms. Brown 20 minutes to calm Emily down and help her join her peers in the classroom. Ms. Smith, however, is able to soothe Emily immediately every time that she attempts to soothe her. Recently, Emily has become defiant, and has begun refusing to participate in certain activities; the refusal is often followed by an outburst of temper tantrums.

Antecedents

Antecedents are events, conditions, and situations that take place prior to the occurrence of a behavior. Antecedents usually trigger the occurrence of a behavior. In the example above, Emily's temper tantrums sometimes happen in the mornings during the arrival times, while other times they occur during transitions from one activity to the next. Antecedents are sometimes things that others do or say. For example, Ms. Smith's announcing that it is time for small group activities is sometimes the antecedent that triggers Emily's behavior.

Antecedents are not always immediately noticeable. For example, ecological conditions, such as temperature, noise level, and other sensory stimuli in the environment, can trigger challenging behaviors in children who have sensory issues. Other antecedents can include physiological conditions, like hunger, pain, lack of sleep, tone of adults' voices or types of demands, etc. Antecedents can trigger challenging behaviors immediately, or they can be temporally and geographically removed and therefore trigger behaviors over time. Therefore, the discovery of the antecedent or function of the behavior takes careful observation and record keeping so that patterns may be distinguished and addressed effectively. Once the antecedents are identified, the PBS can begin and the antecedents can be manipulated.

The process of identifying and manipulating the events in PBS is the concept of *setting events*, used to describe temporally removed antecedents that might have triggered a behavior slowly and over time. Examples of setting events are home and family situations, anxiety-producing events, community and neighborhood conditions, cultural issues, etc. Setting events can add to the immediate triggering effects of an antecedent, as well as to the frequency or severity of a behavior. Setting events and antecedents are closely related to each other, and often work hand in hand in causing or triggering challenging behaviors. In a positive behavior support framework, understanding antecedents and setting events is a crucial part of assessment and intervention.

Looking at the example above, a setting event contributing to Emily's current behavior is a situation that Emily's family is dealing with at home. Emily's mother has recently been diagnosed with a serious illness, which requires Emily's parents' frequent visits to a hospital and doctor's offices. Emily's parents are dealing with the stressors of this new situation in addition to the typical day-to-day stressors that all families face. Furthermore, Emily's parents have not been able to spend the usual amount of time they would otherwise spend with Emily, relying on their extended family to care for Emily while they are in the hospital. Another important piece of information about the setting events surrounding Emily's behavior is that Ms. Brown, the preschool assistant, has only recently joined the teaching team of Emily's preschool. When we consider this information, we see that many changes have occurred in Emily's home and classroom environments and are likely to produce anxiety for Emily and to contribute to the frequency and severity of her challenging behaviors. A plan must then be made for Emily to adjust the setting events and to address the antecedents and providing appropriate and positive consequences for positive behaviors to decrease her challenging behavior.

Consequences

Consequences are events that occur after and often as a result of a behavior. Consequences usually (but not always) consist of reactions of others (e.g. what others do or say). Consequences are not always straightforward. That is, the consequence must be meaningful to the individual with the challenging behavior. Discovering the meaning to the individual may take several attempts to find the right consequence to change the challenging behavior.

So, according to behavioral principles, if a consequence of a behavior is positive from the perspective of the child, the behavior is reinforced, or likely to occur again under the same antecedent conditions. However, if a consequence of a behavior is not desirable from the perspective of the child, the behavior is *extinguished*. Extinction is a term that behaviorists use to explain when a behavior is gradually eliminated, due to the negative effects of a given consequence. A consequence that causes this negative effect is called an *aversive* or a *punisher*.

In an FBA, it is important to have enough ABC data to determine the recurring antecedents and consequences. This is necessary so that a hypothesis can be made about the child's function for the behavior. ABC data is usually collected in a table format, where the *A*ntecedent, *B*ehavior, and *C*onsequences of the child's challenging behaviors are clearly described for further study and analysis. An illustration of ABC data regarding Emily's behavior is presented in Table 7.1.

Looking at Table 7.1, it can be hypothesized that the function of Emily's temper tantrums and defiance is to receive attention from her teachers. Using the setting event information regarding Emily's family situation and classroom environment, it can further be concluded that Emily's behavior is exacerbated by uncertainty and by changes in her caregiving environments. An effective intervention plan for Emily may include changing antecedents (in this case, providing a safe environment for Emily through altering the teachers' responses and giving positive attention to Emily throughout the day; changing the classroom routine to include individual play and small group lessons with Emily), as well as changing the consequences (giving Emily a lot of attention and encouragement for appropriate behaviors only). In this way, the teachers are reinforcing behaviors that they wish to support so Emily's challenging behaviors will diminish.

Table 7.1 ABC Data Table for Emily

Date/Time	Antecedent	Behavior	Consequence	Notes
Monday, 11/12/13 8:45 am	Emily's grandmother says goodbye and leaves. Ms. Brown greets Emily and tells her to go to find her name card on the sign-in table.	Emily begins crying, saying, "I don't want to go to the table."	Ms. Smith is busy greeting a child. She turns around and says, "Emily, you need to go to the sign-in table."	Students are arriving. Teachers greet children and direct each child to go to a "sign in" table to either find their name cards on the table, or print their names on a card.
8:45 am	Ms. Smith says, "Emily, you need to go to the sign-in table."	Emily continues to cry louder, and refuses to go to the table.	Ms. Brown goes to Emily: "When you calm down, you can go to the sign-in table."	
10:30 am	Ms. Smith announces, "It is circle time."	Emily jumps up and down, screaming, "I want to read! I want to read!"	Ms. Smith tells Emily to stop screaming and join the group.	
10:40 am	Teachers are busy with getting everyone to circle time.	Emily continues to refuse to come to the circle time: "No. No."	Ms. Brown takes Emily by the hand: "It is time to join the group."	
	Ms. Brown takes Emily by the hand: "It is time to join the group."	Emily begins crying and pulls on Ms. Brown's hand: "I don't want to come to the circle."	Ms. Smith says, "Emily, if you do not stop crying, you will have to go to timeout."	
10:45 am	Children and teachers are engaged in the circle time.	Emily continues to cry in the "timeout chair."	None.	

Reinforcements

The reinforcements that FBA researchers identify and describe are the three functions to a child's challenging behavior: positive reinforcements, negative reinforcements, and automatic reinforcements. Reinforcements are conditions that follow a behavior and are likely to strengthen or increase the reoccurrence of that behavior. A *reinforcer* is a reinforcing object, action, event, or stimuli. In nontechnical literature, reinforcers are commonly referred to as *rewards*. With rare exceptions, reinforcers are almost always valued and highly preferred from the perspective of the recipient.

Not all seemingly rewarding events and objects are equally reinforcing to all children. That is, while something might be reinforcing to one child's behavior, it may not be the same for another child. For example, Joshua, a second grader, receives a good grade on a completed homework assignment. Joshua is gratified and proud of his good grade. He is, therefore, likely to complete a future homework assignment in order to receive another good grade. In this case, getting a good grade is a reinforcer to Joshua. This may not be the case for another child who does not value good grades or who cannot achieve at a "high" level.

Types of Reinforcements

Reinforcements can be conditions or objects that are gained, or they can be conditions or objects that are avoided. When reinforcements are gained, they are called *positive reinforcements*. When situations or actions are avoided (for example, avoiding demanding tasks), they are called *negative reinforcements*.

Positive Reinforcement

If the function of a child's challenging behavior is positive reinforcement, it means that the child resorts to this behavior because he seeks to receive or gain something. In the examples of Emily and Joshua, the functions of their behaviors are to gain the teacher's attention for Emily, and to receive good grades for Joshua. Thus, the teacher's attention and good grades are positive reinforcers for these children.

There are three general types of positive reinforcers: 1) *social reinforcers*; 2) *tangible reinforcers*; and 3) *learned reinforcers*. Social reinforcers are socially and culturally valued conditions that are mediated by other people, such as parents, teachers, peers, etc. Examples of social reinforcers are praise, approval, and attention. Tangible reinforcers are objects and object-related events that the child likes and highly prefers, such as food, toys, and objects, and object-related activities, like reading books or playing with computer games. Learned reinforcers are objects that on their own do not have a value, but the child learns to associate a particular value to them, or the objects may be exchanged for a reinforcing object. Examples of learned reinforcers are tokens, coins, or stars that teachers and parents sometimes use as a part of a reward system. For example, tokens may be collected and exchanged for a reinforcing prize or privilege.

Negative Reinforcement

The concept of negative reinforcement may be confusing, because of the word "negative." Many mistakenly believe that a negative reinforcement is a punishment. However, this is not the case. On the contrary, a negative reinforcement is actually a positive consequence, or reward. The word negative is used to apply to events or stimuli that one prefers to avoid. In other words, a negative reinforcement relieves or rewards the person from a condition that the person prefers to avoid. To clarify this concept, let us consider an example:

Sophia is a two-and-a-half-year-old child who has an auditory sensitivity. Sophia usually cries and covers her ears when there are loud noises in the environment. Sophia screams when she is taken to a crowded and noisy place. When Sophia indicates discomfort by such behaviors, her parents respond by taking her to a quiet and secluded place, where Sophia usually begins to calm down quickly. In this case, being taken away from the crowded and noisy place serves as a negative reinforcement for Sophia, in that it takes away sensory stimuli that are painful to her.

Negative reinforcement may be thought of as an *escape* from an unwanted or disliked condition. The effects of a negative reinforcement are identical to those of a positive reinforcement, in that both are reinforcements that strengthen a behavior.

Automatic or Sensory Reinforcement

Automatic or sensory reinforcement is inherent in the behavior itself. For example, the act of smelling a rose on its own is pleasing (at least to most people). A person is likely to repeat the behavior of smelling a rose, because that behavior has an inherent or automatic reinforcement in it. Some behaviors that children exhibit may have an automatic reinforcement function. A common example is stereotyped behaviors in some children with certain neurodevelopmental disorders, like ASD. These behaviors are repetitive behaviors such as hand flapping or body rocking. Many stereotypical behaviors as such have automatic reinforcement functions for children who exhibit them, in that the act itself provides an automatic sensory input, which comforts the child.

In an individual behavior intervention plan, positive, negative, and sensory reinforcements are used to change an inappropriate behavior and teach a replacement behavior. The three types of reinforcements are also used in ABA and other behavioral approaches to teach cognitive and adaptive skills to children with disabilities. One more approach that is used in some situations is the application of aversive consequences to the appearance of a challenging behavior.

Using Aversives

The concept of *aversive* is synonymous with punishment, which is the opposite of the concept of reinforcement. Behaviorists prefer to use the term aversive to describe any negative consequence following a behavior that weakens the likelihood of the behavior occurring again – decreasing the behavior or extinguishing the behavior. According to this perspective, an aversive is only definable based on the effects it has on a behavior (Alberto & Troutman, 2013). Similar to the concept of reinforcement, what is considered an aversive or a *punisher* to one person may not be the same to another. There are two basic kinds of aversives in ABA approaches: removing reinforcements and presenting aversives.

Removing Reinforcements

The most common form of this type of aversive is the loss of a preferred object, event, stimuli, or privilege that is usually reinforcing. To use an example, consider Rachel, a seven-year-old, who gets into fights with her three-year-old sister and hits her. Rachel's mother disciplines Rachel by taking away her favorite Nintendo-Wii™ game for one day. If Rachel stops hitting her sister from that point forward, then the loss of her favorite game is clearly a punishment (aversive) for her. Use of timeouts is another form of an aversive, which relies on excluding the person from peers, and thus removing the reinforcement of being with peers and socializing.

Presenting Aversive Stimuli

Another and perhaps a more severe form of punishment is presentation of an aversive stimulus. Aversives usually cause some kind of physical or emotional pain. Inducing physical pain (such as corporal punishment) or emotional pain are two common forms of aversives. In traditional ABA approaches, aversives such as electric shocks were used to reduce aggressive and self-injurious behaviors in children and youth with neurodevelopmental disorders, but as discussed earlier, the use of electric shock is questioned and has fallen out of favor since the 1980s. However there are still some proponents who continue to argue that using aversives, such as inducing electric shocks,[1] are highly effective in reducing dangerous and aggressive behaviors. It is important to note here that behavioral research on this topic is primarily related to children and adolescents with severe developmental disorders, more particularly those with self-injurious and aggressive behaviors. For examples of studies on electroconvulsive therapy see Consoli et al., 2013; and Salvy, Mulick, Butter, Bartlett & Linscheild, 2004; Wachtel et al., 2009.

The use of aversives, particularly using corporal punishment, timeouts, and physical restraints, as discipline strategies in schools is a topic of attention and controversy for the past several years. The issue of current school discipline strategies will be further discussed in the next chapter, but for now I conclude with a final overview of FBA in a PBS system.

Interventions in a Positive Behavior Support Framework

Once a comprehensive functional behavior assessment is conducted, a PBS framework recommends manipulating the variables through four possible types of interventions for addressing challenging behaviors:

1. Altering the antecedents and setting events that contribute to challenging behaviors. Strategies may include: change of classroom schedule; structure and routines; reducing environmental sensory stimuli; changing instructional techniques; altering teachers' responses; expanding choices; planning for transitions; and manipulating other setting events and antecedents through working with the family or other school professionals.
2. Teaching replacement and appropriate behaviors. Appropriate behaviors, that serve the same function as challenging behaviors, might include teaching functional communication, appropriate expression of feelings, appropriate social skills, self-regulation, anger management, friendship skills, etc.
3. Reinforcing appropriate behaviors regularly and consistently. These include use of positive social reinforcers tangible or negative reinforcers to encourage appropriate behaviors.
4. Preventing challenging behaviors from occurring by articulation of rules and clear guidelines with consistent reinforcers. Consequences to challenging behaviors should optimize the safety of all children while supporting learning and respecting the dignity of the child.

Closing Remarks

Despite the promise of positive behavior support (PBS), and research supporting its efficacy, implementing PBS at any of its three levels faces several challenges. The most cited issue affecting implementation of PBS is the absence of appropriate professional development (McLean & Grey, 2012). Successful implementation of a PBS depends on correct understanding of the underlying behavioral principles, refined positive behavioral teaching skills, and a belief in the child's dignity. It is important that teachers and other school professionals have access to professional development in various aspects of functional behavior assessment. Professional development activity includes focus on developing observational procedures for behavioral analysis; understanding behavioral data collection and the analysis of behavior; procedures for interpretation of data;

skill development in forming a behavioral hypothesis; and the design and implementation of a BIP successfully.

Note

1. Judge Rotenberg Center in Massachusetts is a private school and residential facility for children and youth with developmental and behavioral disorders. The center is currently the only facility in the USA that uses electric shocks as a form of discipline strategy. Despite several lawsuits and an outcry from educators and human and disability right activists, the school continues to use a device called a Graduated Electronic Decelerator (GED) to induce electric shock on the skin of children and adolescents who display aggressive behaviors. Children whose parents have given consent wear a backpack carrying the device, which is connected to the different areas of the child's body via wired electrodes. The device is controlled remotely by staff, which monitors the child's behavior through surveillance cameras or direct observation. The child receives an electric shock as a consequence for breaking specific behavioral rules or resorting to aggressive behaviors (for details see Gonnerman, 2007; and CBS news, August 5, 2014, http://www.cbsnews.com/news/controversy-over-shocking-people-with-autism-behavioral-disorders/).

References

Alberto, P. A., & Troutman, A. C. (2013). *Applied behavior analysis for teachers* (9th edition). Upper Saddle River, NJ: Pearson.

Allyon, T., & Michael, J. (1959). The psychiatric nurse as a behavioral engineer. *Journal of the Experimental Analysis of Behavior, 2,* 323–334.

Baer, D. M., Wolf, M. M., & Risely, T. R. (1968). Some still-current dimensions of applied behavior analysis. *Journal of Applied Behavior Analysis, 1,* 91–97.

Bowman, R. A., & Baker, J. P. (2014). Screams, slaps, and love: The strange birth of Applied Behavior Analysis. *Pediatrics, 133*(3), 364–366.

Carr, E. G. (1977). The motivation of self-injurious behavior: A review of some hypotheses. *Psychological Bulletin, 84,* 800–816.

Consoli, A., Cohen, J., Bodeau, N., Guinchat, V., Wachtel, L., & Cohen, D. (2013). Electroconvulsive therapy in adolescents with intellectual disability and severe self-injurious behavior and aggression: A retrospective study. *European Child & Adolescent Psychiatry, 22*(1), 55–62.

Dixon, R., Vogel, T., & Tarbox, J. (2012). A brief history of functional analysis and Applied Behavior Analysis. In J. L. Matson (Ed.), *Functional Assessment for Challenging Behaviors-IV* (pp. 3–24). New York, Dordrecht, Heidelberg, London: Springer.

Dunlap, G., Carr, E. G., Horner, R. H., Zarcone, J. R., & Schwarz, I. (2008). Positive behavior support and applied behavior analysis: A familial alliance. *Behavior Modification, 32,* 325–328.

Dunlap, G., & Fox, L. (2011). Function-based interventions for children with challenging behavior. *Journal of Early Intervention, 33*(4), 333–343.

Gonnerman, J. (Sep/Oct 2007). School of shock. *Mother Jones, 32*(5), 36–90.

Grant, A. (1965, May 7). Screams, slaps, and love. *Life,* p. 87–97.

Hagopian, L. P., Rooker, G. W., Jessel, J., & Deleon, I. G. (2013). Initial functional analysis outcomes and modifications in pursuit of differentiation: A summary of 176 inpatient cases. *Journal of Applied Behavior Analysis, 46*(1), 88–100.

Horner, R. H., Dunlap, G., Koegel, R. L., Carr, E., Sailor, W., Anderson, J., ... & O'Neill, R. E. (1990). Toward a technology of "nonaversive" behavioral support. *Journal of Association for Persons with Severe Handicaps, 15*(3), 125–132.

Individuals with Disabilities Education Act Amendments of 1997 (IDEA '97). (1997). Retrieved from: http://www2.ed.gov/offices/OSERS/Policy/IDEA/index.html

Iwata, B. A., Dorsey, M. F., Slifer, K. J., Bauman, K., & Richman, G. (1994). Toward a functional analysis of self-injury. *Journal of Applied Behavior Analysis, 27*, 197–209.

Larsson, E. V., & Wright, S. (2011). In memoriam: Dr. O. Ivar Lovaas (1927–2010). *The Behavior Analyst, 34*, 111–114.

Lavigna, G. W., & Donnellan, A. M. (1986). *Alternatives to punishment: Solving behavior problems with non-aversive strategies.* New York: Irvington.

Lovaas, O. I. (1987). Behavioral treatment and normal educational and intellectual functioning in young autistic children. *Journal of Consulting and Clinical Psychology, 55*, 3–9.

Lovaas, O. I., Freitag, G., Gold, V. J., & Kassorla, I. C. (1965). Experimental studies in childhood schizophrenia: Analysis of self-destructive behavior. *Journal of Experimental Child Psychology, 2*, 143–157.

McLean, B., & Grey, I. (2012). A component analysis of positive behavior support plans. *Journal of Intellectual and Developmental Disability, 37*(3), 221–231.

Meyer, L. H., & Evans, I. M. (1989). *Nonaversive interventions for problem behaviors: A manual for home and community.* Baltimore: Paul H. Brookes.

Salvy, S., Mulick, J. A., Butter, E., Bartlett, R. K., & Linscheid, T. R. (2004). Contingent electric shock (SIBIS) and a conditioned punisher eliminate severe head banging in a preschool child. *Behavioral Intervention, 19*, 59–72.

Schlinger Jr., H. D., & Normand, M. P. (2013). On the origin and functions of the term functional analysis. *Journal of Applied Behavior Analysis, 46*, 285–288.

Skinner, B. F. (1938). *The behavior of organisms: An experimental analysis.* New York: Appleton-Century-Crofts Inc.

Skinner, B. F. (1965). Review lecture: The technology of teaching. *Proceedings of the Royal Society of London: Series B, Biological Science, 162*(989), 427–443.

Skinner, B. F. (2001). Contingency management in the classroom. *Education, 90*(2), 93–100.

Smith, T., & Eikeseth, S. (2011). O. Ivar Lovaas: Pioneer of applied behavior analysis and intervention for children with autism. *Journal of Autism and Developmental Disorders, 41*, 375–378.

Sturmey, P., & Bernstein, H. (2004). Functional analysis of maladaptive behaviors: Current status and future directions. In J. L. Matson, R. B. Laud, & M. L. Matson (Eds.), *Behavior modification for persons with developmental disabilities: Treatments and support* (Vol. I, pp. 1–32). Kingston: NADD Press.

Sugai, G., & Simonsen, B. (2012). *Positive behavioral interventions and supports: History, defining features, and misconceptions.* Retrieved from: https://fcps.edu/dss/ips/srr/committee/resources/sections/documents/research/PBIS.pdf

Wachtel, L., Contrucci-Kuhn, S., Griffin, M., Thompson, A., Dhossche, D., & Reti, I. (2009). ECT for self-injury in an autistic boy. *European Journal of Child and Adolescent Psychiatry, 18*, 458–463.

Wacker, D. P., & Berg, W. K. (2002). PBS as a service delivery system. *Journal of Positive Behavior Interventions, 4*, 25–28.

Watson, J. B. (1913). Psychology as the behaviorist views it. *Psychology in the Schools, 42*, 737–744.

8

CURRENT DISCIPLINE PRACTICES IN EARLY CHILDHOOD PROGRAMS AND SCHOOLS

Issues, Problems, and Alternatives

A recent U.S. Department of Education Report on *Guiding principles: A resource guide for improving school climate and discipline* (2014) shows that, annually, a significant number of students are disciplined, i.e. expelled or suspended, in schools for small infractions of school or classroom rules. African-American children and children with disabilities are three times more likely to be the subject of school and classroom discipline as compared to other children (U.S. Department of Education, 2014). According to the same report, in one state,[1] about 95 percent of out-of-school suspensions were for very minor disruptions, such as speaking out of turn, in the classroom.

Although not all schools employ discipline strategies that are problematic, some strategies are so excessive that they often produce the opposite of the intended effect; the strategies create unsafe and anxiety-producing environments for children and inadvertently promote negative and ineffective approaches as models to problem solving. For this reason, the topic of discipline in schools is controversial for both families and educators. Suffice it to say there is an array of classroom and school-wide discipline strategies that schools use, and states differ in approved levels and forms of disciplinary procedures. For example, while one state's highest level of school discipline might be expulsion, another state might allow the use of corporal punishment by teachers and school personnel, as well as expulsion.

In this chapter, I will discuss common strategies (from preschool through early elementary grades) that are used at the center, school, and/or classroom level to address challenging behaviors of children. I will explain why some of these strategies are at best ineffective and at worst unethical and abusive. I will present research relating to these strategies and suggest positive alternative approaches to be used.

Common Discipline Procedures in Public Schools Today

Public schools are required to ensure that learning environments are safe, secure, and orderly, so that teachers can teach and children can learn effectively. In order to do so, within a state, each school district devises policies and procedures regarding intervention and disciplines for their students' conduct. These policies are called the *discipline code*. Public schools mirror the community in which they are established, and as such the makeup of their student body, and the disciplinary codes they create are similar to those in their communities (Council on School Health, 2013). Although the Department of Education annually releases a report about school discipline codes and makes recommendations, states have the authority to set the parameters for the disciplinary procedures to be used in their schools.

Most states leave the decision about discipline codes to individual schools or school districts. This practice creates variability in discipline codes and approaches from one school district to the next within the same state. In the following sections, I will focus on four types of classroom and school-wide discipline methods used in the USA. The methods are verbal reprimand, timeout, suspension and expulsion, and corporal punishment. I will discuss issues and possible problems with each of these approaches.

Verbal Reprimands

Verbal reprimands are one of the most common forms of discipline used in the classroom or the principal's office (Alberto & Troutman, 2013). Examples of verbal reprimands range from saying "no" and "don't" to scolding and sometimes even humiliating the child in front of peers and other adults. Verbal reprimands seem to be effective in the short run. However, they are completely ineffectual in the long run, particularly when used repeatedly. In fact, research shows that in many cases, saying "no" or "don't" results in escalating oppositional behaviors in children (Gong et al., 2014; Mace, Pratt, Prager, & Pritchard, 2011).

Problems with Verbal Reprimand

In reality, verbal reprimands sometimes provide good negative reinforcement; the teacher may put an end to a disruptive incident for a short time, giving the teacher an escape from the child's behavior for the time being, while creating an illusion that the reprimand is effective (Alberto & Troutman, 2013). In such a scenario, a verbal reprimand only teaches the adult to use it again and often, but does not necessarily teach the child to stop that behavior. Unfortunately, teachers are apt to use verbal reprimands for children with challenging behaviors so often that these children are at the receiving end of reprimands, even when the behavior does not warrant discipline. In some cases, particularly for children who are labeled as the "problem child," verbal reprimands seem to dominate the adults communication patterns with the child.

Suspension and Expulsion

In-school and *out-of-school suspensions* are two forms of suspension schools use to address inappropriate behaviors of children. The in-school suspension requires a child to spend a specific period of time outside the classroom under the supervision of school staff. In an out-of-school suspension, the child is denied access to the school for a specific period of time, varying according to the perceived threat that the behavior warrants. Expulsion denies the child access to school or childcare center permanently. The rationale for out-of-school suspension and expulsion is that not only the offending act is punished; but also by limiting the influence of the child's behavioral act on others, the school ensures that an acceptable standard of behavior is maintained (Council on School Health, 2013).

The practice of suspension and expulsion became popular with the "zero tolerance" disciplinary policies that were adopted by school districts after the enactment of the Gun-Free Schools Act of 1994. The Gun-Free Schools Act of 1994 (PL 103-882) was enacted as a part of the reauthorization of the Elementary and Secondary Education Act of 1965 (ESEA), in order to address the growing trend of violence involving students. This Act required that each state receiving federal funds under ESEA must have a state law requiring educational agencies to expel (for a period of no less than one year) any student who brought a weapon to school (Gun-Free Schools Act, 1994). Though this legislation was designed particularly to address the issue of weapons, its application in schools soon turned into zero tolerance disciplinary policies. A zero tolerance policy mandates specific and predetermined punishments or consequences for specific school offences (U.S. Department of Education, National Center for Education Statistics, 1998).

In reality the zero tolerance policy used by many school districts in the country leads to suspension and expulsion of a great number of children for minor behavioral infractions. Several scholars argue this practice leads to discriminatory disciplinary actions in schools against African-American children, children with disabilities, English learners, and Native Americans as compared to other children (Council on School Health, 2013; Hoffman, 2014; Whitford & Levine-Donnerstein, 2014). The statistics show that boys are more likely to receive suspension and expulsion than girls (U.S. Department of Education, 2014). African Americans are six times more likely to be disciplined than white students; children with disabilities and English learners are two times more likely to receive out-of-school suspension than other children (U.S. Department of Education, 2014).

The zero tolerance policy particularly leads to suspending and expelling an alarmingly high number of young children from early childhood programs. In these programs boys and African-American children experience the highest rate of suspension and expulsion. The U.S. Department of Education report of 2014 indicates that: 1) African-American children represent 18 percent of preschool children, yet they receive more than 48 percent of out-of-school suspensions; 2) white children represent 43 percent of preschoolers, yet they receive only 26 percent of out-of-school suspensions; 3) boys represent 54 percent of preschool enrollment, while representing 79 percent of children suspended from preschool once, and 82 percent of preschool children who are suspended multiple times (Office of the State Superintendent of Education [OSSE], 2014).

Problems with Suspension and Expulsion of Young Children from Programs

These recent statistics regarding suspension and expulsion of preschool children are disturbing on several accounts. First, implementation of a zero tolerance disciplinary policy at early childhood level is developmentally inappropriate for young children. Second, the disproportionately high number of children from low socio-economic, minority groups, and those with disabilities is counterproductive. For many of these children schools and childcare centers in all likelihood may provide the only safe and stress-free learning environments – in contrast to their home/community environment. Third, as I have discussed earlier, during the early childhood years, children go through many neurocognitive and developmental changes. Taking away children from their learning environment and their peers will put undue stress on them and therefore affect their development. Fourth, early childhood programs have obligations to meet developmental and behavioral needs of children during this time when learning is optimized. Depriving children from appropriate social-emotional learning opportunities is counterproductive to the mission of early childhood education programs. Finally, suspension and expulsion of children from an early childhood education program is highly punitive relative to the behavioral infractions for which these children receive these consequences.

As a reminder, the initial purpose of the zero tolerance policy was to provide guidance regarding the Gun-Free School Act (1994), which was designed to keep weapons and related violence out of schools, and not for keeping young children out of preschool for their challenging behaviors.

Timeouts in Early Childhood and Special Education Classrooms

Timeout is a common classroom discipline practice used in many schools, early childhood classrooms, and in special education classrooms for all grades. Unfortunately, often the concept is misunderstood, and so when timeout is used it is used incorrectly or too frequently and thus loses the potential to effect a change in behavior.

In the typically inappropriate version of timeout for a preschool child, the child is instructed to sit in a corner (in a "timeout chair") for a predetermined period, say 10 minutes. Another inappropriate strategy used in some preschools is when the teacher instructs children to put their heads on their desks (sometimes with lights being turned off) for a short duration, so that the disruptive child or children cannot interact or access learning materials. These practices are not among any forms designed as a timeout, and the origin or rationality of such strategies is not clear.

In special education, children are sometimes put in isolation timeouts for inappropriate behaviors, such as non-compliance, refusal to work, or for aggressive behaviors. Unfortunately, these strategies are ineffective, and currently there is no research evidence to show that timeouts in these ways are effective in reducing inappropriate behaviors of children.

What Is a Timeout?

Timeout is a shortened version of the term *timeout from positive reinforcement*. It is an aversive procedure designed by behaviorists to reduce inappropriate behaviors. In its correct use, the child is denied any opportunity to receive reinforcement for a fixed period of time (Alberto & Troutman, 2013). There are four types of timeouts: 1) inclusion timeout; 2) exclusion timeout; 3) seclusion; and 4) restraint. Seclusion and restraint timeouts are the most restrictive forms of timeout. However, they are often thought of as separate disciplinary procedures than a timeout. I will describe each of these practices and explain their implications.

Inclusion/Non-Exclusionary Timeout

Inclusion timeout is also called *non-exclusionary* timeout. In this approach, all reinforcements are removed from the child, rather than removing the child from reinforcements. The idea behind an inclusion timeout is that the child remains in the classroom and continues to have access to all learning activities and instructions, but is denied any opportunity to receive reinforcement from peers or from adults in the environment (Ryan, Sanders, Katsiyannis, & Yell, 2007). The reinforcements denied include conversation with peers or teacher. There are different variations of inclusion timeout: 1) timeout ribbons; 2) planned ignoring; 3) removing materials; and 4) contingent observations.

Timeout Ribbons

Foxx and Shapiro (1978) developed the timeout ribbons in response to a widespread incorrect use of timeouts in special and general education classrooms – such as children being put for an extended periods in timeout rooms. The timeout ribbons procedure requires that an object, such as a ribbon, a wristband, a piece of yarn, or another similar material be paired with reinforcements (e.g. activities, materials, toys, etc.), which means the child will learn that unless she is wearing her ribbon, she will have no access to any reinforcement. Therefore, removal of the ribbon will be aversive to the child (Foxx & Shapiro, 1978). If a child resorts to an inappropriate behavior, the teacher will remove the timeout ribbon from the child for a predetermined period, which should be relatively short. Teachers may also determine that only in the absence of inappropriate behavior is the ribbon returned to the child. During the timeout, the child is not allowed to escape from educational demands. On the contrary, the child is expected to continue to work (Kostewicz, 2010).

This form of timeout is not very common in typical classrooms, because the success of this procedure depends on correctly pairing the ribbon or another reinforcing object with the reinforcing materials, activities, or with a social reinforcer. Additionally, there needs to be a great number of positive and social reinforcers naturally available in the learning environment that children regularly receive during the daily activities and lessons of the classroom. In reality, not all early childhood professionals utilize positive reinforcements as a regular part of their teaching and classroom management. In this case, implementing timeout ribbons is not practical.

Planned Ignoring

Originally described by Nelson and Rutherford (1983), and further articulated by Wolery, Bailey, and Sugai (1988), planned ignoring is an especially popular concept in parenting and early childhood education literature for the past two decades. In planned ignoring the teacher withholds attention (parents' attention, if at home) from a child following an undesirable behavior, for a predetermined period of time. At the end of the timeout period, the adult then returns the attention to the child (Ryan et al., 2007). Planned ignoring is recommended for non-aggressive yet inappropriate behaviors, such as dropping pencils during class discussions.

Removing Materials

In this type of timeout, if and when the child displays inappropriate behaviors, all materials (often what the child is playing or working with) are removed. This is an appropriate strategy to use when the child is playing with or using materials destructively or inappropriately, for example, when a child throws toys or learning materials around or breaks them. In such cases, the logical action will be to remove all objects and materials until such behaviors cease. For the procedure to be effective, Wolery et al. (1988) suggest that the teacher should withdraw attention from the child along with the materials.

Contingent Observation

In a contingent observation, the child receives a timeout following an inappropriate behavior and is placed in a location in the classroom (like a timeout chair) for a predetermined period of time. The child is to observe the class activities, but is not allowed to participate in class activities or interact with peers. This is the most common form of inclusion timeout currently used in early childhood classrooms.

Exclusion Timeout

In exclusion timeout the child is removed from instructional activities, and is instructed to stay in a designated area inside the classroom. However, the child is required not to watch peers or activities of the classroom. For example, the child is instructed to sit behind a partition or face the wall (Ryan et al., 2007).

Severe Forms of Timeouts: Seclusion and Restraint

Seclusion and restraints are additional forms of timeout. In seclusion, also called *isolation* timeout, the student is removed from the classroom and is confined in a different location. The student is not allowed to leave the seclusion area unless the timeout period is finished. Although this practice is more common in special education, some schools do use the procedure with typically developing children for inappropriate behaviors. Because seclusion is usually used when a child displays an aggressive behavior, restraint is frequently used at the same time. For this reason the term seclusion and restraint are usually used together. Restraint consists of using physical force, mechanical devices, or drugs to limit or prevent physical movement or control behavior (U.S. Department of Education, 2012).

Problems with Various Forms of Timeouts

There are some serious physical and emotional traumatic consequences for implementing seclusion and restraint. There are also issues with implementing the mild forms of timeout. Let us examine some of these issues.

Dangers of Seclusion and Restraint

Seclusions and restraints are dangerous interventions, which have led to death of at least 20 children in the USA in 2013 (Butler, 2014). In 2009, the United States Government Accountability Office (GAO) found that during the past two decades, thousands of public and private school children had been restrained in the years previous to their report. The report stated that hundreds of cases of abuse and death related to the use of restraint and seclusion occurred in the last decade of the report. The cases of seclusion and restraint of children in schools continue to be reported today (Butler, 2014).

Relevant to early childhood settings, the reported example of cases of the past decade include:

- A four-year-old with cerebral palsy and autism being restrained by her teacher in a wooden chair with leather straps for being "uncooperative," who suffered posttraumatic stress disorder.
- A five-year-old girl being tied to a therapy chair with bungee cords and duct tape, who suffered broken bones.

- A seven-year-old boy who died after being held on the floor face-down by the school staff.

- A number of children with disabilities as young as six-years-old in one school district, who were placed in strangleholds, restrained for extended periods of time, and confined to dark rooms, in which they were prevented from using the restroom, causing them to urinate on themselves.

All cases of restraint that led to the death of children involve teachers or school staff using restraint techniques that restricted the flow of air to the children's lungs (Butler, 2014; 2009; U.S. GAO, 2009).

Children with disabilities are by far the largest number of children who are put in locked-up isolations or in restraints. In fact, nine out of ten cases leading to abuse and death are children with disabilities (Butler, 2014; U.S. GAO, 2009). Many of these children are young and non-verbal and are not able to report the events that resulted in restraint and seclusion. Additionally, non-verbal children are not able to express their emotions appropriately. Their frustrations in communication frequently lead to aggressive bouts of temper tantrums, which may be interpreted as "noncompliance," "uncooperativeness," or aggression toward others. Therefore, nonverbal children with disabilities are more likely to become subject to seclusion and restraint in schools. Supplying these children with ways to communicate can reduce the challenging behavior and minimize the risk of inappropriate seclusion and restraint.

Currently, there is no research that indicates that the use of restraint or seclusion leads to a decrease in inappropriate or aggressive behaviors in children with or without disabilities. In fact, they often result in anger, frustration, and further aggression. Due to a lack of evidence with regards to the effectiveness of these methods, using restraint and seclusion is banned in most psychiatric hospitals and residential institutions in Europe and the USA. Additionally, the existing psychiatric research on this topic indicates that seclusion and restraint are not only ineffective but also lead to serious psychological trauma and physical injury (see comprehensive reviews of the literature by Bower, McCullough, & Timmons, 2003; Lindsey, 2009; Nelstrop et al., 2006; and for a research example see Bonner, Lowe, Rawcliffe, & Wellman, 2002). Therefore, an important question to ask is why schools prescribe practices that even psychiatric research deems not only ineffective but also dangerous.

A legal analysis of the current U.S. laws on seclusion and restraint of children in schools, as presented by Butler (2014), shows that in the United States there are currently only 19 states[2] that have laws that meaningfully protect all children from seclusion and restraint; only 32 states provide similar protection for children with disabilities alone; only 20 states prohibit use of restraint that will prevent breathing; only 13 states limit the use of restraint to emergencies posing an immediate risk of harm; only 15 states prohibit use of mechanical restraints, such as duct tapes or bungee cords; and only 30 states require parents to be notified when a child is being secluded or restrained at school. In 2009, after publication of the GAO report, a bill on school seclusions and restraints was introduced to the U.S. Congress, and although the bill passed the House of Representative, it did not pass the Senate and thus did not become a law (Keeping All Students Safe Act, 2011–2013).

Problems with the Common Forms of Timeouts in Early Childhood Classrooms

As I mentioned, contingent observation is the most common use of timeout in early childhood classrooms today. The largest issue with contingent observation is that for some children the timeout actually serves the opposite purpose than intended, in that the timeout itself can be reinforcing or rewarding for the child's inappropriate behavior. This is usually the case when a child prefers to avoid a learning task as a result of a learning problem, social relationship problems with peers, boredom, or disinterest. To illustrate, let us consider the following example:

> Michael is a second-grader who displays some disruptive behaviors particularly during the math period. When children are busy working on their worksheets, Michael throws bunched up pieces of paper around, talks to peers incessantly, or makes noises with his mouth. This happens always during the math period.
>
> Verbal reprimands are not effective with Michael. However, Ms. Piper has found sending Michael to the timeout chair seems to at least keep him quiet during math and allow other children to do their work. Ms. Piper believes she has found the perfect discipline strategy to address Michael's disruptive behavior.

Timeout seems like an appropriate behavior management strategy for Michael for the moment. In reality, however, Michael dislikes the math period. For him, doing a math worksheet is difficult and uninteresting. Michael has learned that his repertoire of disruptive behaviors provides him with a means to escape from this unwanted task. Getting a timeout is exactly what Michael wants. All he has to do next time is to repeat his disruptive behaviors or come up with similar ones. Thus, timeout, when used inappropriately, as with Michael, can become a perfect negative reinforcer or reward for the child's inappropriate behaviors.

Exclusive timeout, in which the child is instructed to sit in a corner with his face away from the class, is also problematic, with an added issue of humiliation or degradation of the child in front of peers, both of which are emotionally traumatizing.

Effective Use of Removal of Play and Educational Materials from Children

Although this type of timeout is a safe way to set limits for children about appropriate use of materials, removing materials will not be effective unless the teacher implements appropriate activity lessons related to this issue. Lessons on the limits and rules of working and respecting materials and space can be taught to children both in small and large group lesson formats explicitly and reviewed regularly. The rules should be posted so that everyone can see them and teachers can review at the beginning of a lesson. For example, the teacher may say, "We are going to listen to a story in our circle now. Remember, we should put away our toys and follow the rules for sitting in the circle. Could you tell me what those rules are?" Such statements could be directed to the whole class, or be addressed quietly to an individual child who may have difficulty with transitions. Limits should be reiterated if a material or toy is removed from a child due to inappropriate usage. Thus, there should be no doubt in the child's mind that materials are removed because the child interacts or plays inappropriately with them.

Effective Use of Planned Ignoring

In general, planned ignoring is an effective strategy for most inappropriate behaviors occurring in the classroom. The problem is that, in reality, the implementers of planned ignoring, teachers and parents, find it difficult to consistently ignore inappropriate behaviors of children as the behaviors are occurring. In the majority of cases, teachers actually show more attention to the child during the time the child is resorting to an inappropriate behavior, for example, calling out to a child who is humming, "Mary, is now the time for humming?" Or they may implement planned ignoring very inconsistently. Inconsistency is counterproductive to the goal of planned ignoring, in that it may teach to the child that if he is persistent in his inappropriate behaviors for a longer duration, the teacher or parent is bound to give in and pay attention to him. For example, a child drops a pencil and the teacher ignores, he drops a book and the teacher says, "Arnold, stop dropping materials on the floor." Therefore, a lack of consistency renders the whole procedure of planned ignoring ineffective. Additionally, planned ignoring is ineffective when the teacher ignores the inappropriate behavior of a child, while the peers in contrast show attention to the child with inappropriate behaviors. They may laugh, for example, when Harry puts a paper hat on his head during the science demonstration. For the procedure to be effective, all persons in the environment, adults as well as peers, should follow planned ignoring. An alternative approach for addressing inappropriate behaviors is *Differential Attention (DA)*, which I will describe in Chapter 9.

In general, the concept of timeout as a disciplinary practice makes the assumption that the community of the classroom and activities within it are typically reinforcing to the child. This means even in its least restrictive form, such as in timeout ribbons, planned ignoring, or removal of materials, the practice of timeout is only effective when the classroom as a whole is positive, and when the instruction is engaging to the community of learners. In this case, the classroom itself is reinforcing to the child, and so receiving a timeout is in fact an appropriate and effective discipline strategy in eliminating inappropriate behaviors because the children want to participate.

Corporal/Physical Punishment

Corporal punishment is defined as "the use of physical force, no matter how light, with the intention of causing the child to experience bodily pain so as to correct or punish the child's behavior" (Gershoff & Bitensky, 2007, p. 232). A form of corporal punishment used in public schools involves battering the backside with a paddle (Mortorano, 2013).

In 1977, the U.S. Supreme Court in *Ingraham v. Wright* ruled that the decision to use corporal punishment in public schools is an issue better left to states (*Ingraham v. Wright*, 1977). Although the practice of corporal punishment in schools is banished in most states in the USA, currently, there are 19 states[3] allowing the use of corporal punishment as a form of discipline strategy in public schools with children. Alabama, Arkansas, and Mississippi have the highest rate of corporal punishment, with Mississippi accounting for 50 percent of physical punishment cases (Farrell, 2014).

Although the principal or a school administrator usually administers physical punishment, a teacher might also (Mortorano, 2013). In most cases, children are hit on their buttocks with a wooden paddle. Some school districts have specifications for the size and shape of the paddle (Gershoff, 2008). Children with disabilities and African-American children are subject to corporal punishment at the highest rates compared to other children (American Civil Liberties Union, 2009; Carr, 2014). Boys are also more likely to be the subject of corporal punishment as compared to girls (Farrell, 2014). There is no age restriction for corporal punishment, and children may be punished beginning from age four for infractions such as breaking school or classroom rules or failing to finish their homework on time (Carr, 2014; Farrell, 2014). Corporal punishment of children leads to many cases of serious physical injury and psychological trauma (Carr, 2014).

Issues with Corporal Punishment of Children in Schools

Despite an increasing body of research indicating that physical punishment is only effective in reducing challenging behaviors for a short time, and in fact as an intervention might do more harm than good (for examples see Knox, 2010; Miller et al., 2014; Gong et al., 2014; and Whitford & Levine-Donnerstein, 2014), corporal punishment continues to exist in today's public and private schools. Private schools may choose to use corporal punishment on religious grounds, even in states where the practice is banned. Similarly, as mentioned in previous chapters, schools may justify use of painful aversives/punishers as effective treatments for children with disabilities.

A debate on the use of various forms of corporal punishment (such as paddling or use of electric shock, discussed in Chapter 7) to address challenging behaviors of children continues. There are a great number of educators, scholars, civil rights advocates, and lawyers on each side of this debate. A detailed examination of issues surrounding this debate is outside the scope of this chapter; however, here, I bring forth some of the most important ethical and legal aspects of this argument. (To read more, consult Teaching Tolerance [2014] on the topic: http://www.tolerance.org/search/apachesolr_search/corporal%20punishment)

Racial Disparities and Corporal Punishment

Discrimination against African-American children in schools is a major and serious concern. As such, some points need to be made in regards to this issue. First, the majority of cases of corporal punishment occur in Southern states, in which public schools have the largest number of African-American children. During 2011–2012 in Mississippi alone – the state with the current highest rate of corporal punishment – African-American children accounted for 64 percent of those being paddled (Carr, 2014). Corporal punishment statutes in these states leave the decision to use this discipline practice to individual schools.

Second, schools are not allowed to use corporal punishment on children without signed consents from parents or guardians, so parents see the method as an appropriate one to employ with their children. Furthermore, school discipline policies usually mirror practices that are valued in the surrounding community of each school. Some have argued that in some African-American communities, corporal punishment may be used in homes as a parenting discipline strategy (Carr, 2014; Farrell, 2014). In fact, some parents and leaders view a decision to allow using corporal punishment in their schools as their civil right (Carr, 2014). Therefore, although the issue of discrimination remains central to this topic, an appropriate discussion of racial disparity and corporal punishment at the very least requires a careful examination of all dimensions involved (e.g. cultural and parenting practices, socio-political and economic history, and the relationship to the existing school laws and policy); this discussion is beyond the scope of this chapter.

Ethical and Legal Issues

There are a number of ethical and legal arguments against the use of corporal punishment with children. Most ethical arguments rely on the research of the past three decades on the negative consequences of physical punishment on the social-emotional and psychological health of children. Though most of this research relates to parental corporal punishment, many have argued that these research findings are generalizable to corporal punishment in schools (Bitensky, 2006; Knox, 2010; McCluskey, 2014). The major points of these arguments based on a review of research show little evidence for physical punishment:

- actually improving children's behaviors
- reducing or preventing aggressive behaviors from occurring in the long run.

On the contrary, the research evidence shows:

- The use of physical punishment puts children at risk for further challenging and aggressive behaviors as well as mental health issues.
- Children who are punished physically are at risk of being physically abused and/or injured.

In addition, notable early childhood scholars argue that corporal punishment induces fear of authority figures, an animosity against adults in children, and gives the message that violence is the correct way of dealing with conflicts and problems (Brazelton & Greenspan, 2000). Corporal punishment can be particularly emotionally traumatic for children who already deal with stressful caregiving and living situations. Finally, corporal punishment in schools creates an overall negative school climate and anxiety-producing experiences in which learning cannot be optimized.

Furthermore, at the societal level, using corporal punishment brings forth the issue of the civil rights of school children. School children's rights are argued through various U.S. Supreme Court cases. Given the purpose of our discussion, a detailed examination of all case laws on this issue is not possible in this chapter. Three important cases, however, set forth the precedence regarding the protection of civil rights of children in schools. All cases involved children being disciplined in their schools.

New Jersey v. T.L.O. *(1985)*

The U.S. Supreme Court held that the Fourth Amendment right against "unreasonable search and seizure" applies to all school children, and that children should expect for their properties to be safe against any unreasonable search and seizure that might be conducted by the school personnel.

Goss v. Lopez *(1975)*

The U.S. Supreme Court held that all school children have the right to a "due process of law" when they are subjected to disciplinary practices or procedures. This includes a right to a notice or a hearing prior to implementation of any punishment, including corporal punishment, suspension, expulsions, etc.

Ingraham v. Wright *(1977)*

The U.S. Supreme Court set that the Eighth Amendment protection against "cruel and unusual punishment" only applies to criminal punishment and not to schools. Thus, school children are not covered under this protection.

Because of the precedence set forth by *Ingraham v. Wright* (1977), currently in the USA schools are the only institutions in which physical punishment is sanctioned.

Physical punishment is not allowed in any other U.S. institutions including in prisons. Thus currently, there are no federal laws prohibiting the use of corporal punishment of children in schools.

Legal scholars (such as Bitensky, 2006; Mortorano, 2013; Wasserman, 2011) continue to raise several important concerns regarding children's rights and corporal punishment in schools. They argue, for example, that: 1) corporal punishment in schools is in fact a cruel and unusual punishment, because according to research it harms children's physical and emotional well-being; 2) because corporal punishment disproportionately targets children with disabilities and African-American children, it violates these groups' civil rights; 3) most countries of the world view corporal punishment as cruel, and consider corporal punishment a human rights issue.

Important international human rights instruments, such as the Convention on the Rights of the Child, recognize the right of the child to respect for her/his human dignity and physical integrity, as well as the child's right to be protected against all forms of corporal punishment in the family, schools, and other settings under the law (UN Committee on the Rights of the Child, 2006). Although 192 countries of the world have ratified the Convention of the Rights of the Child, the United States has not yet signed this important document.

In 2011, the United States Congress introduced the Ending Corporal Punishment in Schools Act against the practice of physical punishment in schools. The bill was reintroduced to the House of Representatives in June of 2014 (Ending Corporal Punishment in Schools Act of 2014). However, the bill was reassigned to a congressional committee, which may consider it before sending it to the House or Senate in upcoming years.

Alternative Approaches: Positive Discipline and School-Wide Positive Behavior Support (SWPBS)

If schools have the goal of developing responsible citizens, then the discipline policies they use should align with this goal (Mayworm & Sharkey, 2014). School discipline policies are designed to help them manage students' behaviors, and teach them problem-solving skills, self-regulation, and self-discipline (Bear, 2010). As we have seen in this chapter, some schools choose negative strategies to do so, and as a result many students may be subject to harsh punishments.

To summarize research results: 1) punishing practices do not promote problem-solving skills nor do they promote self-discipline in children; 2) although punishment of children might be effective in eliminating challenging behaviors in the short run, such practice has no teaching value or positive influence on children in the long run; and 3) punishment of children often leads to negative psychological and physical consequences for them.

For schools to reach their goal of developing responsible citizens, discipline policies need to be safe, positive, child-centered, humanistic, preventive, and proactive. In this sense, applying positive discipline to schools means that schools should not only create a sense of safety, but also a sense of belonging in children, in which they connect with peers and adults and are able to learn successfully (Gfroerer, Nelsen, & Kern, 2013). Positive discipline strategies create a safe learning atmosphere for children, and students are most likely to develop problem-solving skills, self-discipline and self-efficacy.

The term *positive discipline* itself was coined in the 1980s, and was possibly the motivation behind using the word *positive* in the phrase Positive Behavior Support (PBS). In the previous chapter, I described important principles of PBS, which are grounded in behaviorism. Here, I will add that the concept of positive discipline itself embraces a series of strategies that are derived from Adlerian/humanistic individual psychology. The purpose of positive discipline is to help teachers and parents learn discipline strategies that build positive relationships with children, while helping children achieve self-reliance and a sense of belonging at homes and in schools (Nelsen, 2006). Positive discipline is intended to create a sense of connection and significance in children, and support their development of life skills (Gfroerer et al., 2013). Thus, any school-wide PBS approach should have the concept of positive discipline at its core.

There is ample research evidence to show that when humanistic positive discipline principles guide the practices of a school-wide PBS, schools are quite successful in promoting positive climates and in addressing the challenging and aggressive behaviors of children proactively (Marchant, Heath, & Miramontes, 2012; Martens & Andreen, 2013). Specific schools using such approaches have reported to successfully reduce aggressive behaviors and bullying issues (Nese, Horner, Dickey, Stiller, & Tomlanovich, 2014), reduce and in most cases eliminate expulsion, suspension, and exclusion of children with various ethnic backgrounds – with or without disabilities (Vincent & Tobin, 2011), and completely reject a need for resorting to any extreme disciplinary measures (McIntosh, Predy, Upreti, Hume, Turri, & Mathews, 2014). These schools are able to promote culturally responsive practices, which include collaboration and cooperation among school personnel, and between school staff and families (McIntosh et al., 2014).

Closing Remarks

In this chapter I discussed several common classroom and school disciplinary practices that are at best ineffective and at worst abusive, discriminatory, and unethical. In essence, learning environments that resort to these methods can become unsafe, anxiety producing, and dangerous places for children to be in, and as a result deprive students from much needed precious educational resources. This is particularly the case for African-American children, children with disabilities, and English language learners. My purpose in discussing this topic was to bring attention to the negative and in some cases tragic consequences that such ineffective disciplinary practices have on children and youth. Contrary to such practices, there are positive discipline strategies, such as school-wide and classroom-level Positive

Behavior Support, or other similar humanistic strategies, that are not only effective, but also teach valuable lessons of belonging, self-regulation, and self-reliance to children. When there are such strategies available, there should be no reason for using any disciplinary action that results in humiliating, excluding, restraining, isolating, or possibly harming children.

Notes

1. To see details about states visit: http://www2.ed.gov/policy/gen/guid/school-discipline/guiding-principles.pdf
2. Alabama, Colorado, Georgia, Illinois, Indiana, Iowa, Kansas, Kentucky, Massachusetts, Maryland, Maine, North Carolina, Ohio, Oregon, Rhode Island, Vermont, West Virginia, Wisconsin, and Wyoming.
3. Alabama, Arizona, Arkansas, Colorado, Florida, Georgia, Idaho, Indiana, Kansas, Kentucky, Louisiana, Mississippi, Missouri, North Carolina, Oklahoma, South Carolina, Tennessee, Texas, and Wyoming.

References

Alberto, P. A., & Troutman, A. C. (2013). *Applied behavior analysis for teachers* (9th edition). Upper Saddle River, NJ: Pearson.

American Civil Liberties Union. (2009). *Impairing education: Corporal punishment of students with disabilities in U.S. public schools.* Retrieved from: https://www.aclu.org/disability-rights/impairing-education-corporal-punishment-students-disabilities-us-public-schools

Bear, G. G. (2010). *School discipline and self-discipline: A practical guide to promoting prosocial student behavior.* New York, NY: Guilford Press.

Bitensky, S. H. (2006). *Corporal punishment of children: A human rights violation.* Ardsley, NY: Transnational Publishers.

Bonner, G., Lowe, T., Rawcliffe, D., & Wellman, N. (2002). Trauma for all: A pilot study of the subjective experience of physical restraint for mental health inpatients and staff in the UK. *Journal of Psychiatric and Mental Health Nursing, 9*(4), 465–473.

Bower, F. L., McCullough, C. S., & Timmons, M. E. (2003). Synthesis of what we know about the use of physical restraint and seclusion with patients in psychiatric and acute care settings: 2003 update. *Woldview on Evidence-Based Nursing, 10*(1), 1–29.

Brazelton, T. B., & Greenspan, S. I. (2000). *The irreducible needs of children: What every child must have to grow, learn, and flourish.* Cambridge, MA: Perseus Publishing.

Butler, J. (2009). *Unsafe in the schoolhouse: Abuse of children with disabilities.* The Towson, MD: Council of Parent Attorneys and Advocates (COPAA). Retrieved from: http://c.ymcdn.com/sites/www.copaa.org/resource/collection/662B1866-952D-41FA-B7F3-D3CF68639918/UnsafeCOPAAMay_27_2009.pdf

Butler, J. (2014). *How safe is the schoolhouse? An analysis of state seclusion and restraint laws and policy.* Autism National Committee (AutCom). Retrieved from: http://www.autcom.org/pdf/HowSafeSchoolhouse.pdf

Carr, S. (April 28, 2014). Spare the child: A controversy over corporal punishment in public schools has a painful racial subtext. *The Nation,* 18–21.

Council on School Health. (2013). Out-of-school suspension and expulsion. *Pediatrics, 131*(3), 1000–1007.

Ending Corporal Punishment in Schools Act of 2014, H.R. 5005, 113th Cong. (2014). Retrieved from: https://beta.congress.gov/bill/113th-congress/house-bill/5005

Farrell, C. (2014). *Corporal punishment in U.S. Schools*. Retrieved from: http://www.corpun.com/counuss.htm#who

Foxx, R. M., & Shapiro, S. T. (1978). The timeout ribbon: A nonexclusionary timeout procedure. *Journal of Applied Behavior Analysis, 11*(1), 125–136.

Gershoff, E. (2008). *Report on physical punishment in the United States: What research tells us about its effects on children.* Columbus, OH: Center for Effective Discipline. Retrieved from: http://www.nospank.net/gershoff.pdf

Gershoff, E. T., & Bitensky, S. H. (2007). The case against corporal punishment of children: Converging evidence from social science research and international human rights law and implications for U.S. public policy. *Psychology, Public Policy, and Law, 13*(4), 231–272.

Gfroerer, K., Nelsen, J., & Kern, R. M. (2013). Positive discipline: Helping children develop belonging and coping resources using individual psychology. *The Journal of Individual Psychology, 69*(4), 294–304.

Gong, J., Yuan, J., Wang, S., Shi, L., Cui, X., & Luo, X. (2014). Feedback-related negativity in children with two subtypes of attention deficits hyperactivity disorder. *Public Library of Science: PLO ONE, 19*(16), 1–7.

Goss v. Lopez, 419 U.S. 569 (1975). Retrieved from: http://caselaw.lp.findlaw.com/scripts/getcase.pl?court=US&vol=419&invol=565

Gun-Free Schools Act of 1994, 20 U.S.C. §§ 7151 et seq.

Hoffman, S. (2014). Zero benefit: Estimating the effects of zero tolerance discipline policies on racial disparities in school discipline. *Educational Policy, 28*(1), 69–95.

Ingraham v. Wright, 430 U.S. 651 (1977). Retrieved from: http://caselaw.lp.findlaw.com/scripts/getcase.pl?court=US&vol=430&invol=651

Keeping All Students Safe Act, S. 2020, 112th Cong. (2011–2013). Retrieved from: https://www.govtrack.us/congress/bills/112/s2020

Knox, M. (2010). On hitting children: A review of corporal punishment in the United States. *Journal of Pediatric Health Care, 24*(2), 103–107.

Kostewicz, D. E. (2010). A review of timeout ribbons. *The Behavior Analyst Today, 11*(2), 95–104.

Lindsey, P. L. (2009). Psychiatric nurses' decision to restrain: The association between empowerment and individual factors. *Journal of Psychological Nursing, 47*(9), 41–49.

Mace, F. C., Pratt, J. L., Prager, K. L., & Pritchard, D. (2011). An evaluation of three methods of saying "no" to avoid an escalating response class hierarchy. *Journal of Applied Behavior Analysis, 44*(1), 83–94.

Marchant, M., Heath, M. A., & Miramontes, N. Y. (2012). Merging empiricism and humanism: Role of social validity in the school-wide positive behavior support model. *Journal of Positive Behavior Interventions, 15*(4), 221–230.

Martens, K., & Andreen K. (2013). School counselors' involvement with a school-wide positive behavior support intervention: Addressing student behavior issues in a proactive and positive manner. *Professional School Counseling, 16*(5), 313–322.

Mayworm, A. M., & Sharkey, J. D. (2014). Ethical considerations in a three-tiered approach to school discipline policy and practice. *Psychology in the Schools, 51*(7), 693–704.

McCluskey, G. (2014). 'Youth is present only when its presence is a problem': Voices of young people on discipline in school. *Children & Society, 28*(2), 93–103.

McIntosh, K., Predy, L. K., Upreti, G., Hume, A. E., Turri, M. G., & Mathews, S. (2014). Perceptions of contextual features related to implementation and sustainability of school-wide positive behavior support. *Journal of Positive Behavior Interventions, 16*(1), 31–43.

Miller, N. V., Haas, S. M., Waschbusch, D. A., Willoughby, M. T., Helseth, S. A., Crum, K. I., Coles, E. K. & Pelham, W. E. (2014). Behavior therapy and callous-unemotional traits: Effects of a pilot study examining modified behavioral contingencies on child behavior. *Behavior Therapy, 45*(5), 606–618.

Mortorano, N. (2013). Protecting children's rights inside of the schoolhouse gates: Ending corporal punishment in schools. *Georgetown Law Journal, 102*, 481–518.

Nelsen, J. (2006). *Positive Discipline.* New York: Ballantine Books.

Nelson, C., & Rutherford, R. (1983). Timeout revisited: Guidelines for its use in special education. *Exceptional Education Quarterly, 3*(4), 56–67.

Nelstrop, L., Chandler-Oatts, J., Bingley, W., Bleetman, T., Corr, F., Cronin-Davis, J., … & Tsuchiya, A. (2006). A systematic review of the safety and effectiveness of restraint and seclusion and interventions for the short-term management of violence in adult psychiatric inpatient settings and emergency departments. *Worldviews on Evidence-Based Nursing, 3*(1), 8–18.

Nese, R. N. T., Horner, R., Dickey, C. R., Stiller, B., & Tomlanovich, A. (2014). Decreasing bullying behaviors in middle school: Expect respect. *School Psychology Quarterly, 29*(3), 272–286.

New Jersey v. T.L.O., 469 U.S. 325 (1985). Retrieved from: http://caselaw.lp.findlaw.com/scripts/getcase.pl?court=US&vol=469&invol=325

Office of the State Superintendent of Education. (2014). Reducing out-of-school suspensions and expulsions in District of Columbia public and public charter schools. Retrieved from: http://osse.dc.gov/sites/default/files/dc/sites/osse/publication/attachments/OSSE_REPORT_DISCIPLINARY_G_PAGES.pdf

Ryan, J. B., Sanders, S., Katsiyannis, A., & Yell, M. L. (2007). Using timeout effectively in the classroom. *Teaching Exceptional Children, 39*(4), 60–67.

Teaching Tolerance. (2014). A project of the southern poverty law center on corporal punishment. Retrieved from: http://www.tolerance.org/search/apachesolr_search/corporal%20punishment

U.S. Department of Education. (2012). *Restraint and seclusion: Resource document.* Washington, DC. Retrieved from: https://www2.ed.gov/policy/seclusion/restraints-and-seclusion-resources.pdf

U.S. Department of Education. (2014). *Guiding principles: A resource guide for improving school climate and discipline.* Washington, D.C. Retrieved from: http://www2.ed.gov/policy/gen/guid/school-discipline/guiding-principles.pdf

U.S. Department of Education, National Center for Education Statistics. (1998). *Violence and discipline problems in U.S. public schools: 1996–97.* NCES 98-030, by Sheila Heaviside, Cassandra Rowand, Catrina Williams, and Elizabeth Farris. Project Officers, Shelly Burns and Edith McArthur. Washington, DC. Retrieved from: http://nces.ed.gov/pubs98/98030.pdf

UN Committee on the Rights of the Child. (2006). *Convention on the rights of the child: General comments No 8 – The rights of the child to protection from corporal punishment and other cruel or degrading forms of punishment.* Retrieved from: http://srsg.violenceagainstchildren.org/sites/default/files/documents/docs/GRC-C-GC-8_EN.pdf

United States Government Accountability Office (GAO). (2009). *Seclusions and restraints: Selected cases of death and abuse at public and private schools and treatment centers.* United States Government Accountability Office (GAO): Testimony before the Committee on Education and Labor, House of Representative. Retrieved from: http://www.gao.gov/assets/130/122526.pdf

Vincent, C. G., & Tobin, T. J. (2011). The relationship between implementation of school-wide positive behavior support (SWPBS) and disciplinary exclusion of students from various ethnic backgrounds with and without disabilities. *Journal of Emotional and Behavioral Disorders, 19*(4), 217–232.

Wasserman, L. (2011). Corporal punishment in K-12 public school settings: Reconsideration of its constitutional dimensions thirty years after Ingraham v. Wright. *Touro Law Review, 26*(4), 1021–1101.

Whitford, D. K., & Levine-Donnerstein, D. (2014). Office disciplinary referral patterns of American Indian students from elementary school through high school. *Behavioral Disorders, 39*(2), 78–88.

Wolery, M. R., Bailey, D. B. Jr., & Sugai, G. M. (1988). *Effective teaching principles and procedures of applied behavior analysis with exceptional students.* Boston: Allyn & Bacon.

9

BEST PRACTICES

Practical Strategies for Addressing Challenging Behaviors of Children

In this chapter I will present specific recommendations and guidelines to design and implement effective behavior intervention plans that are most likely to promote emotional and behavioral health in children with challenging behaviors in the classroom. These strategies are grounded in research and related theoretical frameworks presented throughout this book. My approach is based on a developmental framework, which views children as capable and resilient. The methods described respect children's dignity, their individual needs and capabilities in their cultural and family contexts

I hope that the information in this chapter will help early childhood professionals develop new, effective strategies and refine their own teaching practices to support children's mental and behavioral health. At the end of the chapter, I present a study of a child with a personalized behavior intervention plan. This study and other examples of children are real. The names of children, teachers, and other professionals involved are changed to protect their privacy.

Underlying Principles of my Approach and Philosophy

Being solidly grounded in a particular theoretical approach is important, whether for an educator or a mental health clinician. A theory provides consistency and predictability in one's practice and helps the child know what to expect from the professional. However, I also believe that a one-size approach does not fit all children or conditions. Given each child's unique neurobiological and physical makeup, family, and cultural background, I believe that solid knowledge of several theoretical approaches is required in order to address the various needs of children. Thus, designing a behavior intervention plan may sometimes involve using more than one intervention method. To reiterate, no matter which type of strategy I recommend, I believe that the philosophy that drives any child intervention practice is first and foremost acknowledging, observing, and respecting the child's dignity and personhood. My work is grounded in positive approaches to guidance and discipline. I believe that under no circumstances should the child be demeaned, humiliated, or at worst be physically or psychologically punished. With this ethical attitude in mind, the next section begins with specifications for addressing challenging behaviors.

A Three-Step Process of Addressing Challenging Behaviors

Thus far, I have presented most of the underlying causes of mental and behavioral issues in children along with appropriate and evidence-based interventions, from child-centered play-based to behavioral approaches. Utilizing the approaches I have discussed in this book, I recommend a three-step process based on positive discipline approaches. Each step has additional subcomponents.

- **Step one: Pay positive attention to all children**
  1. *Process* or *narrative praise* to encourage learning and achievement.
  2. *Follow up praise* for guiding behavior.
  3. *Appreciation praise* to convey meaning, teach values, and promote a sense of belonging in the community.
- **Step two: Build a naturally/positively reinforcing classroom**
  1. Use the best teaching practices.
  2. Use a sound classroom management system.
- **Step three: Design a behavior intervention plan**
  1. Collect ABC data and other information.
  2. Analyze data and make a hypothesis.
  3. Plan, implement, and assess an intervention.

Step One: Pay Positive Attention to All Children

So far, I have examined various consequences that an adult's inattention or lack of warmth might have for a child in early childhood. There are, of course, degrees for experiencing an adult's neglect and inattention. Although not all children develop a pathological condition, all children react negatively when caregivers fail to notice and acknowledge them. The same way that inattention from caregivers may create serious issues for a child at home, consistent lack of appropriate response and positive attention from teachers can cause not only academic or learning issues for the child, but also additional problems with authority.

All children, regardless of biological or developmental characteristics, need attention, validation, and acknowledgment (Yuill, Hinske, Williams, & Leith, 2014). My work with children, with and without special needs, and my study of child development grounds my belief that almost all challenging behaviors occur partly to gain the adults' or peers' attention. Challenging behaviors often serve as a message from the children who resort to them – they require attention from others to take care of their needs, to help them learn, to alleviate their anxiety, to make them feel safe or better, to take notice of them, or to guide them in regulating themselves.

In particular, children who do not receive consistent appropriate and positive attention in their home environments from their parents or caregivers often constantly crave attention from teachers and other children around them in school and childcare settings. Thus, these are the children who resort to challenging behaviors and in response usually receive negative attention. Negative attention is one of the three ways adults and peers respond to a child behavior.

Types of Attention

There are three types of attention. *Negative attention* is actions by adults such as reprimanding or negating the child. *Neutral attention* is giving simple regards, such as looking at the child and describing what the child is doing. *Positive attention* is smiling, making a positive statement, or praising the child. As I mentioned in Chapter 7, positive attention is possibly the strongest positive reinforcement for reducing challenging behavior.

Many early childhood teachers and families complain that children with challenging behaviors often demand their attention and monopolize their time away from other children. Therefore, in reaction, adults' automatic response often includes saying no, reprimanding the child, putting the child in timeout, and in some cases implementing physical or emotional punishment. What most adults fail to see is that by resorting to any of the actions listed above, they are in fact giving these children a good bit of attention for their inappropriate behaviors, even though it is negative attention. For a child who needs it, getting even negative attention is better than receiving no attention at all – that is, being ignored. As a result, this negative attention reinforces that behavior, and the child is more likely to repeat the behavior. To clarify, let us look at this example:

Ms. Kayle, an early childhood teacher, asked me to observe Le, an English language learner (ELL), who had recently moved with his family to the United States from China. Ms. Kayle described him as being "non-compliant and oppositional at all times." She complained that none of her efforts in working with Le had worked, and he continued to have challenging behaviors.

During a classroom session, Le was observed in a two-hour period prior to, during, and after a large group *read aloud* story time. The data I took during the targeted lesson (story time) at the time of observation showed that Le fidgeted in his floor seat frequently, stood up on his knees six times (often to peek over the child in front of him), and stood up completely five times. One time, as he stood up, he blocked the view of a couple of children behind him, who then complained that they could not see. In response to Le's body movement (a total of 11 times), during a 25-minute period, Ms. Kayle called on him, saying, "stop," "sit down properly," "pay attention," "do not ...", some in negative and angry tones, 27 times – more than twice as many times as Le's behaviors might have called for any kind of correction from the teacher.

Without going into further details regarding Le's fidgeting and its reasons, this data presents a clear example of how a teacher can be paying negative attention – to what in her view is inappropriate – at a rate higher than the actual number of target behavior (e.g. Le's behavior occurred 11 times, while Ms. Kayle called on Le 27 times). There were instances when Le sat quietly and appropriately, paying close attention to the teacher and the story.

Unfortunately, these instances, which she can pay attention to and acknowledge, were completely disregarded by the teacher. For example, Ms. Kayle could have praised Le when he was attentive by smiling at Le directly, while saying, "Everyone is sitting appropriately and paying close attention to the story" or "I like the way Le is listening to the story." Such statements are expressions of an adult's positive attention and regard for all children, with a message of acknowledgment and validation of appropriate behaviors. At the same time, statements like this set the parameters for behaviors that are expected of the child. Ms. Kayle also could have placed Le in close proximity to herself, where she could have supervised him closely and provided guidance for him as she read the story. These actions most likely would have prevented Le from too much movement, and thus eliminated any need for further intervention from the teacher. Ms Kayle could also have ignored the movement if it did not interfere with other children's sight line.

Paying positive attention to all children matters, particularly for children who merit attention. In the case of Le, considering that he is just beginning to learn English, and has recently entered a completely new learning and cultural environment, it is particularly important that the teacher is attentive not only to his learning needs, but also to his behavioral and emotional needs. This attention should be positive and descriptive as the situation merits, instead of negative and reprimanding in reaction to minor and small incidences, which can be handled positively instead.

One form of positive attention, which has become an issue of controversy in early childhood education, is *praise*. In the following section, I will look at the issue of praising children and the arguments surrounding it.

Praise Controversy and Appropriate Forms of Praise

Praising children is most common in the form of parental exclamation of excitement and celebration of the child, generally beginning early when the infant begins to show developmental accomplishments. According to Wierzbicka (2004) parental expressions such as "good girl" or "good boy," are essentially Anglo-American in nature, and do not exist in some languages like German, Polish, and French. Historically, parental praise of children became common around the turn of the 20th century, when a more positive and scientific view of children emerged (for a history see Chapter 10), and parents began to notice and celebrate their children's development.

In education settings, praising children is linked to Branden's popular book *The Psychology of Self Esteem,* published in 1969. The book began a movement in psychology, part of which focused on building self-esteem in children (particularly those who are at risk for low academic achievement due to risk factors in their environment) as a way of encouraging not only their psychological health, but also their academic achievement. Over time, praising children became a popular approach for families and teachers to boost the self-esteem of children.

However, during the past two decades various scholars have questioned the virtue or effectiveness of praising children (for a comprehensive review see Baumeister, Campbell, Kreuger, and Vohs, 2003; also Weissbourd, 2009). In fact, current research provides evidence to the contrary, that praising children with low self-esteem can actually backfire and do quite the opposite (Brummelman et al., 2014a; Brummelman, Thomaes, De Castro, Overbeek, & Bushman, 2014b; Pomerantz & Kempner, 2013). These studies suggest that praising children with low self-esteem conveys to them that they should meet very high standards, which they deem unrealistic, or might not be able to reach, and therefore would in turn discourage them from taking on any further challenges (Brummelman et al., 2014a, 2014b; Pomerantz & Kempner, 2013).

The guidelines for Developmentally Appropriate Practices (DAP) recommended by the National Association for the Education of Young Children (NAEYC) indicate that professionals should *encourage* persistence and effort instead of just praising children (for details see NAEYC, n.d.). The term *encouragement* is preferred to the term praise by many early childhood scholars and professionals (Gartell, 2007). Some professionals distinguished encouragement from praise with the clarification that praising a child sets the adult in the power position of judging the child's work, while encouragement promotes child empowerment (Gartell, 2007; Meece & Soderman, 2010).

The term "praise junky" appears several times in the work of Kohn (2001, 2005) an author of popular parenting and education books. He warned early childhood educators that when they praise children, they manipulate them to do the adult's biddings, make children become "praise junkies" who rely on an adult's judgment and evaluation, steal children's pleasure by telling them how to feel, and reduce children's achievement (Kohn, 2001). While I do not dispute the validity of some of these points, I believe that the issue of praise needs to be examined at least from three different perspectives in order to be understood correctly.

First, the act of praising the child should be isolated from any connection to the issue of self-esteem. Instead, praising children should be connected to paying positive attention, conveying a positive regard, and encouraging learning. In this way, there can be three specific kinds of praise: 1) praise to encourage learning and achievement; 2) praise to guide the child's behavior; 3) praise to convey meaning, values, and a sense of belonging in the community.

1. Process or Narrative Praise to Encourage Learning and Achievement

The literature related to praise for academic and developmental learning is mostly related to the research conducted by Dweck (1999, 2006, 2009) on mindset. Dweck (2006) suggests that praising children, such as telling them, "You are so smart," creates a particular negative mindset that discourages children from trying their best; children discern that they should take an easy way out for success and meet the expectation of parents and educators who praise them for their attributes. Thus, praising the child for attributes is neither conducive to learning nor to achievement, according to Dweck.

However, there is an appropriate form of praising children, called *process praise*, which Dweck (2006, 2009) says is actually beneficial to children. Process praise may be thought of as a narrative statement that focuses on the child's work and effort instead of the child's attributes. For example, saying, "You worked really hard," is a statement on process, as opposed to, "You are very smart," which is a praise of a child's attribute. Process praise according to Dweck (2006, 2009) motivates the child to explore, work hard, and have a healthy mindset and outlook about self. Recent research in this area (Brummelman et al., 2014a; Pomerantz & Kempner, 2013; Skipper & Douglas, 2012) confirms Dweck's findings in this regard.

Process praise seems to be what NAEYC guidelines suggest and describe as encouragement. Early childhood professionals use this kind of praise as a way of giving feedback to children and motivating them to explore further and learn. Thus, if praise is given in such a way as to describe the work and effort that the child has put in, it is likely to promote further efforts to explore, learn, and achieve goals. Additionally, according to Dweck (2006), process praise puts children in a positive mindset about themselves and their abilities, encourages them to challenge themselves, and to look for different opportunities to solve problems. Examples of praise to encourage learning and achievement are:

- "I see you are working hard on this painting."
- "You really tried different ways to solve your math problems."
- "You are working so carefully on your tall tower."

2. Follow-Up Praise to Guide Behavior

Research on praise to guide a child's behavior is related to working with children with various kinds of neurological and behavioral special needs, and those with challenging behaviors. This research began with a couple of studies, first by

Zimmerman and Zimmerman in 1962, and by Becker, Madsen, Arnold, and Thomas in 1967. These studies showed that by using praise the interventionists were successful in eliminating challenging behavior and reducing aggressive behaviors in special education elementary classrooms. Studies in this area continue to grow (for an example see Dufrene, Lestremau, & Zoder-Martell, 2014; for a review see Hester, Hendrickson, & Gable, 2009; and Owen, Slep, & Heyman, 2012).

Praising to redirect and guide behavior is called *follow-up praise*. It is a positive, behavior-specific statement that follows and acknowledges an appropriate behavior in a child, and therefore reinforces the reoccurrence of that particular behavior. The rationale is that a positive description of a child's appropriate behavior would give the child positive attention, and at the same time provides a clear framework and guidance for the child about what kind of behavior would receive an attention from adults. As a result, that behavior would be more likely to be reinforced and reoccur. Examples are:

- "I see you are sitting so quietly."
- "It is great that you have your hands to yourself."
- "You are paying close attention to your teacher and your friends."
- "Good sitting so appropriately, and ready for the circle time!"
- "I can see you are angry, but you are taking deep breaths to calm yourself."

3. Appreciation Praise to Convey Meaning, Teach Values, and Promote a Sense of Belonging in the Community

The literature related to this topic examines praising children from a historical and philosophical perspective (Bayat, 2011; Quinn, 2005; Suissa, 2013). From this perspective, the issue of praise and its purpose differs from those presented above. The philosophical argument considers praising children to be not only important, but also essential (both in childrearing and in education) as a way of conveying meaning and values of the community and culture to children. Looking from this aspect, praise is related to the moral development of the child, and its use is rooted in religious teachings, which dates back at least to the 16th century (Quinn, 2005). Praising children has always been a way by which parents have conveyed moral meaning, a sense of right and wrong, and responsibility (Suissa, 2013).

In this sense, praise expresses a sense of appreciation – instead of guidance, encouragement, or approval – when the child demonstrates that he has learned cultural, familial, or community values. This kind of praise is likely to instill a sense of worth and make the child know values that are appreciated by adults (Bayat, 2011). That is, in the same way that a process praise of effort and behavior guides the child to learn and to behave appropriately, praise that describes the ethical and moral values of the child's community – such as cooperation, helpfulness, sharing, honesty, friendship – promotes a healthy social-emotional growth in the child, and helps the child develop a sense of belonging (Bayat, 2011). Examples of this type of praise are:

- "Thank you for cooperating and working together."
- "It is so nice that you gave your place in the line to your friend."
- "Well done, helping your friend learn and solve that math problem."
- "I am so glad that you told the truth."

No matter in what sense praise is used, it is important that it is descriptive, clear, and precise. Praise should never be done meaninglessly, mechanically, or excessively. When done excessively and without a purpose, praise can do the opposite of what it intends to do. Children know if and when they have worked hard or accomplished something. They recognize insincerity and know when their efforts merit attention. Lavishing unconditional praise on children can create cynicism about adults and doubt about self (Weissbourd, 2009).

Step Two: Build a Naturally Positively Reinforcing Classroom

Setting up an appropriate environment whether at home or in the classroom is the key to preventing challenging behaviors from occurring. We saw some model approaches to prevention in the classroom in Chapter 5. Here, I recommend some general strategies early childhood teachers can use to create a positively reinforcing classroom, so that challenging behaviors are less likely to occur.

A *positively reinforcing classroom* is a learning environment where adults pay children positive attention naturally and regularly, make children feel safe to explore, motivate children to learn, and engage them in learning activities that are meaningful. Basic factors that contribute to establishing a naturally and positively reinforcing classroom are directly related to the teacher's knowledge and skills in both instruction and in classroom management. Let us consider these two skill sets.

Use the Best Teaching Practices

It is no surprise that teachers who have the best practices worry less about, and in fact report fewer instances of, challenging behaviors in their classroom. There is, of course, a reason for this. Teachers who use best practices often create environments that are emotionally responsive, highly engaging, and supportive of children, and therefore children either have no need or have no chance to resort to inappropriate behaviors. Some of the important components of best practices in the early childhood classroom that are conducive to appropriate behaviors are as follow:

- *Be in charge and have a positive attitude.* Teachers who are responsive and take charge of their classrooms with a positive attitude create a nurturing atmosphere and communicate a sense of safety and positive regard for all children. These teachers notice and pay attention to all children positively (e.g. with smiles and a positive yet matter-of-fact tone of voice), with sincerity, and show genuine interest in their students.

- *Have meaningful lessons and related activities.* When lessons and daily activities are meaningful to children and are appropriate for the developmental level of children, they automatically attract children's attention and engage their interests. These lessons connect meaningfully to the lives of children and their families in their communities, answer children's natural questions, and fulfill their curiosity.
- *Understand and address learning needs promptly.* When teachers pay close attention to children, their behavioral cues, and their development, they are able to recognize learning difficulties, whether of a social-emotional, cognitive, or academic nature. The best teachers respond to various learning issues promptly by modifying lessons to meet a particular child's learning needs (e.g. use visuals, technology, and objects), designing new lessons to address a particular area of need, and by differentiating instruction and working with a child individually or in small groups regularly.
- *Engage children.* In most cases, lessons that are meaningful and interesting are automatically engaging. Some lessons may need to be taught at a fast pace so as to keep children engaged, while others may need to be instructed at a slower pace. Children who have social-emotional or cognitive special needs may also require additional assistance from the teacher or other professionals in the classroom to be engaged in all the activities of the classroom. The teacher's own interest and enthusiasm in the delivery of lessons also plays an important role. Teachers who are engaging are usually well-animated and eager to work with children.
- *Organize and utilize materials well.* Lack of appropriate materials and having too many materials are both problematic. Not having enough materials for all children can create conflict between them, while having too many materials that are not utilized can create clutter. When materials are lacking, teachers can get children involved in creating learning materials from a variety of accessible and simple materials found in day-to-day use. Creative design and use of materials is another way of engaging children meaningfully in their learning process. On the other hand, classroom clutter can be distracting and may lead to a lack of self-regulation, particularly in children with ADHD. Therefore, having a well-organized classroom is important for creating a calm and organized atmosphere.
- *Interact positively, give feedback, and promote a sense of community.* Teachers who answer children's questions promptly, positively, and in ways to promote further thinking and problem solving automatically provide role models for children for behaviors that they want to see in their classroom community.

Use a Classroom Management System

Classroom management is related to the structure and schedule of the classroom, and the implementation of a community system with values and rules. There are three basic strategies that are conducive to best practices in this system.

- *Establish and follow a routine with visual schedules.* A clear routine, whether at home or in the classroom, gives children some predictability about events and a sense of control over their environment. A clear routine also helps children regulate their own emotions and behaviors prior and according to an event. A lack of understanding regarding what is happening and what might be occurring next creates anxiety in children, specifically in those who have mental or behavioral health issues. Children with special needs, particularly those with cognitive and intellectual disability (ID), ASD, ADHD, and generalized anxiety often resort to inappropriate behaviors because they cannot predict what will come next, and therefore cannot prepare for and self-regulate accordingly. It is not enough to simply have a weekly schedule or a posted daily lesson plan schedule for the classroom. Although each classroom should have a visible and visual daily schedule for the entire class, each child with special needs should also have an individual and interactive visual schedule. Visual signs and pictures for each item on the child's schedule can be created using any of the different software designed for this purpose (e.g. Boardmaker™: http://www.mayer-johnson. com/category/boardmaker-family-3/software) or by using a picture of items representing each activity. In general, all visual schedules either for the whole class or for individual children should leave room for change and flexibility. Pictures should be removable (e.g. fastened by Velcro to schedules), and children can learn to interact with their individual and class schedule by removing and replacing pictures as they go through their daily lessons and activities.

- *Have transition plans and related activities.* Children's individual and classroom schedules should include different transition plans throughout the day. Many behavioral issues occur because change creates anxiety in children, or because some children are not ready to move to the next lesson. Simple and short transition activities that are placed in between lessons help with this. Visual transition notices like signs, timers, and the teacher's verbal notices can be a part of the transition plan and activities during the day.

- *Establish clear rules with consistent consequences.* Having no articulated rules, or having rules with no consistent consequence, creates situations that automatically lead to inappropriate behaviors. Thus, there should be clear rules with articulated reasons and consequences for various situations such as large group lessons, free play time, group and cooperative games, field trips, playing on the playgrounds, hallway, etc. Simply stating rules once or twice, without articulating the reasons, is not enough. Basic rules should be written down, illustrated with pictures when possible, posted in different areas of the school and classroom as appropriate, and be reviewed and reiterated regularly with reasons why following them is important. In learning about rules, it is important that children also learn alternative and replacement behaviors to those that are deemed inappropriate. For example, a poster may illustrate alternative behaviors, like "Don't run in the hallways; walk instead." Coming up with replacement behaviors can be part of the weekly social-emotional lessons and activities. There should be clear and logical consequences for specific instances so there are no doubts as to what consequences follow a particular behavior. Consequences should be logical and fit the infractions instead of being highly punitive and unfair (see Chapter 8 for a discussion of punishment). An example of a logical consequence for throwing a toy at a peer is that the child may not play with that toy and/or with that peer. Consequences should be enforced consistently and immediately once a rule is broken. Similarly, there should be acknowledgements (e.g. follow-up praise and statements) when rules are observed.

• *Provide a safe place (Cozy Corner) and related activities for self-regulation and calming down.* Every environment should have a quiet and safe place that is always available for children to go to in order to calm down and regulate themselves when they need to do so. This place is often called a *Cozy Corner* or a *Calming Center*. A secluded corner of the classroom can easily be converted to a Cozy Corner. The Corner should contain comfort items such as large pillows, or beanbag chairs, and sensory calming items, such as weight vests and belts, squeeze balls, and plush stuffed animals. The Cozy Corner might be used when children have difficulties regulating their emotions (e.g. at signs of or during temper tantrums, crying, anger bouts, etc.), and/or at the beginning of the day and intermittently for children with sensory integration issues. It should not be used in a way to positively reinforce inappropriate behavior, nor should it be used as a punishment. Teachers should plan carefully how best to introduce this center to children. The teacher can guide a child to go to the Cozy Corner when signs of the child's distress are seen, by saying, for example, "Olivia, let's go to the Cozy Corner to calm down." When in the Cozy Corner, the teacher can model examples of activities for calming down (e.g. deep breathing and counting to 10, squeezing pillows, or using sensory materials) to help the child learn self-soothing strategies. The goal is that the child will gradually learn to use the Cozy Corner regularly and independently as a place for self-regulation when she needs to. In addition, various calming activities should be integrated as a regular part of the schedule throughout the day. These lessons include, but are not limited to, controlled movement to slow music, listening and thinking with music, listening and drawing to music, age-appropriate and simple calming physical exercises (e.g. children's yoga), exercises for breathing and focus.

Intervention Strategies

Once challenging behaviors do occur, there are two basic intervention strategies that teachers can use for all challenging behaviors.

Differential Attention (DA) for Challenging but Non-Aggressive Behaviors

As mentioned, giving appropriate attention to all children matters. However, giving the correct kind of attention to the child who seeks attention through challenging behaviors matters even more. An important question to ask is: How can we give appropriate attention to such a child who obviously needs it, but in a way that we do not reinforce his inappropriate behavior? *Differential Attention* (DA) is an effective method for teaching the child that his challenging behavior is not the way to get attention from adults.

DA has its root in a behavioral procedure called Differential Reinforcement of Other behavior (DRO). DRO involves giving a reinforcer (e.g. giving a positive reinforcer) to a child after a period of time in which a targeted inappropriate behavior is absent (Matson et al., 2011). In this technique, a consistent delivery of a reinforcer upon appropriate behavior, while not reinforcing the inappropriate behavior, results in the reduction and gradual elimination of inappropriate behavior.

Differential Attention (DA) (Lavigne, n.d.) is a modified version of DRO in which the adult ignores the child's inappropriate behavior when it occurs, but engages with the child immediately after the inappropriate behavior stops. Turning off attention includes stopping any verbal exchange, avoiding eye contact, and having body language that demonstrates to the child that the adult's attention is not engaged (e.g. turning one's head or body away from the child). Turning on attention includes looking and/or smiling at the child, speaking to the child, having open body language, and using follow-up praise when the child shows appropriate behaviors. The example below demonstrates how DA can be used for a disruptive behavior:

Children in Ms. Daly's kindergarten classroom are waiting for Ms. Daly to begin reading a story. Ms. Daly starts by saying, "Remember, my friends, the rule of our classroom is when you want to say or ask anything, or answer a question I ask you, you should raise your hand, then wait to be called on. When I call on you, then you can speak." She then begins:

Ms. Daly: This book is about a man and his dog. Do any of you have a pet dog? (Children raise their hands.)

Kimberly: (shouts) I have a dog… I have a dog!

Ms. Daly: (Does not look at Kimberly. She turns to Michael who has raised his hand.) Michael, you have raised your hand. Do you have a dog? (While Michael is speaking, Kimberly continues to shout, "I have a dog!" Ms. Daly continues to avoid looking at Kimberly, completely ignoring her shouts.)

Ms. Daly: (After Michael finishes his answer, she turns to Melissa, who has raised her hand.) Melissa, you have your hand raised, do you want to tell us about your dog? (Kimberly stops shouting and raises her hand.)

Ms. Daly: (Immediately looks at Kimberly and smiles.) Kimberly, I see you have raised your hand. After Melissa tells us about her dog, you can speak and tell us about yours. (Melissa tells the class about her dog.)

Ms. Daly: (After Melissa finishes talking) Good waiting, Kimberly! Now tell us about your dog. (Kimberly talks about her dog.)

Differential attention is an effective strategy for harmless, yet often disruptive, behaviors such as whining, uttering inappropriate words, interrupting, or other similar behaviors that do not pose a threat to others. In our experience, adults have a hard time ignoring such behaviors because they find them annoying. Most teachers react negatively to such behaviors or are unable to ignore them completely and consistently. In fact, when children resort to minor disruptions, teachers usually respond by looking at the child pointedly, reminding them about rules, warning them about consequences, or reprimanding them. In such cases, adults inadvertently acknowledge the child's disruptive behaviors and reinforce those behaviors. Additionally, when these behaviors are not ignored completely and consistently, the child learns to insist upon those behaviors, because they have learned that insistence in one or more of those behaviors will ultimately get the adult's attention. Therefore, DA requires practice on the part of the teacher to be implemented consistently and firmly. When done consistently, all children in the classroom learn that only appropriate behaviors receive acknowledgment from the adults.

DA must never be used for dangerous or harmful behaviors, such as physical aggression toward others or self-injurious behaviors. Dangerous behaviors must never be ignored. Instead, they should be stopped and redirected, so that no harm can come to the child or to others.

Addressing Aggressive and Harmful Behaviors

In most physically aggressive children, there are specific behavioral cues that act as warning signs. For example, the child can throw a temper tantrum, cry, scream, or utter inappropriate words. If and when observed, these signs are strong cues for the teacher that the child needs redirection before any aggressive act is committed. At these times, the child can be taken to a designated center, such as a Cozy Corner, and supported by the teacher to use strategies for calming. However, in reality, the teacher can miss behavioral cues of children during the daily classroom activities. In these situations, when a dangerous behavior occurs, it is important that an adult (e.g. the teacher or another professional) follows the following steps:

- Interrupt and stop the child immediately by disengaging the child from the act (e.g. removing any other child who is the target of the aggressive act). Say, "No hitting," or "Stop."
- Guide the child by the hand or direct him to go to the Cozy Corner (e.g. "Let's go to the Cozy Corner to calm down").
- Do not reprimand or engage the aggressor.
- Avoid engaging the aggressor in a conversation.
- Make sure there are no materials that the child can throw or hurt others with in the Cozy Corner.

- Remain close by the Cozy Corner, modeling breathing and counting with a low calming voice.
- Give some time to the child to self-regulate.
- Avoid any conversation until the child is calm.
- Once the child is relatively calm, acknowledge his efforts in self-regulation with a statement, and guide him back to the classroom activities.

It is important to keep in mind that engaging in conversation about the aggressive actions immediately after the behavior might be reinforcing. Instead of doing so, if another child has been the target of an aggression, it is important to give appropriate attention to that child. A conversation about the child's behavior can take place a short period after the incident. Specific social-emotional lessons should be designed around aggression and hurting self and others, especially if a child with aggressive behaviors has developmental special needs. For example, social stories are one way of teaching children with special needs about aggression and anger (see Bayat, 2012 for details).

Step Three: Design Individual Behavior Intervention Plan (BIP)

The first step in planning an intervention for challenging behaviors in a child is to determine and pinpoint the behavior targeted for intervention. As a reminder, a challenging behavior: 1) interferes with the development, learning, and pro-social engagement and interactions of children with their peers and adults; 2) harms or may harm the child or others; and 3) may therefore put the child at risk for later social-emotional or learning problems (Chapter 1). This is important because many of the minor behavioral infractions of children are not in fact challenging and can be addressed by appropriate teaching practices and classroom management strategies. Therefore, a teacher's first step is to ask whether the behavior is frequent and severe enough to warrant designing a behavior intervention plan.

Once the behavior that is targeted for intervention is determined, a BIP can be designed with the following steps: 1) conducting observations; 2) collecting and analyzing data; 3) forming a hypothesis; 4) planning the intervention and assessing its efficacy.

Collect and Graph ABC Data and Gather Other Information

The best way to collect observation data is to create ABC (Antecedent, Behavior, Consequence) tables and take observational notes of the events leading to and following the *target* behaviors of the child within those tables. The first set of observational data, including the *frequency of behavior*, that is collected without manipulating any environmental factors or consequences are called the *baseline data*. The behavior frequency refers to the number of times a challenging behavior occurs within a specific period of time (e.g. a set period of observation, a day, etc.). Recording this frequency before and after intervention is important, because it gives us data to compare with to determine whether or not our intervention was successful in reducing or eliminating the target behavior. To have a visual representation of the change in the frequency of behavior, the behavior frequency could be graphed, using Word or Excel applications (see Figures 9.1 and 9.2).

Other important data are information about the child's development and the setting events (i.e. when the challenging behavior occurs). While information about the child's development may be obtained through direct or indirect assessment methods, details about home environmental setting events and whether or not the behavior occurs at home also are only obtainable through interview with parents or caregivers with their consent. It is important to work with parents and family members to understand what kind of consequences occur at home as a result of the child's behavior. Other setting event data, such as classroom setup, schedule, teacher's attitude and instruction, time and kinds of activities or lessons during which behavior is most likely to occur, should also be recorded for further examination. Academic report of the child from the previous year is also an important source of data that can provide information regarding the learning profile of the child.

Analyze Data, and Make a Hypothesis

Once observation and other data are obtained, they should be studied carefully for patterns to determine the function of the behavior. In the best-case scenario, more than one ABC baseline table should be obtained to see any behavioral patterns as related to antecedent and consequences. After examining all data, a hypothesis should be made about the reason for or function of the child's behavior.

Plan, Implement, and Assess an Intervention

The function of the child's behavior is the driving force behind an intervention. For example, if the function of the child's behavior is to obtain attention, then the plan of intervention should be around implementing Differential Attention and designing play sessions for the child; if the function of the behavior is to obtain a specific sensory input (e.g. tactile sensory input), the plan of intervention should be around providing the needed sensory input throughout the day so that the child's sensory needs are met.

The most effective intervention is the one that includes manipulating all factors in the control of the teacher; that is, changing setting events in the classroom environment as well as changing consequences. For example, manipulating these factors may include adjusting the teacher's attitude or behavior, which might be inadvertently contributing to the child's behavior; changing the child's schedule to address the child's behavior; creating specific targeted social-emotional lessons around the behavior of the child; and using visuals to increase communication and comprehension.

In the following sections, I present a case example of a boy named Jordan who has challenging behaviors. This case illustrates a well-designed and successful behavior intervention plan.

Case Example: Jordan

Jordan is a six-year-old boy in Ms. Williams' kindergarten classroom. Ms. Williams reports that Jordan is frequently non-compliant and gets into conflicts with peers. She reports that when Jordan gets angry, he may become aggressive toward other children. Ms. Williams admits that she sometimes loses patience with Jordan. She is particularly concerned that most of her time is spent in disciplining Jordan for inappropriate or aggressive behaviors and is seeking alternative and more positive ways of addressing Jordan's behaviors.

In terms of Jordan's development, Ms. Williams reports that Jordan has typical cognitive development for his age. He is creative and is able to complete most academic activities successfully, particularly when he is interested in a lesson. Jordan is independent in all areas of adaptive and self-help skills. His language development is generally on par with those of his peers. Jordan is physically healthy and active for his age and enjoys running, jumping, and climbing with his peers. Jordan is strong in the area of fine motor development. Jordan enjoys writing, and shows a great interest in drawing pictures.

In the area of social-emotional development, Jordan falls short of what is typically expected of children his age. Jordan has some difficulties in getting along with his peers during cooperative games or activities. He has difficulties expressing his emotions, and when he gets angry he has a hard time calming down. When getting into a conflict, he displays verbally aggressive outbursts, such as shouting or calling his peers names. On several occasions, Jordan has displayed physical aggression, such as pushing peers, or throwing objects around.

A Behavior Intervention Plan for Jordan

Julie, a graduate student, was assigned to collaborate with Ms. Williams to design a behavior intervention plan for Jordan. After obtaining consent from Jordan's guardian, his grandmother, Julie and Ms. Williams began the process of data collection and intervention.

Data Collection

Ms. Williams and Julie determined three target behaviors for intervention: non-compliance; verbal aggression, like name calling; and physical aggression, like throwing objects at others. After determining the target behaviors, Julie measured the frequency of these behaviors. Julie noted that during the first period of observation, Jordan resorted to verbal and physical aggression four times, and refused to follow the teacher's directions four times, totaling eight times on the first day of observation (Figure 9.1).

Julie also recorded one set of of ABC baseline data. Table 9.1 displays the baseline ABC data taken during the periods of social studies and math in one afternoon.

To understand home and environmental factors that might have contributed to Jordan's behaviors, Ms. Williams decided to have an interview with Jordan's grandmother, with whom Jordan lived. Jordan's grandmother agreed to a phone conversation with Ms. Williams during which Ms. Williams learned that Jordan is exposed to many environmental risk factors (i.e. poverty, parental education below high school, single parenthood). Jordan's single grandmother works two jobs to support her two other children and Jordan. Because Jordan's grandmother works long hours, Jordan is usually at home under the supervision of his teenage aunts.

Jordan's father is in jail for undisclosed reasons. Jordan's mother was a teenager at the time of Jordan's birth. She lost Jordan's custody when he was a toddler due to child physical abuse. Court proceedings resulted in the recommendation for psychiatric help for Jordan's mother, which she began receiving immediately. Recently, Jordan's mother has been granted supervised visits.

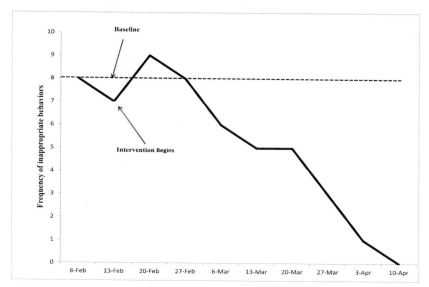

FIGURE 9.1   Frequency of Challenging Behaviors in Jordan at the Baseline and After Intervention. Jordan's Inappropriate and Aggressive Behaviors Decrease Steadily After Intervention, and Stop Completely After a Few Weeks of Consistent Intervention

Table 9.1 ABC Baseline Data for Jordan

Date/Time	Antecedent	Behavior	Consequence
1:30 pm	Teacher asks how many family members are in each child's family.	Michael, one of the students, says, "I have four in my family." Jordan says, "I have three."	Michael says, "No. You don't have three people in your family."
	Michael says, "No. You don't have three people in your family."	Jordan shouts back, "YES I DO TOO, STUPID!"	Ms. Williams tells Jordan to go to the timeout area.
1:32 pm	Ms. Williams tells Jordan to go to the timeout area.	Jordan screams "No," throws his chair on the floor, and stomps out to the timeout chair.	Ms. Williams says to Jordan loudly, "I will talk to you later."
2:15 pm	Ms. Williams asks students "How many pencils do each of you have in your supply box?"	Jordan begins to talk to Maria who sits next to him.	Ms. Williams says, "Jordan, stop talking and pay attention."
	Ms. Williams says, "Jordan, stop talking and pay attention."	Jordan stops talking, but does not look in his supply box.	Ms. Williams says to Jordan, "Jordan, I am going to count to three, while you get ready to look in your supply box. You will go to timeout if you don't. ONE…"
	Ms. Williams counts to three.	Jordan sits without doing anything.	Ms. Williams sends Jordan to timeout.
2:30 pm	Ms. Williams gives students two-digit number cards and asks them to use objects to build those numbers.*	Jordan begins to play with his supply box. He brings out five pencils.	Ms. Williams tells Jordan, "You need to go to the math table to get supplies to build your number." She removes the supply box from Jordan's desk.
	Ms. Williams removes the supply box from Jordan's desk.	Jordan shouts, "These are mine," throws his chair on the floor, and starts screaming, "I hate you. You are stupid!"	Ms. Williams approaches Jordan and takes his hand, leading him to go outside the classroom, saying, "I think we need to leave the class to calm ourselves."
2:35 pm	Ms. Williams approaches Jordan and takes his hand, leading him to go outside the classroom, saying, "I think we need to leave the class to calm ourselves."	Jordan pushes Ms. Williams's hand away, and starts throwing objects from his desk on the floor.	Ms. Williams holds Jordan from behind (in a restraint position), and with difficulty drags him outside of the classroom.**

Note: * Math table has cheerios, counting chips and math manipulatives.

** Jordan is heard continuing to scream and cry from outside of the classroom.

Hypothesis and Plan of Intervention for Jordan

Examining their ABC data (Table 9.1), Ms. Williams and Julie focused on antecedents and consequences and asked themselves the following questions:

1. Are there specific time periods in which Jordan's behaviors occur?
2. Are there specific triggers for Jordan's behaviors?
3. How are consequences effective or ineffective for Jordan's behavior?

Ms. Williams and Julie noticed that the consequences set by Ms. Williams not only maintained Jordan's behavioral outbursts, but also triggered further defiance and aggression. In such instances, consequences became antecedents for a new or repeated inappropriate behavior, creating a cycle (called AB/AB cycle). Thus, those consequences were not only inefficient but also problematic. Additionally, Jordan's behaviors were often in reaction to specific triggers related to his home environment. Given the information received from the interview with Jordan's grandmother, Julie and Ms. Williams made the following hypothesis:

> Given Jordan's home situation, the function of Jordan's challenging behavior is likely a desire to receive positive attention, emotional validation, and support from peers and adults in his environment. In addition, Jordan developmentally lacks social-emotional skills, contributing to his lack of self-regulation.

To address the function of Jordan's behavior, Julie and Ms. Williams brainstormed for a plan of intervention. They came up with the following behavior intervention plan:

1. Set up play sessions with Jordan, in which he can freely express emotions. Play sessions can also give Ms. Williams and Jordan a chance to develop a positive relationship and change the dynamics of their current interactions.
2. Use Differential Attention for defiance or non-compliance.
3. Use various kinds of praise with Jordan to encourage appropriate behaviors throughout the day.
4. Encourage and model the use of the Cozy Corner, along with exercises for calmness and relaxation throughout the day.
5. In case of physical aggression, follow appropriate steps to stop aggressive behaviors, using the Cozy Corner for isolation and calming down.
6. Design and set up small group lesson plans about appropriate expressions of various emotions, such as anger and frustrations (e.g. set up activities in which children can role play anger management and self-regulation).

Setting up Individual Play Sessions with Jordan

Ms. Williams and Julie decided to conduct short play sessions (15 to 20 minutes) with Jordan at the beginning of each day, as children arrived, or toward the end of each day, while children were getting ready to go home. Examples below are selected episodes from three play sessions with Jordan.

* *Session one*

    Jordan and Julie are in the housekeeping center. Jordan picks up a plastic banana from a toy fruit basket, points at Julie and pretends to shoot.

    Julie: My face is not for shooting, Jordan. You can choose to shoot a doll.

    Jordan: (Throws the banana back in the basket, and picks up an apple.) Okay, then I throw this… (He poses to throw the apple at Julie.)

    Julie: Toys are not for throwing. They are also not for hurting others with. If you choose to throw the apple, you choose not to play with me today.

    Jordan: (Seems to think for a few seconds. Then puts back the apple in the basket.)

    Julie: I am glad you made the choice to put back the fruit in the basket, Jordan. (Jordan plays for 15 minutes in the play session without any further episode.)

* *Session two*

    Jordan and Julie are in the Cozy Corner together. Jordan begins to punch the beanbag that is on the floor.

    Jordan: (Punching a beanbag on the floor.)

    Julie: I see you are punching the bean bag. You look like you are angry.

    Jordan: Yes, it is a stupid bean bag!

    Julie: This bean bag is stupid. You are angry at it, so you are hitting it.

    Jordan: (Stops after a few more punches.) I don't want to punch this anymore. Can we make a volcano with clay?

    Julie: Sure. (Jordan and Julia leave the Cozy Corner to get the materials for making a volcano together. The play session ends after 20 minutes.)

* *Session three*

    Jordan and Ms. Williams are in a play session together. Jordan decides to draw a picture.

    Ms. Williams: I see you are drawing a picture.

    Jordan: I am drawing a picture of you.

    Ms. Williams: Wow, you decided to draw a picture of me?

    Jordan: Yes.

    Ms. Williams: (Smiles) I see you are really focused on your drawing … It looks like you are drawing my hair now.

    Jordan: Aha. (Continues to draw.) When it is finished, it is for you!

    Ms. Williams: Thank you very much, Jordan! (Ms. Williams begins to write in her notebook.) I will write my notes while you are drawing, okay?

Jordan: Okay. (Jordan finishes the picture after a while, and hands it to Ms. Williams.)

Ms. Williams: This is very nice Jordan. I am going to take it home with me and put it on my refrigerator.

Jordan: (Smiles) Okay.

Assessment of Intervention

Together, Ms. Williams and Julie implemented Jordan's behavior intervention plan for a period of four weeks and took ABC data of their intervention. After consistent implementation of all elements of the plan, Jordan's aggressive behaviors and non-compliance began to decrease and gradually stopped completely. Table 9.2 represents a sample of ABC intervention data with Jordan, using DA and praise.

Table 9.2 Intervention with Jordan Using Differential Attention for Defiance, and Process/Follow-Up Praise for Appropriate Behavior and Work

Date/Time	Antecedent	Behavior	Consequence
March 13			
9:07 am	Ms. Williams announces Morning Meeting.	Jordan wanders around the classroom.	Ms. Williams ignores and continues with Morning Meeting.
9:08 am	Julie asks Jordan to come sit down on the rug.	Jordan comes over to his spot on the rug and sits down.	Julie praises Jordan for following directions. Ms. Williams looks and smiles at Jordan.
9:09 am	Teacher announces Literacy Station, rotation.	Jordan continues to sit on the rug.	All adults ignore Jordan.
9:10 am	Children are at their literacy stations. Teacher begins instructing them to create cards for someone they would like to show their appreciation to.	Jordan walks to his small group station and sits at the table.	Ms. Williams looks at Jordan, smiles and says, "Jordan, I am glad you are joining your station."
10:05 am	Sharing time: Children have transitioned to large group, and are taking turns to share the cards they created with the class. It is Jordan's turn to share his card.	Jordan lifts his card. "I made a card for my grandmother."	Ms. Williams says, "Jordan you worked hard on your card. Wow! You drew a big heart, and wrote: *For Grandma!*"
10:05 am	Ms. Williams says, "Jordan you worked hard on your card. Wow! You drew a big heart, and wrote: For Grandma!"	Jordan smiles, and says, "I am going to give it to my grandma."	Ms. Williams says, "That's wonderful! I think your grandma will like it."

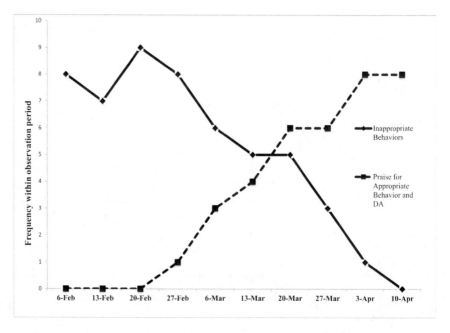

FIGURE 9.2   Change in Frequency of Challenging Behaviors in Jordan in Relationship to Increase of Praise and Differential Attention (DA). The figure illustrates that consistent positive attention for appropriate behaviors and ignoring inappropriate behaviors results in a steady decrease in, and complete elimination of, challenging behaviors.

Figure 9.2 represents a graph indicating a steady decrease in Jordan's challenging behaviors throughout the intervention period.

Looking at the intervention data, it is obvious that Ms. William's positive attention to Jordan worked well in encouraging Jordan to express his emotions appropriately, get along with his peers, and follow teachers' directions. After her experience with Jordan, Ms. Williams made positive changes in her own attitude and behavior toward the children. She also made the Cozy Corner, along with social-emotional lessons and related activities, important features of her classroom activities.

Closing Remarks

Most challenging behaviors of children can be addressed using simple strategies. In this chapter, I discussed some of these strategies. I believe that effective strategies are those that are positive, respect and acknowledge the dignity of the child, and reinforce the child's appropriate bids for attention regularly and consistently. On the other hand, when children's environments lack limit setting and behavioral guidelines, children have no firm frame of reference or guidance to regulate their own behaviors. In this situation, children often form their own behavioral rules by pushing adults' limits and challenging an authority when faced with it. Therefore, an appropriate intervention includes addressing various aspects of the classroom, teaching instruction, and the teacher's attitudes and behaviors toward children. The case example presented in this chapter showed how changing relationship dynamics between the teacher and students can address some very challenging behaviors simply and effectively.

References

Baumeister, R. F., Campbell, J. D., Krueger, J., & Vohs, K. D. (2003). Does high self-esteem cause better performance, interpersonal success, happiness, or healthier lifestyles? *Psychological Science in the Public Interest, 4*, 1–44.

Bayat, M. (2011). Clarifying issues regarding the use of praise with young children. *Topics in Early Childhood Special Education, 31*(2), 121–128.

Bayat, M. (2012). *Teaching exceptional children*. New York: McGraw Hill.

Becker, W. C., Madsen, C. H., Arnold, C. R., & Thomas, D. R. (1967). The contingent use of teacher attention and praise in reducing classroom behavior problems. *Journal of Special Education, 1*, 287–307.

Branden, N. (1969). *The psychology of self-esteem*. New York, NY: Bantam Books.

Brummelman, E., Thomaes, S., De Castro, B. O., Overbeek, G., & Bushman, B. J. (2014b). "That's not just beautiful – That's incredibly beautiful!": The adverse impact of inflated praise on children with low-esteem. *Psychological Science, 25*(3), 728–735.

Brummelman, E., Thomaes, S., Overbeek, G., De Castro, B. O., & Van den Hout, M. A. et al. (2014a). On feeding those hungry for praise: Person praise backfires in children with low self-esteem. *Journal of Experimental Psychology: General, 143*(1), 9–14.

Dufrene, B. A., Lestremau, L., & Zoder-Martell, K. (2014). Direct behavioral consultation: Effects on teachers' praise and student disruptive behavior. *Psychology in the Schools, 51*(6), 567–580.

Dweck, C. S. (1999). *Self-theories: Their role in motivation, personality and development*. Philadelphia: Taylor and Francis.

Dweck, C. S. (2006). *Mindset: The new psychology of success*. New York: NY: Random House.

Dweck, C. S. (2009). Boosting achievement with messages that motivate. *Education Canada, 47*(2), 6–10.

Gartell, D. (2007, May). Guidance matters. *Beyond the Journal: Young Children on the Web*. Retrieved from: http://www.naeyc.org/files/yc/file/200705/GuidanceMatters.pdf

Hester, P. P., Hendrickson, J., & Gable, R. A. (2009). Forty years later – The value of praise, ignoring, and rules for preschoolers at risk for behavior disorders. *Education and Treatment of Children, 32*(4), 513–535.

Kohn, A. (2001). Five reasons to stop saying, "good job!" *Young Children, 56*(5), 24–30.

Kohn, A. (2005). *Unconditional parenting*. New York: Atria Books.

Lavigne, V. (n.d.). *Tuesday's child parent training manual*. Chicago: Tuesday's Child.

Matson, J. L., Shoemaker, M. E., Sipes, M., Horowitz, M., Worley, J. A., & Kozlowski, A. M. (2011). Replacement behaviors for identified functions of challenging behaviors. *Research in Developmental Disabilities, 32*, 681–684.

Meece, D., & Soderman, A. K. (2010, September). Positive verbal environments: Setting the stage for children's social development. Reprinted from *Young Children*. Retrieved from: http://www.naeyc.org/files/yc/file/201009/MeeceOnline0910.pdf

National Association for the Education of Young Children (NAEYC). (n.d.). *10 Effective DAP teaching strategies*. Retrieved from: http://www.naeyc.org/dap/10-effective-dap-teaching-strategies

Owen, D. J., Slep, A. M., & Heyman, R. E. (2012). The effect of praise, positive nonverbal response, reprimand, and negative nonverbal response on child compliance: A systematic review. *Clinical Child Family Psychology Review, 15,* 364–385.

Pomerantz, E. M., & Kempner, S. G. (2013). Mothers' daily person and process praise: Implications for children's theory of intelligence and motivation. *Developmental Psychology, 49*(11), 2040–2046.

Quinn, N. (2005). Universals of childrearing. *Anthropological Theory, 5,* 477–516.

Skipper, Y., & Douglas, K. (2012). Is no praise good praise? Effects of positive feedback on children's and university students' responses to subsequent failures. *British Journal of Educational Psychology, 82,* 327–339.

Suissa, J. (2013). Tiger mothers and praise junkies: Children, praise and the reactive attitude. *Journal of Philosophy of Education, 47*(1), 1–19.

Weissbourd, R. (2009). *The parents we mean to be: How well intentioned adults undermine children's moral and emotional development.* New York, NY: Houghton Mifflin Harcourt.

Wierzbicka, A. (2004). The English expressions *good boy* and *good girl* and cultural models of child rearing. *Culture and Psychology, 10,* 251–278.

Yuill, N., Hinske, S., Williams, S. E., & Leith, G. (2014). How getting noticed helps getting on: Successful attention captured doubles children's cooperative play. *Frontiers in Psychology, 5*(418), 1–10.

Zimmerman, E. H., & Zimmerman, J. (1962). The alteration of behavior in a special classroom situation. *Journal of Experimental Analysis of Behavior, 5*(1), 50–60.

10

PARENTING, CULTURE, AND DISCIPLINE

Throughout this book, I have emphasized the important role parents and caregivers play in the emotional and behavioral health of children. Parenting involves a complex set of attitudes, skills, and behaviors. All of these behaviors are influenced by a multitude of factors, both individually related, such as a parent's health and developmental history, and environmentally-related, such as a parent's culture, education, and socio-economic status. Parenting is related also to the child's developmental and behavioral characteristics. Thus, parenting beliefs and practices vary among individuals and families in different social-cultural situations and personal histories.

Without question, in the last two decades there has been an unprecedented growth in the diversity – in ethnic and socio-economic backgrounds as well as family structures – of families. Children attending early childhood programs and schools in the USA reflect this diversity. Therefore, understanding parenting beliefs and behaviors can help professionals teach and relate to parents, caregivers, and children more effectively.

In this chapter, I will look at the history of parenting in the USA, and will describe the more dominant parenting beliefs and practices in a number of cultures represented extensively in the USA. I acknowledge, however, the danger of stereotyping a group's behaviors when describing their cultural practices. I respect the vast diversity and variations that exist within each culture, society, and group of people. Thus, I ask readers to keep in mind that my discussion of parenting practices is offered in the spirit of the belief that individuals in our society do not function in a static state. That is, people change with experience, age, geographic location, economic circumstances, and a host of other variables.

The Science of Parenting

Parenting requires many skills as well as demanding an incredible amount of emotional investment. While education and various media offer guidance on parenting, the lived experience requires nimble adaptation to unexpected events and challenges. In particular, contemporary parenting seems to be more demanding and stressful than at any other time in history. Parents increasingly find themselves faced with pressures and stressors on a daily basis:

> [T]he truth is there's little even the most organized people can do to prepare themselves for having children … Prospective parents have no clue what their children will be like; no clue what it will mean to have their hearts permanently annexed; no clue what it will feel like to second-guess so many seemingly simple decisions, or to be multitasking even while they're brushing their teeth, or to have a ticker tape of concerns forever whipping through their heads. Becoming a parent is one of the most sudden and dramatic changes in adult life.
>
> *(Senior, 2014, p. 3)*

Terms such as "hyper parents," or "helicopter parents," are used to describe middle-class Western parents who strive to give their children every possible opportunity and to fill their free time with enrichment activities, sports, and lessons (Mintz, 2004a). Such parents seem to deal with much anxiety related to planning and directing their children's activities. What is the origin of this hyper-vigilance and anxiety?

Parenting and its science are influenced by changes in the way a society views children and childhood, as well as by changes in society. For example, throughout the history of the USA, parenting beliefs, concerns, and behaviors changed along with the socio-political, economic, historical, and cultural developments that were taking place. In the following section, I will briefly describe some of the major changes in the USA and how they impacted views on childhood and parenting. The overview presented in this chapter is not comprehensive, nor does it examine all social and economic developments in the country. The overview highlights trends influencing parenting ideas in a social-historical context as an illustration of thinking about our current reality and as a reminder to consider the dynamic nature of social-cultural variables in thinking about parenting.

A Brief History of Parenting in the United States

From colonial America to contemporary USA, views of children in general, and parenting behaviors in particular, saw a dramatic change. Major historical and economic developments in the USA were often catalysts for change determining the role of children in the family and in society. Depending upon the view of parenting and responsibilities of children in the family, childrearing practices varied accordingly (Mintz, 2004a).

Colonial Parents

In colonial America, religion played an important influence on parenting and on childhood education (Carper, 2000). For example, in the Middle Colony, Quakers treated children with gentleness to nurture each child's "Light Within" (Mintz, 2004a). Colonial parents saw themselves as not only responsible for their children's health, but also for their souls, thus, they taught children to reflect upon their morality as well as to have a useful piety (Mintz, 2004a). Puritan parents, on the other hand, thought their newborn infants "filthy" and as soon as they were born, babies were considered sinners (Zuckerman, 2006). Puritan parents talked about death frequently and took their children to hangings, so that they might fear the consequences of their sinful actions and retributions (Mintz, 2004b).

Colonial children were considered "adults-in-training," and responsible for obeying the elders who trained them without question (Mintz, 2004a). They were watched closely for infantile corruption and any assertion of will by the child was crushed immediately (Zuckerman, 2006). Families were generally large, with at least seven to ten children (Mintz, 2004b). Fathers were the major authority in childrearing and implementers of discipline within the family (Zuckerman, 2006; Hiatt-Michael, 2008; Mintz, 2004b). Children did not have a long period of schooling, and often after a few years, when they were physically able, they were put to work in the farms and fields (Zuckerman, 2006). In working- and middle-class families, it was a common practice to send children away to relatives around age 10 or 11 to work in their relatives' homes while in affluent families it was customary to send their children to other countries for education (Zuckerman, 2006).

Parents of the American Revolution

The American Revolution brought a shifting of ideas, from patriarchy to liberty and freedom. This view accordingly influenced parenting practices. During this period, patterns of precocious autonomy began to emerge in young adolescents (Mintz, 2004b; Zuckerman, 2006). Children and youth were caught up in the socio-political conflict and many of them as young as nine or ten years old participated in various events leading up to the American Revolution (Mintz, 2004b). A shift in parenting responsibilities occurred from fathers to mothers, who took over teaching children civility, self-restraint, and literacy along with the democratic values of the new republic (Mintz, 2004a). Children became more independent and left home early, and by half a century later, by the time of the American Civil War, many children as young as nine or ten years old (African Americans or whites) left their homes to participate in the war as drummer boys, messengers, or fighters (Mintz, 2004b). During the years following the Civil War, the freedom to determine personal destiny, gained by adolescents continued as families reconstituted their lives and the great westward expansion of the country began.

Parents in 19th-Century America

By the 19th century the young country experienced rapid industrialization, commercialism, immigration from China (to build the railroads) and Europe (to escape poverty and war), as well as a new economy in the USA. The economic change brought in a new attitude toward children. Middle-class parents found more opportunities to increase financial resources, and thereby allowed an extended period of childhood and schooling for their children; whereas working-class parents looked at their children's utility function, and child labor became an important source of capital and income for the family (Hiatt-Michael, 2008; Mintz, 2004b). Working parents who could not afford to have their children in school for more than a few years, if that, put both boys and girls as young as six or seven years old to work in mines, textile mills, factories, farms, or as servants in middle-class or affluent households (Mintz, 2004b; Saad, 1989). As well, society was influenced by disease due to poor sanitation and nutrition and the absence of effective medications to combat disease. Babies were most affected by these conditions; the infant mortality rate reached its peak in the 19th century at about 18 percent (Mintz, 2004b, Zuckerman, 2006). Adults fell victim to disease as well, resulting sometimes in abandoning children to the streets in cities when relatives or strangers refused care. In rural situations, children might become "premature" adults, i.e. managing the farm, becoming the breadwinner for younger siblings.

In urban slums the effect of poverty and disease led to the establishment of institutions for children, as many poor families abandoned their children to institutional care either temporarily or permanently (Mintz, 2004b). Many adolescents left home willingly to go to orphanages or asylums. At the turn of the century about 200,000 abandoned children or teenagers left their parents' homes and were transported by the "orphan train" to rural areas to serve in the households of other families or to work on farms (Hammel, 1982; U.S. Department of Health and Human Services, 2012).

All of these social and economic changes led to an important development for parenting ideas at the turn of the century. Following the societal emphasis on science and industrialization of cities, the new popular science of psychology brought the idea of scientific study of the child, called "child study." *Child study* was initiated by G. Stanley Hall, an American psychologist and educator in the 1880s. Hall, who was influenced by psychological and educational developments in Germany, advocated for a scientific study of children as a basis for designing educational curricula and pedagogy (Metchling, 2004). He invited parents and teachers to join the scientific community in a study of their children by sending out questionnaires to collect observational records of development (e.g. physical, cognitive, and behavioral) (Metchling, 2004). The child study movement gradually resulted in the design of developmental and intelligence testing instruments in the following years, and it also created a view of parenting as a science, or a vocation grounded in one's firm scientific knowledge of one's child (Bigelow & Morris, 2001).

Another influential development at the turn of the century was the American eugenics movement. The eugenics movement advocated the elimination of the "unfit" as a way to fix the ills of society (American Eugenics Archives, n.d.). The eugenics movement resulted in various public phenomena; among the influences of this movement were the creation of laws restricting marriage and immigration, as well as sterilization of more than 60,000 individuals with intellectual disabilities (Lombardo, n.d.). Because eugenics argued the determinacy of heredity, it advocated for certain parenting practices. Starting in 1908, the movement provided "Fitter Families" and "Better Baby" competitions for the general public through a variety of family activities, in state fairs and after-church activities (Selden, n.d.). The competitor families submitted a record of their family traits and a team of doctors conducted physical and psychological examinations of family members. The family scoring the highest grade received a silver trophy. The Fitter Families contests not only gave rewards to "fit" families, but also provided advice on parenting (American Eugenics Archives, n.d.). Though the eugenics movement is considered an influential factor in the social history of the American society, its exact influence on parenting has not been determined (Golden, 2011). While child study remains an important tool for research of childhood and parenting practices, the influence of the eugenics movement faded due to the absence of empirical support. The evolution of the scientific method applied to the study of parenting and parenting practice took a turn toward increased respect for childhood as a valued phase in human development.

Parenting as a Science in the 20th Century

So, the end of the 19th century saw the beginnings of an era of advocacy for children. With it, a shift occurred in the public view of children. This view parallels the early 20th-century involvement of women in the suffragette movement, social reform advocacy, and in professions such as teaching and social services (e.g. Jane Addams, Hull House). Women were key drivers of this wave of advocacy for child welfare and child labor laws in the United States (Day, 2013; U.S. Department of Health and Human Services, 2012). An important development of the 20th century was the creation of the federal Children's Bureau in 1912. The idea of creating a Children's Bureau was conceived in 1903 by two settlement women activists, Lillian Wald, an author and nurse, and Florence Kelly, a social and political reformer. Julia Lathrop, a friend of Jane Addams at Hull House, was appointed to head the Children's Bureau in 1912 (Bradbury & Oettinger, 1962). The United States Children's Bureau was the first organization that was run and staffed completely by women (U.S. Department of Health and Human Services, 2012). The Children's Bureau focused on the well-being of children and mothers and had multiple missions.[1] However, its most important missions were to reduce the infant mortality rate and to improve children's welfare, health, and development (Golden, 2011). By the late 1920s, the Children's Bureau's efforts resulted in reducing infant mortality by about 50 percent (Mintz, 2004b). For the next two to three decades the organization became a source of research on infant mortality, infant care, child advocacy, child labor laws, child health and development, professional childcare training, and dissemination of information to parents (U.S. Department of Health and Human Services, 2012). Thus, from this early beginning, the protection of children created an ethos of care and cherishing.

An illustration of this ethos is the keeping of personal and commercial baby books, beginning in 1910 and finding a mass market as a result of the popularity of the home versions (Golden, 2001). Personal baby books were books made by mothers in which they recorded details about their infants' development, photographs, gifts, religious ceremonies, and holiday traditions (Golden & Weiner, 2011). Commercial baby books, on the other hand, were for sale and ranged from fancy and large volumes to small, cheaply printed pamphlets designed to advertise the Children's Bureau's recommendations and information on healthy child development, hygiene, and care (Golden & Weiner, 2011). A popular baby character who appeared in the commercial baby books was a toddler by the name of Charlie Flood. Charlie Flood's escapades often resulted in calamities like burns, swallowing buttons, or catching a nail in his foot; and so his mother detailed these adventures and gave advice on how to address these problems (Golden & Weiner, 2011). Baby books were, in fact, vehicles for giving culturally prescribed guidance to parents about raising their children (Golden & Weiner, 2011).

In addition, the U.S. Children's Bureau distributed developmental advice to parents in the form of a popular series of pamphlets and brochures called *Prenatal Care, Infant Care,* and *Child Care,* published between 1913 and 1914 (Bradbury & Oettinger, 1962). The Children's Bureau received thousands of letters on a daily basis from parents asking questions and seeking advice about their children (Day, 2013; Golden, 2011). Though the idea of the federal government giving advice and telling people how to raise their infants may be startling to many people today, parents valued and turned to the Children's Bureau in that era. In the years following the publication of childrearing pamphlets, *Infant Care* became the U.S. government's "bestseller" (Bradbury & Oettinger, 1962, p. 10).

By 1925, the Children's Bureau had distributed three million copies of this pamphlet; by 1965 the *Infant Care* booklets had been translated into eight languages, and another 60 million had been distributed by the late 1970s (Bigelow & Morris, 2001; Reed, 1980). The childrearing advice provided by the Children's Bureau covered topics ranging from practical advice on infant and child's hygiene, feeding, and toilet training, to advice on establishing daily routine, discipline, and addressing "bad habits" (Reed, 1980). Besides the far-ranging impact of the Children's Bureau, focusing on child welfare, the science of childhood increasingly influenced social attitudes and practices with the research of major theorists such as Benjamin Spock, whose influence began in the post-World-War-II period.

Benjamin Spock: "Trust Your Instincts, Love Your Baby"

In the years prior to World War II, mainstream childrearing advice was for parents not to show too much affection and love to their children, because parental affectionate behavior might create anxious and fearful children who are overly dependent on their parents (Bigelow & Morris, 2001). Behaviorist John Watson regularly wrote a series of short articles in the women's magazine *McCall's*, which gave similar childrearing advice (Bigelow & Morris, 2001). Watson advised parents to establish a regular four-hour schedule for feeding babies, and recommended for the children not to be hugged or kissed too often, and not to be put on one's lap; he also recommended for children to be punished if and when they misbehaved (Caulfield, 1999).

In 1946, Benjamin Spock, a pediatrician who studied psychoanalysis and believed in emphasizing the psychological aspects of children's development (Caulfield, 1999), published *Common Sense Book of Baby and Child Care*. Spock also wrote a series of childrearing advice essays in *Redbook* and *Parents* magazines beginning in the 1950s. Spock's ideas about parenting were quite opposite to the mainstream childrearing advice of the day. He told parents they knew more than they thought they did, and advised them to trust their own instincts, to feed babies according to their needs, to talk to, play with, love, and gently touch their babies (Spock, 1946). Spock also advocated for parents to allow their children to explore objects and ideas, and to have freedom of movement and choice (Spock & Parker, 1998).

Spock's childcare book, the bestselling book of the 20th century, had sold over 50 million copies by the time of his death in 1998, and to date the book has been reprinted several times; it has also been translated into 42 languages (Parry, 2011). However, by the middle of the 1970s, several social and political groups began to criticize Spock's childrearing ideas as being too permissive (Baumrind, 1966). Spock's parenting advice was blamed for a generation of "hippies" of the Vietnam era (Caulfield, 1999) who believed in "live and let live," free speech, and free love, among other values. Although Spock modified and adjusted his views over time in new editions of his book and in other publications, the basic tenets of his parenting advice remained the same.

Benjamin Spock is one of the most influential figures in parenting and parenting ideas of the 20th century. In fact, one study of American mothers conducted in the late 1950s found that at the time, two-thirds of all American mothers had read Spock's book and over 80 percent of mothers referred to his advice at least twice a month (Lewkonia, 1998).

Variations of Parenting Styles

During the 1950s and 1960s, the influence of child-centered parenting (e.g. of Spock and others) along with contemporary theories in developmental psychology (such as cognitive learning, attachment theory, and social learning theories) began to influence the views of and attitudes toward children and their development and learning. Thus, these child-centered views weakened the dominance of behaviorism in mainstream culture. At the same time, studying parenting behaviors became of interest to some scholars.

In 1966, Diana Baumrind, a developmental psychologist, undertook a study of a group of preschool children and their parents using interviews and observations to investigate variations in parenting behaviors. Baumrind (1966, 1967) identified two aspects or dimensions of parenting, *parental responsiveness* and *parental demandingness*. Parental responsiveness refers to "affective warmth and autonomy support (actions that intentionally foster individuality and rationality by involving children in decision making)" (Baumrind, 2013, p. 420). Parental demandingness is "parents' readiness to confront a defiant child and to require mature behavior and compliance with parental directives" (Baumrind, 2013, p. 420).

Baumrind found that there are four general styles of childrearing that exist in most parents' repertoire (for details see Baumrind, 1966, 1967, 1968, 1971, 2012, 2013): 1) authoritarian; 2) authoritative; 3) permissive; and 4) neglectful. Many families use one style exclusively while others use them in combination. Sometimes mothers and fathers employ distinctive styles that are not in concert with each other. These styles extended across the two basic aspects of parental behavioral dimensions (i.e. responsiveness, and demandingness). Parenting styles may accompany specific parenting practices, and although each parenting style tends to have particular parenting practices and behaviors accompanying it, the styles can overlap from one to the next. For example, parental discipline is a singular parenting practice, and while each parenting style is likely to adhere to use a particular discipline strategy with children (for example, authoritarian parents are likely to use corporal punishment), it does not follow that other parenting styles do not use the same strategy (in that authoritative parents may on occasion use corporal punishment as well). Baumrind's parenting styles are applied around the world in studies of parenting and are one of the most well-known and frequently cited studies in child development and parenting. Let us briefly describe these four styles of parenting.

Authoritarian Parenting

Authoritarian parenting is a restrictive, controlling, and punitive style of parenting. Authoritarian parents are highly controlling. They set strict limits and rules on their child's behaviors and verbal exchanges and enforce rules rigidly. They believe using force, threat, and punishment is more effective in shaping their child's behavior than reasoning. Authoritarian parents are concerned with their power status and are usually angered by disobedience or a lack of conformity. Therefore, they usually use corporal punishment and other coercive methods to manage misbehavior. Authoritarian parents do not reason or make explanations to their child, and therefore they usually use power assertion without warmth or reciprocal communication (Baumrind, 2013). Baumrind (1966, 1967) explained that children of authoritarian parents are likely to be unhappy, fearful, anxious, or aggressive. They may be immature and less independent, since they are not allowed to challenge the authority of the parental figure.

Authoritative Parenting

Authoritative parenting is a more democratic form of parenting. Authoritative parents set limits for their child, and control their child's action through the observance of limit enforcement. However, they allow a high amount of verbal give-and-take and explanations with their child. Authoritative parents set clear expectations for their child, and demand maturity and independence of their child as she grows up. Although they maintain control on the child when the child is young, they gradually cease control and allow for more autonomy as the child gets older. Although authoritative parents enforce rules and directives, they provide explanations for their child and engage him in discussion of rules. Authoritative parents typically do not use corporal punishment. However, they will deter non-compliance by forceful demand or with punishment if arguments and reasoning do not suffice to persuade their child to follow rules (Baumrind, 2013). Authoritative parents tend to maintain close relationships with their child. Baumrind (1966, 2012) believed that children who have authoritative parents tend to be happy, have better self-regulation, and be self-reliant and achievement oriented. These children tend to maintain good relationships with their peers and adults, as well as with their siblings and parents.

Permissive/Indulgent Parenting

Permissive/indulgent parenting is a highly involved style of parenting. Permissive parents place few demands on their children. They believe their child should regulate his own behavior, so they set few, if any, firm limits, and do not enforce strict rules. Indulgent parents are warm and highly responsive to their child's wants. They rarely assert power over their child. Children of permissive parents seem to be creative and confident. However, they tend to have difficulties regulating their own behaviors, may be non-compliant, and have problems with peer relationships.

Neglectful Parenting

Neglectful parenting is an uninvolved form of parenting. Neglectful parents do not show consistent warmth toward their child. Generally, they are not very responsive, nor do they put much demand on their child (e.g. let the child do as she wants). In some extreme cases, neglectful parents may be rejecting of their child. Children who have neglectful parents tend to have a sense that they are not important in their parents' lives. They often have problems with social competence and self-esteem and tend to be immature. They are likely to form negative relationships with their parents or become alienated from them as they grow up. Although these styles of parenting are still observed in society today, there are various social nuances that shape today's perception of parenting practices.

Modern Western Parenting of Today: Helicopter Parenting

The socio-political, economic, and cultural landscape of the USA dramatically changed between colonial times and the beginning of the 20th century. In the 21st century, change continues in an era of information technology, media-driven ideology, increased transparency of information, as well as economic and cultural diversity. Ideas and information (whether research-based or otherwise) are disseminated and exchanged quicker than they are completely articulated. In addition, rapid globalization makes cultural boundaries a thing of the past. It is either as a result of, or in reaction to, this increased social complexity that parenting seems to have become more intricate than ever before.

Both scholarly and popular literature and media describe a rise in (middle-class) parental anxiety (Cucchiara, 2013). Either accurately or inaccurately, parents are portrayed to be in a state of constant panic over their children (e.g. their development, health, self-esteem, achievement and success, etc.). Media focuses on specific parenting behaviors, which are perceived to be dominant in most middle-class parents in Western and developed countries. One such focus is on a commonly cited contemporary parenting style called *helicopter parenting*.

Helicopter Parents

The term *helicopter parenting* was coined by Cline and Fay (1990) in a popular parenting book and soon found its way to media. Helicopter parenting is also called "overinvolved parenting," "intensive parenting," and "over parenting." Helicopter parents are those who continually "hover" over their children's head, constantly communicating with them, directing and intervening in their affairs (even when they are older and should be autonomous), making decisions for them, removing obstacles from their paths, and investing in their children's personal goals (Locke, Campbell, & Kavanagh, 2012; Odenweller, Booth-Butterfield, and Weber, 2014). Overinvolved parents also seem to arrange multitudes of after-school activities for their children when they are young, in an effort to improve their children's developmental skills and perhaps make them happier.

Research on helicopter parenting is just beginning to emerge. Some studies show that children's involvement with too many activities has no link to either better skills development or increased happiness (Schiffrin, Godfrey, Liss, & Erchull, 2014). Other studies established that helicopter parenting of children raised in 1980s and 1990s (also called millennials) may lead to creating poor outcome for these now young adults. Common negative outcomes are cited as poor resilience, a sense of entitlement, poor life skills to cope with difficulties, reduced sense of responsibility, high anxiety, and depression (Locke et al., 2012; Nelson, 2010;

Padilla-Walker & Nelson, 2012; Odenweller et al., 2014; Pomerantz & Moorman, 2007; Sergin, Woszidlo, Givertz, Dauer, & Murphy, 2012).

It is not quite clear where helicopter parenting fits in Baumrind's topography of parenting styles. In one study (Sergin et al., 2012), the style of helicopter parenting seemed to have several elements in common with all three styles of parenting. For example, both permissive and helicopter parents remove obstacles from their children's path and are highly involved, both authoritarian and helicopter parents are highly controlling of their children, and both authoritative and helicopter parents feel responsible for managing their children's moods and feelings.

In a more recent study, Odenweller et al. (2014) found that although the helicopter parenting style is more benevolent in nature than authoritarian parenting (e.g. helicopter parents have healthy parental behaviors such as advice giving and emotional support), the common negative results for children in both of these styles show a strong positive relationship between these parenting styles than others. Both authoritarian and helicopter parenting styles are highly controlling styles. They both tend to impair children's healthy social-emotional development and reasoning by not allowing the child to develop independent healthy reasoning and decision making. Although helicopter parenting may have a positive short-term effect for the child, in the long run the child's unaccustomed mentality to failure will have very negative results for social and emotional functioning and well-being in adulthood.

Influence of Cultural Upbringing on Parenting Styles

Parenting is probably the most important way a culture is reproduced and transmitted from one generation to the next. Children get a sense of their culture, values, and daily practices through their ongoing interactions with their parents from the day they are born (Cauce, 2008). Similarly – though it is by no means the only influential factor – culture influences how individuals parent their own children, what kind of parenting practices they adhere to, and how they communicate and interact with their children on a daily basis. It is difficult to tease apart the exact influence and extent of culture on parenting, mostly because one's culture is shaped not only by one's own upbringing and ethnicity, but also by one's own developmental history, including: environment, neighborhood, education, economic resources, religion, as well as unique personal contextual and psychological background. To add to the complexity, as I mentioned at the beginning of this chapter, culture is not a monolithic entity, and there are variations of culture – sometimes quite vast – in each group of people. Therefore, parents come to have an overall style, and choose particular parenting practices, depending on a variety of complex cultural and non-cultural factors. For example, the child's own development, temperament, and behavioral characteristics influence parenting styles and practices as well.

Since Baumrind's studies, numerous cross-cultural studies have examined the influence of culture on parenting styles and practices (for examples see Bornstein et al., 1998; Harkness & Super, 2002; Hulei, Zevenbergen, & Jacobs, 2006; and Im, Kim, & Sung, 2014). These studies articulate that parents form their worldview regarding parenting based on their cultural socialization. For example, parents teach their children skills to be successful based on the standards by which their specific culture defines success (Harkness & Super, 2002). In many cultures (e.g. Chinese, African, Middle Eastern, etc.), combined spiritual/religious and cultural philosophies together influence parenting styles and practices.

Certain styles of parenting seem to be more compatible with and prevalent in certain cultures as compared to others. For example, in collectivist cultures, in which members of families and communities are interdependent (e.g. Asian and East Asian, Middle Eastern, African, Latin American, etc.), authoritarian styles of parenting seem to be more compatible with their cultural goals and therefore are more prevalent (Choi, Kim, Kim, & Park, 2013). In individualistic cultures (e.g. European, U.S., other Western developed countries), on the other hand, where cultural goals center around a person's independence, authoritative parenting style seems to be more prevalent (Choi, Kim, Kim, & Park, 2013; Deater-Deckard et al., 2011). In general, these are the certain themes that are documented in the research related to diverse groups. In the following sections, I will describe some of them.

Themes on Parenting in African-American Families

Like all parents, African-American parents go through day-to-day tensions, problems, issues, and anxieties of parenting. However, due to a history of discrimination, African-American parents face much higher levels of stressors, tensions, and difficulties as opposed to the majority culture in the USA. I cannot put it any better than Moore and McDowell (2014) put it: that compared to other parents, African-American parents feel like their children are under a two-ton car, whereas other parents only have to lift a toy car to protect their children:

> Many of the issues that African Americans face in parenting are rooted within the social and structural inequities found in laws, politics, cultural ethos, and history. Until these issues are addressed, when teaching their children responsibility, discipline, awareness, and commitment, African American parents will continue to feel as if they are picking up a two-ton car instead of a toy car without the proper tool.
>
> *(Moore & McDowell, 2014, p. 124)*

Because women often head most African-American households in the USA, research on parenting among African Americans has focused mostly on mothers. African-American mothers are characterized as being at a cumulative disadvantage (Arditti, Burton, & Neeves-Botelho, 2010; Greene & Garner, 2012). Cumulative disadvantage is characterized by multiple risk factors that are relative to parenting, such as living in a poor neighborhood, single-parent households, parental unemployment, having physical and/or mental health problems, having three or more children, or being a member of a racially, ethnically, or socio-economically disadvantaged group (Arditti et al., 2010). Studies show that African-American mothers are faced with higher levels of stress as compared with their white counterparts (Greene & Garner, 2012). This is particularly so for African-American mothers who are from lower-income households as compared to African-American mothers from middle-income or high-income families (Christie-Mizell, 2006).

African-American parents raise their children to face many challenges that they know they will face. Most African-American parents are adamant that their children should be able to follow an adult's directives and rules. In fact, traditionally and historically, there is a large emphasis and strong attitude on the child's obedience of adults, more so than any other aspect of parenting and family life (Christie-Mizell, 2006). African-American parents are more likely to say that their parenting is shaped by their religion and by the way they were raised and parented themselves (Spicer, 2010).

One repeated theme in the literature is that African-American parents often adhere to physical punishment and coercive methods of discipline. However, it is not established whether this is because African Americans believe physical punishment is the most appropriate method of addressing misbehavior, or because they follow a more traditional parenting idea (Greene & Garner, 2012). Research shows that African-American parents who are under increasing stress and who deal with lack of economic resources are more likely to use corporal punishment (Westbrook, Harden, Holmes, Meisch, & Whittaker, 2012). It is argued that African-American parents who use coercion or physical punishment may not necessarily display negative emotions in their overall interactions with their children, or withdraw their affection from their children, and so their children may not interpret physical discipline as parental rejection (Arditti et al., 2010). The emphasis on social conformity in the African-American parenting style may have grown in particular due to the parents' own experience with discrimination and institutionalized racism, for they know that the cost of misbehavior in the larger social context may create dire consequences for their children.

It is important to note that African Americans are a heterogeneous group, and not all African-American parents use or deem corporal punishment or other coercive methods effective modes of discipline (Greene & Garner, 2012). It is also important to clarify here that using physical punishment does not necessarily mean that these parents have an authoritarian style of parenting. Although it is established that African Americans tend to have an authoritarian parenting style, other parenting styles exist among them as well, despite the mode of discipline they might use.

Immigrant Families

Migration is part of the reality of many families around the world. In some parts of the world (e.g. in Europe and the United States), immigrant families form a considerable portion of the population. Aside from possibly facing new views of children and childrearing, immigrant families deal with other new issues (such as a different language and/or religion, social structure, employment, etc.), which influence parenting as well as child development. Racial, ethnic, religious, and cultural diversity is greatest among the children from immigrant families compared to children of non-immigrant families (Hernandez, Denton, & Macartney, 2008).

Immigration sometimes means that parents find parenting ideas and practices of the host culture to be in conflict with those of their own. This adds an additional layer of complexity and stress to the daily interactions between immigrant parents and their children. Thus, for immigrant families parenting acculturation involves ongoing negotiation between the parenting practices of the host and heritage culture (Bornstein & Lansford, 2010). In fact, discords and conflicts between the parents and the child are stronger when the immigrant parents adhere to parenting practices that are related to their original cultural values in a host culture, which has a totally different set of values that their child adopts. In this situation conflicts between parents and children, particularly during adolescence, are common and cause serious issues. Studies show that in such situations, children of immigrant families may end up having a host of emotional and behavioral issues, such as peer problems, psychological distress, anxiety, and depression (Daglar, Melhuish, & Barnes, 2011; Hernandez et al., 2008). Some immigrant parents, on the other hand, may adjust to the demands of the new context to maintain a balance between their traditional parenting values and the host culture's parenting values. Here, I will briefly examine some of the common themes that the literature has identified regarding parenting in immigrant families.

Latino Cultures

Latino populations come from different countries including those in North, South, and Central America, as well as the Caribbean islands. In the USA, Latinos form the largest and fastest growing ethnic group of immigrants (Galzada, Huang, Anicama, Fernandez, & Brotman, 2012; Leidy, Guerra, & Toro, 2012). Most Latino families migrating to the USA come from Spanish-speaking countries (except for Brazilian and some Caribbean populations) with predominantly Roman Catholic backgrounds (Hernandez et al., 2008).

Latinos are a highly heterogeneous group in terms of socio-economic and ethnic makeup. However, Latino cultures have many similarities, which may be related partly to their common colonial legacy. Latino cultures are collectivist and put a high value on extended family and community membership, and interdependence of all members (Leidy et al., 2012). Latino parents are often characterized as being warm, nurturing, and responsive, displaying open physical and verbal affections and expressions; but they are also perceived as being controlling (Fagan, 2000; Galzada et al., 2012). Latino parents often seek proximity to their children, frequently engage in verbal interactions, and use modeling and visual cues in teaching and socializing their children (Fagan, 2000; Jabagchourian, Sorkhabi, Quach, & Strage, 2014). Parenting styles of Latino immigrants are diverse, with fathers tending to be more permissive as compared to mothers (Jabagchourian et al., 2014). However, some authoritarian parenting practices (e.g. controlling behaviors, verbal and corporal punishment) might overlap in all prevalent styles of parenting (e.g. authoritative or permissive) among Latino families (Perez & Fox, 2008).

Latino immigrant families historically faced many social and economic issues, such as discrimination based on ethnicity and legal status, unemployment or illegal employment, language barriers, and acculturation (Leidy et al., 2012). A difference in the level of acculturation between parents and their children sometimes leads to a power imbalance between parent and child. Given that Latino parents usually lose their extended family by coming to the States, they find themselves struggling with parenting issues along with all the other social and economic barriers which they have to face (Leidy et al., 2012). Therefore, the families do not have the traditional extended family support enjoyed in their home countries.

Asian Cultures

Traditional Asian cultures (including East Asian) are collectivistic, with an emphasis on interdependence, conformity, emotional control, and humility (Choi et al., 2013). The sense of obligation to family is high in Asian traditions, and obedience to parents and elders is valued (Chao & Tseng, 2002). Asian-American parenting has often been portrayed as authoritarian, harsh, and controlling, with little expression of emotion. Asian parents are highly achievement oriented and put a great value on social and economic success (Chao & Tseng, 2002; Im et al., 2014).

Chinese immigrant families are currently the largest number of Asian immigrants in the USA (Cheah, Leung, & Zhou, 2013). Chinese parenting is influenced by Confucian values on filial piety; honor; obedience toward parents; self-reliance; and emotional constraint (Cheah et al., 2013; Lau, 2010). The term *tiger parenting* became popular with Chua's (2011) book, *Battle Hymn of the Tiger Mother*. Chua described her experience as a second-generation Chinese-American parent, which emphasized a rigorous schedule and expectation of excellence in all school and leisure pursuits. Tiger parenting is now used to refer to a style of Asian parenting; it is an authoritarian, intense parenting style with a reliance on firm and harsh punishment (Chua, 2011; Lau, 2010; Lui & Rollock, 2013). Despite their own experience with strict parenting, Asian-American parents seem to acculturate to Western parenting styles successfully for the most part, combining practices from authoritative and authoritarian parenting styles (Cheah et al., 2013).

Middle Eastern Cultures

Middle Eastern cultures are located around the Persian Gulf, between Saudi Arabia and India, and consist of heterogeneous groups of people (Arabs, Afghans, Israelis, Persians/

Iranians, Armenians, and Turks) with different religions such as Islam, Judaism, Christianity, and Zoroastrianism. Middle Eastern immigrants have settled in the USA since the 19th century, although partly due to their small population, their parenting and other related issues are not of special interest to the West. Since 2011, terrorism, war, and political conflict brought the cultures of the Middle East, particularly those of Islamic nations, to the public's attention in the USA and other countries of the world.

Studies on parenting practices and styles in Middle Eastern groups are scarce. One study conducted in the different regions of Middle East (Dwairy et al., 2006) found that three clusters of parenting styles exist across various societies in the Middle East, and that each of these clusters indicates a wide range of orientation. These clusters are: 1) controlling orientation parenting, a combination of authoritarian and authoritative styles; 2) flexible parenting, a combination of authoritative and permissive parenting; and 3) inconsistent, a combination of two opposite styles of authoritarian and permissive parenting (Dwairy et al., 2006). With some exceptions (e.g. Ali & Fredrickson [2010] which examined Pakistani parenting practices in the UK), very few studies have examined parenting practices of immigrant Middle Easterners.

Parental practices of Muslim Middle Eastern parents are dominated by the Islamic identity and culture (Oweis, Gharaibeh, Maaitah, Gharaibeh, & Obeisat, 2012). Parenting values influenced by Islam revolve around respect for elders, obedience to parents and rules, and strict gender roles. These gender roles often dictate different socialization goals for boys and girls in Middle Eastern parenting practices. Mothers are responsible for the upbringing of children, and discipline practices may include corporal and verbal punishment (Ali & Fredrickson, 2010).

African Traditions

The adage, "it takes a whole village to raise a child," has its origin in the African traditions. Within most African philosophies and traditions, what constitutes a family structure is not only the parents and children, but also grandparents, uncles, aunts, cousins, and close neighbors in the village or community, with each member having a specific role in childrearing (Bledsoe & Sow, 2011). For example, siblings have a substantial role in the socialization of younger siblings, and neighbors and extended family members take on implementing discipline, supervising, or taking care of the child as needed. An authoritarian parenting style seems to be the most prevalent, with the father and elders in the family having the most authority. African traditions put an emphasis on instilling discipline and establishing family and community expectations in their children (Renzaho, Green, Mellor, & Swinburn, 2011).

African families immigrating to Western countries face a tension between the old collectivist and the new individualist culture, and parents therefore have to adjust their roles and expectations accordingly (Renzaho et al., 2011). For example, traditionally Africans adhere to a gender-specific and hierarchical structure in the family, with the father being at the head of the family, and the mother and sons sometimes consulted with (Bledsoe & Sow, 2011). Therefore, changes in the roles between husband and wife and conflict between parents and children are common after immigration (Renzaho et al., 2011).

Some West African parents, who migrate to the Europe or the USA, are concerned about what they see as the "Western tendency to coddle and spoil children and to restrict parents' access to the discipline they may deem necessary for bringing a child into line" (Bledsoe & Sow, 2011, p. 748). In such cases, particularly when the child shows some discipline concerns, these parents may send their child back to Africa to live in an extended family household – for certain durations, often a few years – as a way to protect the child against the host cultural values (Bledsoe & Sow, 2011). In general, African immigrant parents tend to remain authoritarian, expect obedience from the child, monitor and supervise their child very closely, and use both punishment and rewards to control their child's behavior.

Closing Remarks

From the beginning of the nation's inception, parenting in the USA has had a colorful history and evolution. In contemporary USA, parenting practices are as diverse as the socio-economic and ethnic, religious, and racial groups that make up the population of the nation. In this chapter, presented with some attention to historical context, I reviewed some of the more prominent and common parenting styles and practices among the major groups of people in the country. I do not claim that this chapter is a comprehensive review of parenting in the USA; however, I hope that this focus will be a good beginning for additional discussion and study of the science of parenting and the influences parenting practices have for early childhood professionals' and parents' collaboration.

Note

1. Currently, the Children's Bureau is part of the United States Department of Health and Human Services' Administration for Children and Families. The work of the Bureau today is focused on prevention of child abuse, foster care, and adoption.

References

Ali, S., & Fredrickson, N. (2010). The parenting dimensions of British Pakistani and White mothers of primary school children. *Infant and Child Development, 20,* 313–329.

American Eugenics Archives. (n.d.). *Virtual exhibits: Image archives on the American Eugenics movement.* Retrieved from: http://www.eugenicsarchive.org/eugenics/list2.pl

Arditti, J., Burton, L., & Neeves-Botelho, S. (2010). Maternal distress and parenting in the context of cumulative disadvantage. *Family Process, 49*(2), 142–164.

Baumrind, D. (1966). Effects of authoritative parental control on child behavior. *Child Development, 37*(4), 887–907.

Baumrind, D. (1967). Child-care practices anteceding three patterns of preschool behavior. *Genetic Psychology Monographs, 75*(1), 53–88.

Baumrind, D. (1968). Authoritarian vs. authoritative parental control. *Adolescence, 3*(11), 255–272.

Baumrind, D. (1971). Current patterns of parental authority. *Developmental Psychology Monograph, 4*(1), 1–103.

Baumrind, D. (2012). Authoritative parenting revisited: History and current status. In R. E. Lazelere, A. S. Morris, and A. W. Harist (Eds.), *Authoritative parenting: Synthesizing nurturance and discipline for optimal child development* (pp. 11–34). Washington, DC: American Psychological Association.

Baumrind, D. (2013). Is a pejorative view of power assertion in the socialization process justified? *Review of General Psychology, 17*(4), 420–427.

Bigelow, K. M., & Morris, E. K. (2001). John B. Watson's advice on child rearing: Some historical context. *Behavioral Development Bulletin, 1,* 26–30.

Bledsoe, C. H., & Sow, P. (2011). Back to Africa: Second chances for the children of West African immigrants. *Journal of Marriage and Family, 73,* 747–762.

Bornstein, M. H., Haynes, O. M., Azuma, H., Galperin, C., Maital, S., & Ogino, M., et al. (1998). A cross-national study of self-evaluations and attributions in parenting: Argentina, Belgium, France, Israel, Italy, and the United States. *Developmental Psychology, 34,* 662–676.

Bornstein, M. H., & Lansford, J. E. (2010). Parenting. In M. H. Bornstein (Ed.), *Handbook of cultural developmental science* (pp. 259–277). New York: Psychology Press.

Bradbury, D. E., & Oettinger, K. B. (1962). *Five decades of action for children: A history of the Children's Bureau.* U.S. Department of Health Education and Welfare, Social Security Administration. Retrieved from: http://www.mchlibrary.info/history/chbu/2628.PDF

Carper, J. C. (2000). Pluralism to establishment to dissent: The religious and educational context of home schooling. *Peabody Journal of Education, 75*(1&2), 8–19.

Cauce, A. M. (2008). Parenting, culture, and context: Reflections on excavating culture. *Applied Developmental Science, 12*(4), 227–229.

Caulfield, R. (1999). "Trust yourself": Revisiting Benjamin Spock. *Early Childhood Education Journal, 26*(4), 263–265.

Chao, R. K., & Tseng, V. (2002). Parenting of Asians. In M. H. Bornstein (Ed.), *Handbook of parenting* (Vol. 4, pp. 59–93). Mahwah, NJ: Erlbaum.

Cheah, C. S., Leung, C. Y., & Zhou, N. (2013). Understanding "tiger parenting" through the perceptions of Chinese immigrant mothers: Can Chinese and U.S. parenting coexist? *Asian American Journal of Psychology, 4*(1), 30–40.

Choi, Y., Kim, Y. S., Kim, S. Y., & Park, I. J. K. (2013). Is Asian American parenting controlling and harsh? Empirical testing of relationships between Korean American and Western parenting measures. *Asian American Journal of Psychology, 4*(1), 19–29.

Christie-Mizell, C. A. (2006). The effects of traditional family and gender ideology on earnings: Race and gender difference. *Journal of Family and Economic Issues, 27,* 48–71.

Chua, A. (2011). *Battle hymn of the tiger mother.* New York: Penguin Press.

Cline, F. W., & Fay, J. (1990). *Parenting with love and logic: Teaching children responsibility.* Colorado Springs, CO: Pinon.

Cucchiara, M. (2013). "Are we doing damage?" Choosing an urban public school in an era of parental anxiety. *Anthropology & Education Quarterly, 44*(1), 75–93.

Daglar, M., Melhuish, E., & Barnes, J. (2011). Parenting and preschool child behavior among Turkish immigrant, migrant and non-migrant families. *European Journal of Developmental Psychology, 8*(3), 261–279.

Day, N. (2013). *The U.S. Children's Bureau: Parenting advice from Uncle Sam.* Retrieved from: http://www.slate.com/blogs/how_babies_work/2013/04/23/history_of_parenting_advice_the_u_s_children_s_bureau.html

Deater-Deckard, K., Lansford, J. E., Malone, P. S., Alampay, L. P., Sorbing, E., Bacchini, D., ... Al-Hassan, S. M. (2011). The association between parental warmth and control in thirteen cultural groups. *Journal of Family Psychology, 25*, 790–794.

Dwairy, M., Achoui, M., Abouserie, R., Farah, A., Ghazal, I., & Fayad, M. et al. (2006). Parenting styles in Arab societies: A first cross-regional research study. *Journal of Cross-Cultural Psychology, 37*(3), 1–18.

Fagan, J. (2000). African American and Puerto Rican American parenting styles, parental involvement, and Head Start social competence. *Miller-Palmer Quarterly, 46*(4), 592–612.

Galzada, E. J., Huang, K. Y., Anicama, C., Fernandez, Y., and Brotman, M. (2012). Test of a cultural framework of parenting with Latino families of young children. *Cultural Diversity and Ethnic Minority Psychology, 18*(3), 285–296.

Golden, J. (2011, September). *Science of parenting* [Video Recording]. Keynote presented at Monitoring Parents: Science, Evidence, Experts, and the New Parenting Culture. Canterbury, UK: University of Kent. Retrieved from: https://www.youtube.com/watch?v=Ex5dg_gNoaM

Golden, J., & Weiner, L. (2011). Reading baby books: Medicine, marketing, money and the lives of American infants. *Journal of Social History, 44*(3), 667–687.

Greene, K., & Garner, P. W. (2012). African American mothers' disciplinary responses: Associations with family background characteristics, maternal childrearing attitudes, and child manageability. *Journal of Family Economic Issues, 33*, 400–409.

Hammel, E. A. (1982, September). *The value of children during industrialization: Childhood sex rations in nineteenth century America.* Paper presented at the Annual Meeting of the American Sociological Association, San Francisco, CA.

Harkness, S., & Super, C. M. (2002). Culture and parenting. In M. H. Bornstein (Ed.), *Handbook of parenting: Vol. 2. Biology and ecology of parenting* (2nd ed., pp. 253–280). Mahwah, NJ: Erlbaum.

Hernandez, D. J., Denton, N. A., & Macartney, S. E. (2008). Children in immigrant families: Looking to America's future. *Social Policy Report, 22*, 3–23.

Hiatt-Michael, D. (2008). Families, their children's education, and the public school: An historical review. *Marriage & Family Review, 43*(1/2), 39–66.

Hulei, E., Zevenbergen, A. A., & Jacobs, S. C. (2006). Discipline behaviors of Chinese American and European American mothers. *Journal of Psychology, 140*(5), 459–475.

Im, H., Kim, E., & Sung, K. (2014). Korean working mothers' parenting style in Korea and in the United States: A qualitative comparative study. *Journal of Cultural Diversity, 21*(1), 36–43.

Jabagchourian, J. J., Sorkhabi, N., Quach, W., & Strage, A. (2014). Parenting styles and practices of Latino parents and Latino fifth graders' academic cognitive, social, and behavioral outcomes. *Hispanic Journal of Behavioral Sciences, 36*(2), 175–194.

Lau, A. S. (2010). Physical discipline in Chinese American immigrant families: An adaptive culture perspective. *Cultural diversity and ethnic minority psychology, 16*(3), 313–322.

Leidy, M. S., Guerra, N. G., & Toro, R. I. (2012). Positive parenting, family cohesion, and social competence among immigrant Latino families. *Journal of Latino Psychology, 1*(S), 3–13.

Lewkonia, R. (1998, September 5). Benjamin Spock: The public pediatrician. *Lancet, 352*, 825–826.

Locke, J. Y., Campbell, M. A., & Kavanagh, D. (2012). Can a parent do too much for their child? An examination by parenting professionals of the concept of overparenting. *Australian Journal of Guidance and Counseling, 22*(2), 249–269.

Lombardo, P. (n.d.). Eugenics laws against race mixing, Eugenics sterilization laws, Eugenics laws restricting immigration. *American Eugenics Archives, virtual exhibits: Image archives on the American Eugenics movement*. Retrieved from: http://www.eugenicsarchive.org/eugenics/list2.pl

Lui, P. P., & Rollock, D. (2013). Tiger mother: Popular and psychological scientific perspectives on Asian culture and parenting. *American Journal of Orthopsychiatry, 83*(4), 450–456.

Metchling, J. (2004). Child-rearing advice literature. In P. S. Fass (Ed.), *Encyclopedia of children and childhood: In history and society*. New York & London: Macmillan Reference USA. Retrieved from: http://www.faqs.org/childhood/Bo-Ch/Child-Rearing-Advice-Literature.html

Mintz, S. (2004a). Parenting. In P. S. Fass (Ed.), *Encyclopedia of children and childhood: In history and society*. New York & London: Macmillan Reference USA. Retrieved from: http://www.faqs.org/childhood/Me-Pa/Parenting.html; https://cb100.acf.hhs.gov/history

Mintz, S. (2004b). *Huck's raft: A history of American childhood*. Cambridge: Belknap Press of Harvard University Press.

Moore, N., & McDowell, T. (2014). Expanding Adlerian application: The tasks, challenges, and obstacles for African American parents. *Journal of Individual Psychology, 70*(2), 114–127.

Nelson, M. (2010). *Parenting out of control: Anxious parents in uncertain times*. New York: University Press.

Odenweller, K. G., Booth-Butterfield, M., & Weber, K. (2014). Investigating helicopter parenting, family environments, and relational outcomes for Millennials. *Communication Studies, 65*(4), 407–425.

Oweis, A., Gharaibeh, M., Maaitah, R., Gharaibeh, H., & Obeisat, S. (2012). Parenting from a Jordanian perspective: Findings from a qualitative study. *Journal of Nursing Scholarship, 44*(3), 242–248.

Padilla-Walker, L. M., & Nelson, L. J. (2012). Black hawk down?: Establishing helicopter parenting as a distinct construct from other forms of parental control during emerging adulthood. *Journal of Adolescence, 35*, 1177–1190.

Parry, J. M. (2011). Benjamin Spock: Pediatrician and anti-war activist. *American Journal of Public Health, 101*(5), 802–803.

Perez, M. E., & Fox, R. A. (2008). Parenting Latino toddlers and preschoolers: Clinical and nonclinical samples. *Hispanic Journal of Behavioral Science, 30*(4), 481–491.

Pomerantz, E. M., & Moorman, E. A. (2007). The how, whom, and why of parent's involvement in children's academic lives: More is not always better. *Review of Educational Research, 77*, 373–410.

Reed, J. (1980, January–February). Infant care: Then and now. *Children Today*, 16–20.

Renzaho, A. M., Green, J., Mellor, D., & Swinburn, B. (2011). Parenting, family functioning and lifestyle in a new culture: The case of African migrants in Melbourne, Victoria, Australia. *Child and Family Social Work, 16*, 228–240.

Saad, A. I. (1989, June). Schooling and occupational choice in nineteenth century America. *The Journal of Economic History, 49*(2), 454–457.

Schiffrin, H. H., Godfrey, H., Liss, M., & Erchull, M. J. (2014). Intensive parenting: Does it have the desired impact on child outcome? *Journal of Child and Family Studies*. Advance online publication. doi:10.1007/s10826-014-0035-0

Selden, S. (n.d.). Eugenics popularization. *American Eugenics Archives, virtual exhibits: Image archives on the American Eugenics movement*. Retrieved from: http://www.eugenicsarchive.org/eugenics/list2.pl

Senior, J. (2014). *All joy and no fun: The paradox of modern parenthood*. New York, NY: Harper Collins.

Sergin, C., Woszidlo, A., Givertz, M., Dauer, A., & Murphy, M. T. (2012). The association between overparenting, parent–child communication, and entitlement and adaptive traits in adult children. *Family Relations, 61*, 237–252.

Spicer, P. (2010). Cultural influences on parenting. *Zero to Three, 30*(4), 28–32.

Spock, B. (1946). *The commonsense book of baby and child care.* New York: Duell, Sloan & Pearce.

Spock, B. & Parker, S. J. (1998). *Dr. Spock's baby and child care* (7th ed.). New York: Pocket Books.

U.S. Department of Health and Human Services. (2012). *Children's Bureau centennial: Children's Bureau timeline.* Retrieved from: https://cb100.acf.hhs.gov/childrens-bureau-timeline

Westbrook, T. R., Harden, B. J., Holmes, A., Meisch, A. D., & Whittaker, J. V. (2012). Physical discipline use and child behavior problems in low-income, high-risk African American families. *Early Education and Development, 23,* 877–899.

Zuckerman, M. (2006). Coming of age in the age of the American revolution. *European Journal of Developmental Psychology, 3*(4), 402–414.

11

EDUCATORS AND FAMILIES PARTNERING TOGETHER FOR CHILDREN

This chapter will focus on the issue of partnership between education professionals and families. Working and partnering with families has been the hallmark of best practices in early childhood education and special education. Early childhood education and special education have traditionally honored working with and supporting families as an important part of a young child's education. In fact, the guidelines for developmentally appropriate practices (DAP), published by National Association for the Education of Young Children (2009), requires establishing reciprocal relationships with families and involving them in the learning process as one of the necessary standards of early childhood professional practice in the field. Similarly, all amendments of U.S. special education laws (i.e. IDEA) mandate working with families as a necessary and important component of education of children with special needs. Just as in NAEYC's standards, the current ethical principles developed by the Council for Exceptional Children (2010) requires that special education professionals develop relationships with families that are based on mutual respect and actively involve families in the educational decision making of the child.

In this chapter, I will look at issues related to families, the tradition of partnering with them in early childhood education and special education, and recommend guidelines for working successfully with all families. Because this book has focused on children with challenging behaviors and mental health needs, it is particularly important that various aspects of working with families of these children are presented.

Role of Families in the Child's Education

There is little dispute about the important role of parents in the education and development of children. Statements such as "Parents are children's first teachers," or "Parents are the best role models for children," are not only common, but also in some cases the motivation behind some national parenting education organizations in the USA (e.g. Parents as Teachers™; for details see http://www.parentsasteachers.org/).

Both parents and educators want children to succeed in learning. This common goal should naturally compel the two to work and collaborate with one another to achieve this shared goal. In fact, *parent–teacher partnerships* or *family–professional partnerships* are common phrases to describe a process of *collective empowerment* and parent–professional *collaboration* to achieve the best outcome for the child. However, in practice, parents and educators do not always work successfully together. Before I present issues related to partnership between families and professionals, it is important to briefly mention some factors related to the family processes that influence these relationships.

Growing Diversity and Complexity of Families

Rapid social and economic changes in the last century have led to the creation of families that are both diverse and complex in their structure and in their daily functioning and processes (Walsh, 2012). *Family structure* refers to family membership, or who is in the family. No longer are the nuclear and extended families the most commonly cited family structures. Rather, today there are a number of different family structures, such as those that Derman-Sparks and Edwards (2012) describe. For example:

- *Nuclear families*: Consisting of biological parents and children.
- *Extended families*: Consisting of parents and children with grandparents and other kin (such as uncles, aunts, cousins, etc.).
- *Adoptive families*: In which there are parents and one or more adopted children.
- *Blended/step-families*: In which there are members from two or more previous families.
- *Gay, lesbian, or transgender families*: Consisting of single-sex parents with their children.
- *Single-parent families*: Consisting of one parent and children.
- *Co-custody families*: In which there are divorced parents with legal arrangement to share childrearing responsibilities.
- *Kinship/foster families*: In which there is a temporary or long-term family which has the legal responsibility for care of one or more children.
- *Separated families*: In which a separation of one or more family members from the rest of the family occurs. This could be due to a variety of reasons, such as employment, immigration, divorce, military service, hospitalization, etc.
- *Immigrant families*: Consisting of families who live in a different country from their home country, with children who might or might not have been born in the new and adoptive country.
- *Families on the move*: Consisting of families who are on the move to different locations, due to parents' seasonal employments, or job situations which require the family's frequent travel.

In addition to diverse family structures, economic conditions continue to widen the gap between the rich and the poor, affecting the daily functioning of families. The latest U.S. federal survey of consumer finances released in September 2014 reported that as the income of the wealthiest 10 percent of Americans increased by 10 percent from 2010 to 2013, the U.S. families in the bottom 40 percent saw a decline in their income over the same period, and the middle-class families' income fell by 5 percent during this same period (Board of the Governors of the Federal Reserve, 2014). In fact, by 2013, while the top 3 percent of American families held 54 percent of all wealth – an increase of 44.8 percent from 1989 – the bottom 90 percent of American families held only 24.7 percent of wealth – a decrease of 33.2 percent from 1989 (Leubsdorf, 2014). The implication for this growing wealth inequality is clear. Today, more children are born in families stricken by poverty in comparison to the last two to three decades.

Putting aside these issues, each family has a very unique culture in which it constructs day-to-day and worldview meanings, considers its resources, meets the needs of its members, and raises its children. The growing complexity of the families of today creates numerous implications for family–professional partnership in the education of young children. The most important implication is that not all parents or guardians will be able to equally meet the health, developmental, and educational needs of their children. In fact, due to the issues discussed above, an increased number of families face extreme pressure and therefore require support from educators to meet the needs of their children on a daily basis. To add to this issue, when a family has a child with challenging behaviors or special needs, stressors begin to pile up; these might inextricably influence a family's functioning. For these families, it is even more important to have the partnership of the educators to appropriately address the needs of their children. This idea of supporting families to meet their needs has its roots in the *systems theory of development*.

Systems Theory and Working with Families

During a series of congressional hearings on poverty in 1964, the developmental psychologist Urie Bronfenbrenner testified before the U.S. Congress about the adverse effects of poverty on the development of the child. His testimony led to his further involvement in policy for education of young children, which gradually resulted in the creation of the Head Start program and its focus on family involvement and support services. Bronfenbrenner's system theory of child development (1979) changed the way psychologists, educators, and policy makers viewed children's development.

From Bronfenbrenner's systems theory's perspective, it is not only the context of family that influences a child's development, but also the school, the community, the larger society and culture, and the historical and socio-political developments that occur over time. Bronfenbrenner (1979) articulated five complex and interactive systems which influence and shape development: 1) *microsystem*, the child, including his biological makeup, and the child's family system (e.g. daily functioning, structure, and subsystems); 2) *exosystem*, the surrounding community and members within; 3) *mesosystem*, the interactions between the family system and the surrounding community; 4) *macrosystem*, the larger society with its laws, cultural values, and beliefs; 5) *chronosystem*, patterns of events over time, including the socio-historic and political conditions.

Bronfenbrenner (1979, 1986) argued that programs that emphasize the family and the child together and also support both are most successful in promoting a child's development and functioning. Over the past decades, systems theory has been applied as a framework for early intervention, special education, child and family therapy, and counseling. Even before Bronfenbrenner's ideas promoted the importance of parents and professionals working together, the tradition of early childhood education put a premium on parents' involvement in the education of children.

A Tradition of Parent–Teacher Camaraderie in Early Childhood Education

The history of parent involvement in early childhood education is best understood through an examination of the collective work of early childhood historians, such as Dorothy Hewes (1985, 1997a, 1997b, 1998, 2010) and Feeney, Moravick, and Nolte (2013). According to Hewes (1997a), the first Froebelian kindergarten of record in the USA was established in 1856, in Wisconsin, by Margaret Meyer Schurz and her husband (Hewes, 1997a). The Schurz kindergarten was a family model of kindergarten, a playgroup for Schurz children and their cousins under the supervision of Carl and Margaret Schurz. Elizabeth Peabody, who was an educator and reformer, met the Schurzs in Boston and was impressed enough to open her own kindergarten in 1860 (Hewes, 1997a).

As kindergartens became common in the USA in the late 19th century, European early childhood pioneers, like Maria Montessori in Italy, and social activist sisters Margaret and Rachel McMillan in England, began calling attention to the importance of preschool education for children younger than kindergarten age. Margaret and Rachel McMillan put forth the concept of *nursery school* and established the first *open-air nursery school and training center* in England in 1914. Their concept of nursery school differed from kindergarten in that it paid more attention to health and play in fresh air, free exploration, and nurturing emotional development of the child as compared to cognitive development (Feeney et al., 2013; Hewes, 1997b). The McMillans' ideas of nursery school were brought to the USA and thus preschools were established in different cities.

It is little known, however, that some of the most important preschool programs established at the time were formed as programs of partnership between parents and educators. In 1916, the first of many parent cooperative nursery schools was established by a group of University of Chicago faculty wives in Chicago (Parent Cooperative Preschools International, 2014). These mothers wanted to have preschool education for their children, an education for themselves, and childcare so that they could participate in social activities like the Red Cross (Hewes, 1998). The difference between cooperatives and other preschool programs of the time (and even today) was that parents and teachers shared in the responsibility of educating children. Parents were required to assist in the execution of the daily preschool programs, and thus the tradition of parent–teacher partnership was established.

Though other important early childhood institutions were being established at the time, with the exception of the cooperative nursery schools, parents and educators operated none other jointly. Some important programs that also provided parental education were:

- Yale University's Clinic of Child Development, today known as Yale's Child Study Center, which was established in 1911. Its affiliated early childhood program, Comer Child Development Center, provides parent education as a part of its program today.
- Iowa Child Welfare Research Center, established in 1917. Cora Bussey Hills, a woman who had established a Mother's Club, was elemental in advocacy and establishment of this center. The institute closed in 1974.
- In 1916, Lizzy Pitts Merrill Palmer left a bequest to establish the Merrill Palmer Institute in child development. The mission of the center was to educate men and women in child development. Edna Noble White, the first director of the center, provided "motherhood training," which later established the center as one of the most notable parent education centers in the USA.

Looking back at the cooperative nursery schools and their unique parent–teacher partnership, one thing is distinguishable from models above and those that are common today: the cooperatives arranged parent education based on what the parents themselves saw as important to learn (Hewes, 1998). Although a great focus of the cooperative nursery schools' parent education program was on the study of early childhood development and education, parents arranged and invited guest lecturers on other different topics, such as law or finance, as well (Hewes, 1997b, 1998). Aside from these, cooperative preschools also provided leadership training for women and their preschool teachers. In fact, several U.S. pioneers and influential figures in early childhood education, such as Lilian Katz, got their first start in cooperative preschools (Hewes, 1997b).

After World War II, the increase in the number of women entering the workforce created a childcare crisis, and cooperative preschools, with their relaxed and hands-on approach to education and parent-based values, became widespread (Hewes, 1998). Although cooperative preschools continue to exist today, their influence and number began to decline in the 1970s. Today, very little literature is available on the history of cooperative preschools, and thus there is little appreciation for the success of this model with its spirit of camaraderie between parents and teachers.

Although the relationship between parents and educators in the history of early education of children with typical development is marked by camaraderie, the history of relationship between professionals and families of children with developmental disabilities and challenging behaviors is quite different.

The Evolution of Research and Practice Related to Families of Children with Disabilities

Until the last few decades, when parents of children with disabilities began to raise their voices, tell their stories, and advocate against the dominant negative characterization of their lives, the research that described their experiences was dominated by themes such as a profound loss, grief, burden, and coping. In fact, this negative portrayal, which was most often sketched by professionals, continues to dominate the narratives related to the lives of these families and their children and contradicts the accounts of actual experiences provided by families themselves (Bayat, 2007; Ferguson, 2002; Lalvani & Polvere, 2013; Taunt and Hastings, 2002).

The reasons for such a negative portrayal in research are complex and multidimensional. For example, different historical developments and socio-cultural changes which influence views of disability in general, and direction of research in particular, play important roles in maintaining an assumption that families of children with disabilities struggle to overcome difficulties and insurmountable obstacles (Lalvani & Polvere, 2013).

Examination of the complex issues in research and practice related to families is beyond the scope of this chapter. However, I will describe some of the important themes in the literature while outlining the relationship between families and professionals to date. Based on this review, I argue that family–professional relationships can be distinguished by six themes since the early 20th century. These are: 1) separating children from parents; 2) blaming and pathologizing parents; 3) sharing in the grief with parents; 4) training parents; 5) becoming family-centered professionals; and 6) forming partnerships with families. Let us look at each of these themes separately.

Separating Children from Parents (the 19th and Early 20th Century)

In the 19th and early decades of the 20th century, influenced by the eugenics movement on one hand and advances in psychology and social work on the other, the best form of care for children with any kind of developmental disability and/or challenging behaviors was to commit them to asylums, institutions, or training schools for the "feeble-minded." The birth of a child with any kind of disability, particularly with an intellectual disability, was considered as a "tragedy" for the family.

The medicalization of disability, beginning in 1890, brought with it the *rehabilitation movement*, which advocated that the source of the disability was in the body, and therefore the child with the disability should be treated separately from the family and society (Lalvani & Polvere, 2013). Beginning in the late 19th century, it was understood that the best thing that could be done for the family was to take away the child and place him in an institution for life.

In 1889, during the National Conference on Social Welfare, Henry Dechert of Philadelphia said:

> Experience shows that a large proportion of our criminals, inebriates, and prostitutes are congenital imbeciles; and yet, in a very large degree, these children are allowed to grow up unrestrained and without any attempt to improve them ... Can we do anything to prevent these evils, but especially can we do anything which will improve these mentally defective children? The answer is twofold. Actual separation from the other members of the family and the community alone will prevent these evils. When present in the family circle and sheltered by parents, either rich or poor, they are frequently a menace to the peace and happiness of parents, brothers, sisters, and neighbors.
>
> *(Dechert, 1889, p. 84)*

Thus began a culture of disability, and a relationship between professionals and families of children with disabilities, which continues to be problematic to this day. Reform schools and institutions became places for children with any kind of intellectual disability or challenging behaviors to be treated in isolation, and the paternalistic professionals advised parents to stay away and leave the care of their children to experts who knew how to help them (Ferguson, 2002).

Blaming and Pathologizing Parents (1920s to 1960s)

In the early 20th century, researchers began to shift their focus from a dysfunction in the child to a dysfunction in the parents. Influenced by the psychoanalytical views of the time, parents began to be viewed as neurotic or psychotic. It was damaged parents who created damaged children. It was what the parents did or did not do that led to the disability in the child. The infamous label of "refrigerator mothers," coined by Bruno Battleheim in 1967, which referred to mothers who caused autism in their children by their coldness toward their infant, followed these parents for years to come.

During this period, research endeavored to catalogue evidence of parental pathology and find interventions that would help the child (Ferguson, 2002). The solution was simple – provide psychotherapy or similar treatments for parents. Thus in the 1960s it was common for mothers to undergo treatment along with the child so that their child might improve (Turnbull, Turbiville, & Turnbull, 2000). The residue of this view remains to this day. In fact, in some European countries, such as France, psychotherapy for parents (particularly mothers) is a part of treatment for children with some disorders, like ASD.

Though not many continue to openly blame parents for the disability of their child, research is still interested in discovering the possible pathology of parents of children with disabilities. Indeed, a good body of research to date examines various mental health issues, such as depression, anxiety, neuroticism, or similar problems in parents of children with different kind of disabilities (Lalvani, 2011). It is important to note that in most of such research, there is little acknowledgment of other contextual and environmental factors. For example, depression, anxiety, or other mental health issues could exist in a family regardless of whether or not the family has a child with a disability (Lalvani & Polvere, 2013). Thus, most existing research decontextualizes experiences of families of children with disabilities from other factors in their lives, and focuses instead on problems that it considers results from the disability in the child – where in fact those problems could be common in any family.

Sharing in the Grief with Parents (1970s to Present)

Not too long ago, the *stage of grief theory* was taught as part of teacher training programs in special education to help professionals understand the experiences of parents of children with disabilities. According to such a view, in response to disability parents moved through certain *stages of grief* similar to those followed by receiving news of a terminal illness, described by Elizabeth Kübler Ross in 1969 in her book, *On Death and Dying*.

In one application of Kübler Ross's *stages of grief* to families of children with disabilities, Moses (1987) articulated the different stages that these parents go through (although not necessarily in the same order). These were denial, anxiety, fear, guilt, depression, and anger. Moses recommended professionals to share in and experience parents' grief as a way of working successfully with them. Drawing on this kind of thinking, professionals have recommended guidelines for working with families that are based on an empathetic understanding of grief and coping (Lalvani & Polvere, 2013).

The notions of "profound loss," "burden," "chronic sorrow," "grief," "coping," and "guilt" continue to exist in the literature as a way of characterizing the negative experiences of parents of children with disabilities. In the last three decades, scholars have raised questions about the validity or generalizability of this theory to all families. Families of children with disabilities have themselves been very vocal against such a negative portrayal and characterization of their experience (for details see Bayat, 2007; Ray, Pewitt-Kinder, & George, 2009; Scorgie & Wilgosh, 2009, 2012; Taunt & Hastings, 2002).

More recently, some scholars (such as Patterson, 2002; Ulrich & Bauer, 2003) have proposed models of *adaptation* and *adjustment* instead of "grief" and "coping," in which families of children with disabilities adjust to the demands and stressors of disability over a period of time. According to these models, families of children go through a process in which they learn to weigh the demands of disability against the resources available to them and gradually adjust to these demands. The quality and time period in which families go through this process of adjustment differs and depends on the family's particular characteristics, structure and functioning, resources, and the severity and developmental characteristics of the child with special needs himself.

Training Parents (1970s to Present)

Influenced by the behavioral approaches as well as the systems theory in psychology, the idea of professionals teaching parents to teach their children gained ground in both private and public programs starting in the late 1960s. The Head Start program, for example, built its model on parental involvement and education as a way of improving a child's development. Teaching parents to work with their children continues to be recommended not only for children with disabilities, but also for typically developing children who might be at risk, and parent training organizations and programs continue to exist and operate successfully today.

Becoming Family-Centered Professionals (1980s to Present)

Advocated by special education scholars such as Dunst, Trivette, and Deal (1988), the family-centered approach promoted a model of *empowerment* and collaboration between professionals and parents of children with disabilities. The most important change in this model from the previous models of parent–professional relationship was the acknowledgment of the family, not just the parents, in the life of the child. A family's choice in decision-making regarding its own strengths, needs, and wishes is central in this model. Focusing on the strengths of the family instead of its weakness means the professionals are required to work with the family members closely in a collaborative capacity. As such, the professional role is to *empower* parents to meet their family's goals.

The family-centered framework builds its premises on *inclusion* of the child. Beginning in the 1970s, advocacy of families of children with disabilities and individuals with disabilities themselves brought the attention of the public to the rights of children and adults with disabilities to be included in all aspects of society equally along with their peers. The inclusion movement questioned the validity of looking at the child and/or the family as the sources of disability. It argued that the meaning of a disability is something that is negotiated between the individual and the society. And thus, since the society had viewed individuals with disabilities and their families as dysfunctional, the existing societal structures in place were handicapping instead of enabling. Societal structures and services, accordingly, should support and empower both the child and the family from the outset. Family-centered practices could be considered to be an inevitable result of the inclusion movement.

Thus, influenced by the inclusion movement, part C of the special education law (IDEA), which concerns early intervention services for infants and toddlers, requires involvement of families of children with disabilities based on the family-centered perspective. Today, the early intervention programs are required to be family-centered, and programs are expected to meet outcomes related to both the family and the child together.

Forming Partnerships with Families (2000s to Present)

A model of *family–professional partnership* was promoted by Turnbull and her colleagues initially in 2000 and recently advanced further as an ideal model (e.g. Turnbull, Turnbull, Erwin, Soodak, & Shogren, 2010, 2015). The major point of difference between this and the family-centered model is that in this approach, instead of professionals empowering the family members, the family and professionals share a *collective empowerment* through a synergy of power from all parties (Turnbull et al., 2010, 2015). The family and professionals work together on an equal footing and in a *partnership* to achieve shared goals. An underlying assumption is that each family has something to bring to the table and partner with professionals in an equal footing. The family's contribution must be determined by the family itself, on its own terms, based on the priorities it defines, and should be appreciated and valued by the professionals (Turnbull et al., 2015).

Having looked at the evolution of research and professional practice related to families of children with disabilities, I now examine the special education laws and their provisions related to the family.

Special Education Laws and the Family

Since the inception of Public Law 94-142, the first legislation regarding the education of children with disabilities in 1975, Congress emphasized participation of families in their children's education and intervention, and the protection of their rights. In the subsequent amendments to this law – the most recent amendment of which is known as the Individuals with Disabilities Education Improvement Act (IDEA, 2004) – Congress extended the law to include additional family-related provisions to ensure successful partnership between families and service providers. The key points of IDEA in regard to involving families are:

- an acknowledgment of the unique needs of each child and their families, including the diversity of cultural background and language in both the child and the family
- an acknowledgment of the rights of families to participate in the decision making, related to all matters, such as the educational process and the treatment of their child
- the requirement for the service providers and educators to develop and implement culturally competent and family-friendly services to establish collaboration and partnership with family members and caregivers, including the family members who do not speak English
- the requirement for the intervention programs to involve families: to participate in design, planning, and implementation of the *Individualized Family Service*

Plan (IFSP) for infants and toddlers, and the *Individualized Education Plan (IEP)* for preschoolers and older students

- the protection of the rights of parents or guardians through a specific provision of the law, called *procedural safeguards*, which articulates parents' rights to include:
    - having an independent educational and/or developmental evaluation conducted for their child
    - receiving prior written notice to participate in IFSP or IEP of their child
    - being informed and instructed about parents' rights as articulated by the law
    - having access to all educational and treatment records of their child
    - taking a complaint to mediation or to the court through due process of law
    - presenting and resolving their complaints as well as being informed and instructed about the time period in which to make their complaints
    - having the availability of mediation
    - having the school resolve conflict
    - being informed and instructed about the placement of their child during the due process period and related procedures
    - having a due process hearing and all procedures relating to it.

As it is obvious from this multifaceted provision, over almost half a century of development, IDEA has become one of the most comprehensive laws articulating not only the educational rights of children with disabilities, but also ensuring that families of children with special needs actively participate, and are involved in the education process of their child. The USA's early intervention/special education system is unique in its mandates and provisions for parent–professional partnership; in that although the U.S. Department of Education issues recommended guidelines for public schools to form partnerships and collaborations with families of children without special needs, there is no law in general education that mandates parent–professional partnership between families of typically developing children and educators.

Contemporary Issues Related to Families of Children with Disabilities

As we have seen, because each family is unique due to the complex processes and diverse issues that it faces, it is difficult to standardize the lived experiences of families of children with disabilities. However, research that captures the experiences of these families in an unbiased way is emerging. There are certain identified lifecycle themes, pinpointed by research, which I will explain in the following sections.

Diagnosis

Diagnosis of a child with a disability usually creates a period of intense emotion. Each family is different in the way it responds to this process. Some families may feel overwhelmed, confused, or frightened, while others may begin to gather information about the disability, and learn all they can to care for and work with their child. Some families may begin to advocate for their child to receive the best service options available, while others may decide to wait. No matter what a family decides to do, a diagnosis of a disability creates a challenging period for the family, and dealing with this challenge differs from one family to the next.

Meaning Making

Each family makes meaning of the disability in its own unique way. Parents may ask questions like: What does it mean for our family to have a child with a disability? What does it mean for me as a parent to have this child? How are we to deal with this disability? How will our other children deal with this issue? What will my child be like as he/she grows up?

The process of meaning making depends on how the society views and treats children with disabilities and how each family weighs its own stressors as well as demands of disabilities against its resources (Patterson, 2002). Family resources are not necessarily financial. Rather, families rely on their spiritual resources and faith, family members' personal strengths, and a family's cohesion and structure (Walsh, 2012). The way a family considers all of its resources and challenges and makes sense of their child's disability is elemental in forming what has been termed as *family resilience* (Walsh, 2011). Resilient families are those who withstand and rebound from stressful life challenges, strengthened and more resourceful (Walsh, 2011). Many families of children with disabilities are indeed resilient families (Bayat & Schuntermann, 2012). Thus, realistic and positive meaning making is key to the promotion of resilience in families.

Advocacy and Securing Services

It is common for families to spend the first years after the diagnosis of their child in securing educational and related treatment services. It is, of course, natural for all parents to want the best services for their children. However, not all parents will become strong advocates. Some parents find a new network of friends in other families of children with disabilities and get involved in broader advocacy efforts whether locally or nationally (Bayat, 2007; Scorgie and Wilgosh, 2009). Some families may go through personal and professional transformations and become professionals in the field of disabilities (Taunt & Hastings, 2002), while other families may choose not to become as involved.

Most families face various stressors on the way to securing appropriate services. Professionals who make an effort to form strong and positive relationship with parents and form partnership with them from the outset of diagnosis, play an important role in alleviating the level of stress for the family members (Fowler et al., 2012). Strong alliance with professionals not only alleviates stress at home but also plays a strong role in determining future parental involvement in the education of the child (Turnbull et al., 2015).

Adjustment at Home

The period of adjustment at home depends to a great extent on the quality of secured services and how satisfied families are with those services. Generally, when all the services are secured, and as the child learns to become more independent (e.g. self-care, hygiene, and daily living interactions), parents may experience a period of calm. That child's capabilities and independence, as well as continued partnership with school and educators, contributes to the level of adjustment (Turnbull et al., 2015). For example, raising children with challenging behaviors is particularly demanding on all parents' time, specifically on working parents. When most of the time of the family is consumed by addressing the challenging behaviors of their child, parents and other family members will experience conflict and unusual strain (Breevart & Bakker, 2011). Added to this strain is receiving discipline notifications from their child's school, instead of having a parent–professional team collaboration to successfully support and address the challenging behaviors of their child. There is evidence that when parents receive support from professionals regarding the challenging behaviors of their child, they are able to support their child, create a calm environment at home, participate in the community, and have a better quality of family life (Breevart & Bakker, 2011; Summers et al., 2007).

Transition and Looking into the Future

Parents of children with disabilities seldom stop to wonder what will happen to their child with a disability when they are no longer around (Bayat & Schuntermann, 2012; Turnbull et al., 2015). Various times of transition beginning from early childhood are particularly stressful times for families: 1) transition from infancy and early intervention services to early childhood special education; 2) transition to elementary special education; 3) transition to adolescence and high school special education and vocational training; 4) transition to adulthood vocations or appropriate college. Each transition period requires careful planning that necessitates successful working with professionals to plan for skills learning and education that is realistic and relevant to the child's capabilities, interests, and the child's and family's wishes. Professionals who work with families successfully during these transition times alleviate stress levels and help with a smooth transition to the next lifecycle event (Turnbull et al., 2015).

Recommendation for Establishing Family–Professional Partnerships

Except for some disorders which might be detectable at birth (e.g. Down syndrome), most developmental issues or challenging behaviors are identified later. Early childhood educators are usually the first responders when a challenging behavior occurs or a developmental problem is suspected. Similarly, early childhood teachers are usually the first people who break the news to parents about the possibility of behavioral or mental health issues in their children. Although each family is different in the way they respond to, interact, and work with early childhood educators, there are certain recommendations for professional practice which would help early childhood professionals to establish and maintain a successful partnership with families from the outset. As recommended by Turnbull et al., 2015, these include:

- *Commitment:* Without a firm commitment to children and families, there is little hope that professionals will gain the competence to partner with families successfully. Early childhood educators should go above and beyond the call of duty when necessary and demonstrate that they are committed to the success of each child and family. When families realize the commitment of early childhood educators, they are more apt to listen to what professionals have to say.
- *Respect:* No partnership can be successful without the respect and regard of the parties for one another. Respecting families include respecting the family's culture, behaviors, attitudes, and opinions, and accept the family as it is. Professionals who treat families with dignity and respect are likely to be respected in return and therefore be trusted by the family.
- *Professional competence:* Early childhood educators who are highly competent, hold high expectations for children, and provide a high quality education for each child they work with are the ones who are most likely to share the same goals with the family and gain the partnership and support of the family in their own work with children.
- *Equality:* Teachers, other education professionals, and family members are all equal partners in the education of children. When families and educators regard each other as equally powerful and are willing to share power in an equal footing, they work successfully with each other. Partnership means that each party regards the other's knowledge, skills, as well as feelings as equally important and is willing to explore options together.
- *Trust:* Families entrust their children to educators. Educators must be mindful of the value of the family's trust in them. Maintaining confidentiality and respecting the family's privacy is one way of demonstrating this trust. Families whose trust is honored learn to reciprocate this trust and maintain a positive relationship with their child's educators.

Closing Remarks

The history of the parent–professional relationship has not always been a positive one, particularly as it relates to working with families of children with challenging behaviors or disabilities. The experiences of families of children with disabilities have usually been portrayed negatively, and the relationship of professionals with families has been influenced by this portrayal. Gradual changes in the demographic of the families, and in the socio–political and economic landscape of the nation, has compelled promotion of different, more humanistic views of families. A model of collective empowerment and family–professional partnership is currently one of the best practice models recommended for early childhood educators and other professionals. This model is based on working on an equal footing toward a shared goal. Professionals who go above and beyond the call of duty to establish a positive relationship with families and work in equal partnership with them from early on not only promote resilience in the family but a higher quality of life for the child and the family.

References

Bayat, M. (2007). Evidence of resilience in families of children with autism. *Journal of Intellectual Disability Research, 51*(9), 702–714.

Bayat, M., & Schuntermann, P. (2012). Enhancing resilience in families of children with autism through meaning making and mentalization-based therapy. In D. Becvar (Ed.), *Handbook of family resilience* (pp. 409–424). New York: Springer.

Board of Governors of the Federal Reserve System. (2014). *Changes in U.S. family finances from 2010 to 2013: Evidence from the survey of consumer finances.* Retrieved from: http://www.federalreserve.gov/pubs/bulletin/2014/articles/scf/scf.htm

Breevaart, K., & Bakker, A. B. (2011). Working parents of children with behavioral problems: A study on the family–work interface. *Anxiety, Stress, & Coping, 24*(3), 239–253.

Bronfenbrenner, U. (1979). *The ecology of human development: Experiments by nature and design.* Cambridge, MA: Harvard University Press.

Bronfenbrenner, U. (1986). Ecology of the family as a context for human development: Research perspectives. *Developmental Psychology, 22*(6), 723–742.

Council for Exceptional Children (CEC). (2010). *Special education professional ethical principles.* Retrieved from: http://www.cec.sped.org/~/media/Files/Standards/Professional%20Ethics%20and%20Practice%20Standards/Ethics%20Translations/CEC_Ethics_English.pdf

Dechert, H. (1889). Care of idiotic and feebleminded children. *Proceedings of National Conference on Charities and Corrections, 16*, 83–86. Retrieved from: http://quod.lib.umich.edu/n/ncosw/ACH8650.1889.001/126

Derman-Sparks, L., & Edwards, J. O. (2012). *Anti-bias education for young children and ourselves* (2nd ed.). Washington, DC: National Association for the Education of Young Children.

Dunst, C., Trivette, C., & Deal, A. (1988). *Enabling and empowering families: Principles of guidelines for practice.* Cambridge, MA: Brookline Books.

Feeney, S., Moravick, E., & Nolte, S. (2013). *Who am I in the lives of children? An introduction to early childhood education* (9th ed.). Upper Saddle River, NJ: Pearson.

Ferguson, P. (2002). A place in the family: An historical interpretation of research on parental reactions to having a child with a disability. *The Journal of Special Education, 36*(3), 124–130.

Fowler, C., Rossiter, C., Bigsby, M., Hopwood, N., Lee, A., & Dunston, R. (2012). Working in partnership with parents: The experience and challenge of practice innovation in child and family health nursing. *Journal of Clinical Nursing, 21*, 3306–3314.

Hewes, D. W. (1985). *Compensatory early childhood education: Froebelian origins and outcomes.* School of Family Studies and Consumer Sciences: San Diego: San Diego State University. Retrieved from: http://eric.ed.gov/?id=ED264980

Hewes, D. W. (1997a, November 14). *Fallacies, phantasies, and egregious prevarications in ECE history.* Paper presented at the Annual Conference of the National Association for the Education of Young Children, Anaheim, CA.

Hewes, D. W. (1997b, March 15). *California's cooperative nursery schools: Perspectives from past.* Keynote address presented at the 48th Annual Convention of the California Council of Parent Participation Nursery Schools (CCPPNS), San Mateo, CA.

Hewes, D. W. (1998). *It's the camaraderie: A history of parent cooperative preschools.* Davis, CA: Center for Cooperatives, University of California.

Hewes, D. W. (2010, July). Fostering individuality, valuing uniformity – learning from the past to engage in tomorrow. *Young Children, 65,* 60–62.

Individuals with Disabilities Education Act (IDEA), 20 U.S.C. § 1400 (2004).

Kübler-Ross, E. (1969). *On death and dying.* New York: Collier.

Lalvani, P. (2011). Constructing the (m)other. Dominant and contested narratives on mothering a child with Down syndrome. *Narrative Inquiry, 21*(2), 276–293.

Lalvani, P., & Polvere, L. (2013). Historical perspectives on studying families of children with disabilities: A case for critical research. *Disability Studies Quarterly, 33*(3). Retrieved from: http://dsq-sds.org/article/view/3209/3291

Leubsdorf, B. (2014, September 4). Fed: Gap between rich, poor Americans widened during recovery. *The Wall Street Journal.* Retrieved from: http://online.wsj.com/articles/fed-gap-between-rich-poor-americans-widened-during-recovery-1409853628

Moses, K. (1987, Spring). The impact of childhood disability: The parent's struggle. *WAYS Magazine.* Evanston, Illinois. Retrieved from: http://www.pent.ca.gov/beh/dis/parentstruggle_DK.pdf

National Association for the Education of Young Children (NAEYC). (2009). *Developmentally appropriate practice in early childhood programs serving children from birth to age 8: A position statement of the National Association for the Education of Young Children.* Retrieved from: http://www.naeyc.org/files/naeyc/file/positions/PSDAP.pdf

Parent Cooperative Preschools International. (2014). *The history of PCPI.* Retrieved from: http://www.preschools.coop/v/history/

Patterson, J. (2002). Integrating family resilience and family stress theory. *Journal of Marriage and the Family, 64,* 349–360.

Ray, J. A., Pewitt-Kinder, J., & George, S. (2009, September). Partnering with families of children with special needs. *Young Children, 64,* 16–22.

Scorgie, K., & Wilgosh, L. (2009). Including a care-ful journey: A parent's perspective. *Developmental Disabilities Bulletin, 37*(1–2), 203–220.

Scorgie, K., & Wilgosh, L. (2012). Parents' experiences, reflections, and hopes as their children with disabilities transition to adulthood. *Rivista di Studi Familiari, 2,* 55–72.

Summers, J. A., Marquis, J., Mannan, H., Turnbull, A. P., Fleming, K., Poston, D., and Wang, M. et al. (2007). Relationship of perceived adequacy of services, family–professional partnerships, and family quality of life in early childhood service programs. *International Journal of Disability, Development and Education, 54*(3), 319–338.

Taunt, H. M., & Hastings, R. P. (2002). Positive impact of children with developmental disabilities on their families: A preliminary study. *Education and Training in Mental Retardation and Developmental Disabilities, 37,* 410–420.

Turnbull, A. P., Turbiville, V., & Turnbull, H. R. (2000). Evolution of family–professional partnership models: Collective empowerment is the model for the early 21st century. In J. P. Shonkoff & S. Meisels (Eds.), *The handbook of early childhood intervention* (2nd ed.) (pp. 630–650). New York: Cambridge University Press.

Turnbull, A., Turnbull, R. H., Erwin, E. J., Soodak, L. C., & Shogren, K. A. (2010). *Families, professionals, and exceptionality: Positive outcomes through partnerships and trust* (6th ed.). Upper Saddle River, NJ: Pearson.

Turnbull, A., Turnbull, R. H., Erwin, E. J., Soodak, L. C., & Shogren, K. A. (2015). *Families, professionals, and exceptionality: Positive outcomes through partnerships and trust* (7th ed.). Upper Saddle River, NJ: Pearson.

Ulrich, M. E., & Bauer, M. A. (2003). Levels of awareness: A closer look at communication between parents and professionals. *Teaching Exceptional Children, 35*(6), 20–24.

Walsh, F. (2011). *Strengthening family resilience* (2nd ed.). New York: Guilford Press.

Walsh, F. (2012). The new normal: Diversity and complexity in 21st-century families. In F. Walsh, *Normal family processes: Growing diversity and complexity* (4th ed.) (pp. 3–27). New York: Guilford Press.

INDEX